Thank you for being a part of Evansville's Freedom Festival!

Kris Proctor
Evansville Freedom Festival

Mayor Russell G. Lloyd
City of Evansville

Gary L. McDowell
Liason

EVANSVILLE

CROSSROADS OF THE MIDWEST

EVANSVILLE

CROSSROADS OF THE MIDWEST

By Maggie Greenwood-Robinson

Profiles by Barbara Stahura

Featuring the photography of L. Kent Whitehead

Produced in cooperation with the Metropolitan Evansville Chamber of Commerce

WISCONSIN
MAY 29. 1848

IOWA
DEC. 28. 1846

TEXAS
DEC. 29. 1845

FLORIDA
MAR. 3. 1845

MICHIGAN
JAN 26. 1837

EVANSVILLE

CROSSROADS OF THE MIDWEST

By Maggie Greenwood-Robinson
Corporate Profiles by Barbara Stahura
Featuring the photography of L. Kent Whitehead

Community Communications, Inc.
Publisher: Ronald P. Beers

Staff for *Evansville: Crossroads of the Midwest*
Acquisitions: Henry S. Beers
Publisher's Sales Associate: Mike Bartow
Editor in Chief: Wendi L. Lewis
Managing Editor: Kurt R. Niland
Profile Editor: Mary Catherine Richardson
Editorial Assistant: Mandy Lunsford
Design Director: Scott Phillips
Designer: Matt Johnson
Photo Editors: Kurt R. Niland and Matt Johnson
Contract Manager: Christi Stevens
National Sales Manager: Ronald P. Beers
Sales Assistant: Sandra Akers
Proofreader: Kari Collin Jarnot and Heather Ann Edwards
Accounting Services: Sara Ann Turner
Print Production Manager: Jarrod Stiff
Pre-Press and Separations: Artcraft Graphic Productions

Community Communications, Inc.
Montgomery, Alabama

David M. Williamson, Chief Executive Officer
Ronald P. Beers, President
W. David Brown, Chief Operating Officer

TABLE OF CONTENTS

CHAPTER NINE

9 NETWORKS 140

The area's transportation, communications, and energy firms keep people, cargo, information, and power circulating inside Evansville and surrounding communities.

CHAPTER TEN

10 MANUFACTURING & DISTRIBUTION 150

Producing goods for individuals and industry, manufacturing firms provide employment for many Evansville area residents while research, engineering, scientific, and technical firms plot tomorrow's technologies today.

CHAPTER ELEVEN

11 THE BUSINESS COMMUNITY 160

Evansville's business, insurance, and financial communities offer a strong base for the city's growing economy

CHAPTER TWELVE

12 PROFESSIONS 184

From law to accounting, architecture to advertising, and consulting to public relations, Evansville's professional firms are recognized as leaders in their fields.

CHAPTER THIRTEEN

13 REAL ESTATE & DEVELOPMENT 194

From concept to completion, Evansville's building and real estate industries shape tomorrow's skyline and neighborhoods.

CHAPTER FOURTEEN

14 EDUCATION & HEALTH CARE 202

Evansville's educational and medical institutions work hard to ensure that Evansville residents enjoy the highest quality of life possible.

CHAPTER FIFTEEN

15 THE MARKETPLACE 222

The area's retail establishments and service industries vitalize the economic life of the treasure valley.

Foreword

A quality, culturally diverse family environment; a winning spirit; and an ideal home for business. That's Evansville.

On behalf of Metropolitan Evansville Chamber of Commerce and its local businesses, we present this book to the Evansville community.

Within these beautiful pages, it is our sincere hope that you will experience the quality, texture, and healthy pulse of this dynamic city. We are rich in wonderful people, progressive partnerships, and exciting opportunities. As you enjoy this book, you will come to understand why our future is so bright.

With the approach of the new century, it's an exciting time in Evansville. Those of us who live here know and appreciate the warmth and friendliness of our people, respect our traditions and heritage, and look forward to many opportunities for a prosperous future.

We are proud to share with you a glimpse into the heart and soul of Evansville, the crossroads of the Midwest and a great place to live, work, and do business. But most of all, a place simply to enjoy.

Metropolitan Evansville Chamber of Commerce

Preface

At age 21, I spent a Thanksgiving in Indiana. It was my first—and what I thought would be my only—visit to the middle of America. I had grown up in the East, never knowing much about the Midwest. But nearly 10 years later, as a result of corporate transfer, I relocated to a place called Evansville, Indiana, smack in the middlemost part of the country. I have lived here for more than 20 years now—longer than I ever lived anywhere, in fact. As a so-called Navy "brat," my family moved every few years, and I never had any roots or a real hometown, until Evansville.

It was in Evansville that I met my wonderful husband of 17 years, made the best friends of my life, experienced career fulfillment beyond measure, and found spiritual hope and purpose for the first time ever.

And so when I think of Evansville, I don't think first of the bending, mighty Ohio, the verdant fields and forests, the constancy of the beautifully changing seasons, or the never-ending things to do—although these are certainly joys to treasure. I think of people: My friends who bring comfort, support, and laughter into my life. My pastors who strengthen me in my faith. My co-workers who challenge and encourage me. My neighbors who care and share.

For all these people are what give a place its unalterable worth. You see, a city is defined less by its buildings or businesses, by its highways or institutions. A city is ultimately defined by its people. Whether you have lived here all your life or for just a few weeks, it is in Evansville that you will find among the very best, and blessed, of all humanity.

I am grateful for all who worked on this wonderful book. I would specifically like to thank my friend Arden Harris, a talented artist who suggested me for this project; Gina Walker and Harmony Otahal of the University of Southern Indiana Archives who assisted me in securing historical photos; and Carol Bartlett, an archivist at Willard Library, whose assistance was invaluable in locating additional historical photographs. In addition, it was a privilege to work with the talented photographer L. Kent Whitehead, who is home again in Evansville after living in California for many years.

Maggie Greenwood-Robinson

CHAPTER ONE
FOUNDING

Carving Out a Community

From a Riverbank Wilderness

The Ohio River was, and still is, Evansville's reason for being.
(University of Southern Indiana/University Archives/
Special Collections)

In places, its water appears ivy-green; elsewhere, like coffee abounding with cream. It has the most undulating bends, the longest straightaways, and the gentlest flow. A great river indeed is the Ohio River. Nature on a grand scale, to be sure.

Then it is no wonder that the French named it *La Belle Rivière*, translated "the beautiful river," derived from an Iroquois word for river, *OYO*, which also means "beautiful." Significantly, it was not just another beautiful river to the French, but *the* beautiful, as if there were no other.

Of course, the river was, and still is, Evansville's reason for being.

But before there was an Evansville, an ancient community of prehistoric people lived along the riverbank. Called the Mississippians, they were a part of an advanced culture that thrived in the Mississippi River Valley from 900 to 1600 A.D. The Mississippians are also known as the "Mound Builders" because they erected earthen mounds as platforms for elevated buildings. The prehistoric site near Evansville is today called Angel Mounds, named after Mathias Angel, a farmer who owned the land.

Numbering 1,000-3,000 in all, the mound-building people cultivated corn and other crops, hunted animals, gathered plants, and fished in the river. Originally, the town covered 103 acres and served as an important religious, political, and trade center for people living within a 50-mile radius.

Archaeologists believe the Mound Builders abandoned their homes on the Ohio sometime before 1700, although the reason for their desertion remains a mystery. Thereafter, the riverbank was home to forest-dwelling, semi-nomadic tribes of Native Americans, including the Miami, Delaware, Kickapoo, Potawatomi, and Shawnee.

By 1700 French and English explorers had "discovered" the storied river. They began trading with the Native Americans who inhabited the region and established forts and trading posts all along the Ohio Valley.

At the close of the Revolutionary War, the new United States was formed and extended westward to the Mississippi. Land north of the Ohio—which included Indiana—was designated as the Northwest Territory by the Northwest Ordinance of 1787. There was fierce opposition by Native American tribes to white settlement, but eventually, treaties established peace with various tribes.

Property in the new Indiana territory was placed on the market for $2 an acre. Attracted by the rich, fertile, and inexpensive land bordering the sweeping river bend, a few families, traveling by flatboats, purchased land and built log cabins on land that would eventually become Evansville.

The Ohio riverfront has long held a fascination for people of all ages. (University of Southern Indiana/University Archives/Special Collections)

The Morning Star mail boat helped deliver the mail to and from Evansville around the turn of the century. (University of Southern Indiana/University Archives/Special Collections)

The city, it can be said, was born out of a romance. A young man named Hugh McGary, Jr., whose family had settled in Princeton, Indiana, frequently traveled back and forth to Henderson, Kentucky, to court a young woman who had caught his eye. Every time he crossed the Ohio River, McGary was captivated by its beauty and the land that hugged its shores. He dreamed of building a town there.

His dream materialized, and Evansville grew from a pioneer settlement, to a town, to a city in no time at all. Or so it seemed.

On March 27, 1812, McGary purchased 200 acres of land from the government and built a small log cabin on what is now Main Street and Riverside Drive. Early on, he wanted the town to become a big city. And so, McGary sought the help of an influential attorney who just happened to be territorial legislator—Robert M. Evans.

McGary believed that it would be in the town's best interest to have it officially designated as the county seat of justice. Evans saw that it was. In gratitude, McGary proposed that the town be named Evansville after Evans. Later, on January 7, 1818, Vanderburgh County was created and named after an early Indiana Territory judge, Henry Vanderburgh.

Meanwhile, McGary was busy selling lots, but without much success. In those days, there was little industry in the pioneer town. In poor health and nearly bankrupt, McGary—the town's first citizen, first postmaster, first president of the town council—left Evansville in 1825 to spend his remaining years with a married daughter in Tennessee.

Several years later, the town's prospects brightened. In the spring of 1834, Evansville learned that it would be the terminus of the Wabash and Erie Canal, the longest canal in the United States. Construction in Evansville began in 1836. Whole new sections of the town were platted and advertised for sale in newspapers as far away as Washington, D.C. New people came to town, often choosing Evansville over St. Louis or Chicago.

The town expanded commercially, and by 1837, Evansville was home to a cabinet-making shop and a sawmill, driven by the first steam power used in town. Other local firms manufactured agricultural implements, built steamboats, produced tobacco, and made iron castings and stoves. By January of 1847, the town was chartered as a city.

The canal was completed in 1853, but the excitement was short lived. The project was fraught with problems: competition with railroads, lack of revenue from canal tolls, and vandalism, among others. Soon, it was abandoned altogether.

A group of workers in 1900. (University of Southern Indiana/ University Archives/Special Collections)

Despite the canal's colossal failure, Evansville was resilient. The project had put the city in the national spotlight, and as a result, Evansville experienced its first great population boom. During the 1840s, many Germans seeking escape from turmoil and revolution in Europe had immigrated to the United States. A large number relocated to Evansville, bringing with them good solid work ethics and many trade skills that are still with us today.

Prior to the Civil War, Evansville was situated on one of the major routes of the Underground Railroad, which helped blacks escape the bonds of slavery. Several prominent townspeople smuggled hundreds of runaway slaves across the river. They hid the fleeing slaves, and passed them from one sympathizer's home to another on their way to freedom in the north. Anti-slavery sympathizers included Willard Carpenter, who harbored runaways in his cellar; James G. Jones, Evansville's first mayor, who assisted Carpenter; and Samuel McCutchan, who hid slaves under bales of hay and helped cart them northward.

When the Civil War arrived, Evansville served as a major supply depot, and more than 3,000 brave Evansville men fought in the Union army. After the war, the population in Evansville again swelled. Many freed slaves moved to Vanderburgh County. River commerce increased dramatically. Coal was discovered nearby, providing a lucrative new industry. Mule-drawn street cars were a frequent sight on city streets by 1867. In the 1870s, mules were replaced by horses. Culture was officially in full swing with the opening of the

Electric-powered trolleys appeared on the scene in 1892. (University of Southern Indiana/University Archives/ Special Collections)

Showboats brought entertainment to the city in the 1900s. (University of Southern Indiana/University Archives/ Special Collections)

Evansville Opera House on September 9, 1868. Additional portions of the county were annexed, and by 1870, Evansville had become the second largest city in Indiana.

The city continued to grow and modernize at an unprecedented pace. Electricity came to town in 1882, and electric-powered trolleys began to replace horsedrawn streetcars in 1892. The very first electric lights were used in a local brewery.

Life was fun in Evansville. Showboats never failed to dock in the city. The German community had established the Liederkranz and Germania Mannerchor singing festivals. People were entertained by opera, drama, vaudeville, and concerts. Saloons outnumbered churches by 300 to 75.

By the turn of the century the city had become a major commercial center—home to more than 300 iron, steel, textile, and woodworking companies. Evansville could boast the world's largest furniture factory. One of the city's most famous brand-name products at the time, Swans Down Cake Flour, was manufactured by the Igleheart Brothers Mill. Further, Evansville represented the nation's biggest tobacco market.

Horseless carriages—which were standard buggies equipped with one-horsepower gasoline engines and steering gear—were being replaced by automobiles. The first Evansville-built car to have a name was the Zentmobile. Unfortunately, lack of marketing shut down production in the early 1900s. The Evansville Automobile Company manufactured a car called the Simplicity, which had a transmission instead of the usual chain drive. The system was far better than anything yet on the market, but because it would not run in wet weather, the car was a failure. Undaunted, the company introduced another model called the Traveler. It also failed—for two reasons. Bad publicity generated by the Simplicity affected Traveler sales, and customers complained that the Traveler could not climb hills.

By 1906 moving pictures had arrived in Evansville, and the first commercial movie theater was opened in 1907 on Main Street. Within two years, there were 20 movie theaters in town, offering one-reelers for a five-cent admission.

In 1916 E. Mead Johnson moved his company, Mead Johnson, to Evansville. The company produced Dextri-Maltose®, hailed as the first effective carbohydrate milk modifier to help infants suffering from often-fatal food intolerances.

When the United States declared war on Germany in 1917, more than half the population of Evansville was German. Anti-German sentiment in Evansville simmered. The teaching of German ceased, and the *Evansville Demokrat* (a German newspaper) went out of business.

Amidst this, the flame of patriotism was fanned throughout the Evansville community. Approximately 4,000 men and women from the area enlisted and left for active duty. An Evansville chapter of the American Red Cross was mobilized, and 6,671 people enrolled in just one week. The chapter prepared surgical dressings, made supplies for hospitals, and fed troops who passed through the city.

The Mueller family, like some Evansville families, motored about in cars like the Hupmobile, produced in Detroit. (University of Southern Indiana/University Archives/ Special Collections)

By the turn of the century, Evansville had become a major center for furniture production, thanks to the abundant hardwood forests that grace Ohio Valley. (University of Southern Indiana/University Archives/Special Collections)

Corporal James Bethel Gresham of Evansville was the first American soldier to die in World War I. His grave is located in Locust Hill Cemetery. Photo by L. Kent Whitehead.

In 1917, silent screen actor Douglas Fairbanks visited Evansville and sold war bonds at the McCurdy Hotel. (University of Southern Indiana/University Archives/ Special Collections)

The first American to die in World War I—Corporal James Bethel Gresham—was from Evansville. After laying in state in the rotunda of the State Capitol in Indianapolis, Gresham's body was returned to Evansville and came to rest in Locust Hill Cemetery.

The end of the war in 1918 ushered in the roaring twenties, and with them, Prohibition, speakeasies, the Jazz Age, and the radio. Evansville roared right along with the rest of the country.

While society underwent drastic changes, so did local industry. Depletion in hardwood forests hurt the city's furniture manufacturing companies. People were starting to smoke cigarettes instead of cigars. The city's once-thriving cigar industry began a decline. The increasing popularity of central heating and the use of gas and electric ranges for cooking all but obliterated the market for cast-iron stoves, causing factories to shut down.

The twenties, however, brought a new industry—refrigeration, which would dominate Evansville's economy by the mid-1920s. A man named James Howard Dennedy came to town in 1922 with an idea for a new refrigeration system—a silent compressor that would pump refrigerant through coils placed in the ice compartments of existing ice boxes. The innovation eliminated the daily visits of the iceman. The new product was manufactured in Evansville and marketed by a Detroit company.

In 1929 the stock market crashed, and the Great Depression followed. The community was hit hard. During a three-month period, eight banks closed. People were out of work, hungry, and begging for food at doorsteps. Few were ever turned away. In a sacrificial act of kindness that cost some their livelihood, neighborhood grocery stores gave away free food to those who could not afford it. This spirit of greathearted charity lives on in the community today.

The hardships of the Great Depression were eased somewhat with the discovery of oil in the area in the early 1930s. Many major oil companies located their offices in Evansville.

There was more good news in 1935 when the Chrysler Corporation announced that it would produce its Plymouth line of cars here. The company purchased two plants owned by businessmen Joe, Bob, and Ray Graham. One plant, at Stringtown and Maxwell Avenue, had originally been built to manufacture Graham trucks; the other, at East Columbia Street, had produced a passenger car, called the Graham-Paige. Within a few months, Chrysler had employed 3,000 workers and was paying them the highest wages in the industry. By 1937, Plymouth sales soared.

That same year, the city was devastated by the Great Flood of 1937, when the Ohio River rose to 53.74 feet and practically immersed downtown. Houses floated downriver, dead animals hung from trees, and people were rescued from rooftops. No one died, thankfully, but all told, property loss was tallied at $20 million.

Gearing up for the war effort revitalized Evansville's economy in the wake of the Depression. In 1942, the Evansville Shipyard was established to build Landing Ship Tanks (LSTs), the Navy's largest self-beaching landing crafts. The football field-sized LSTs could carry tanks, trucks, soldiers, gasoline, ammunition, and other material through shallow waters right onto beaches. During the war, the Evansville Shipyard produced more sea-going military ships than any inland shipyard in the nation.

Elsewhere in the city, factories were converted to help build airplanes for the war effort. Republic Aviation built a $16-million plant in Evansville to produce P-47 fighter planes known as Thunderbolts. The plant today houses the Evansville operations of Whirlpool. Other industries in the city made ammunition and clothing, grew food, and printed government manuals. Much of the 2,000 tons of the track on which electric trolleys used to run was taken up and used to make tanks during the war. Local employment swelled from 21,000 to 64,000 in a matter of months.

After World War II, the Evansville area grew steadily. The insatiable demand for automobiles, household appliances and farm equipment helped to maintain high levels of employment in the city. The city was known as the "Refrigerator Capital of the World."

But in the late 1950s, Evansville and the area which it hubbed became a worried place. The prosperity it had shared with the rest of the nation in the wake of World War II was losing its luster. The 1957 closing of its largest employer—Servel—a gas appliance and air conditioning plant, had crippled the city's economy. Twelve thousand people had suddenly and hopelessly found themselves without jobs.

The St. Joseph crew was one of many rescue teams that aided flood victims during the Great Flood of 1937. (University of Southern Indiana/University Archives/ Special Collections)

During the Great Flood of 1937, the Ohio River rose to 53.74 feet and practically immersed schools, homes, and businesses. (University of Southern Indiana/University Archives/ Special Collections)

The Justrite Drilling Company was among the companies that took advantage of the area's oil boom, which began in the thirties. (University of Southern Indiana/University Archives/ Special Collections)

Main Street in downtown Evansville was the center of business and retail activity. (University of Southern Indiana/ University Archives/Special Collections)

And if things were not already bad enough, the Chrysler Corporation closed the doors of its two then-aging Plymouth plants and consolidated its operations in a state-of-the-art automated factory in St. Louis. Six thousand jobs were lost.

But while some companies were moving out, others were moving in, bringing a diversification and resiliency to the local economy still enjoyed today. One of these was Whirlpool, which bought an International Harvester refrigeration plant in 1955 and Servel's facilities in 1958. Whirlpool eventually became one of Evansville's largest employers.

In 1956, it was announced that the Aluminum Company of America (ALCOA) would build a huge plant in neighboring Warrick County. The giant aluminum producer had chosen Southern Indiana for its new plant because of the region's rich and vast natural resources, the plentiful coal, the navigable river, and the availability of the most important resource of all, its people. The plant began operating in 1960.

That same year, General Electric opened the Lexan Polycarbonate plant 20 miles west of Evansville, near Mt. Vernon, Indiana. By the 1970s, Evansville had become home to numerous plastics companies, thanks in large part to the pioneering efforts of plastics innovators such as Thomas J. Morton, Jr. and Robert Morehouse. Considered the father of decorative molded plastics, Morton established Hoosier Cardinal Corporation. His was the first company to manufacture a high-volume injection-molding product—refrigerator shelf studs for Sears, Roebuck, and Company. Morehouse was one of four men who founded the former Kent Plastics

in 1945 after leaving Hoosier Cardinal. He played an important role in Evansville's becoming a force in the plastics industry. Today, the city has a large number of plastics-related businesses, earning it the nickname "The Plastics Valley."

With the arrival of the Toyota Motor Manufacturing plant in nearby Gibson County, the region was back in the business of making vehicles. The $700-million plant produced its first Tundra pickup trucks in 1998.

Today, Evansville's growth as a regional center is evidenced by the location of two major hospitals, two full-service universities, and a vibrant retail and banking community. Evansville is now the third largest city in Indiana, with a core population of more than 126,000 people, but serves as a commercial and medical center for approximately one million people in 24 counties in Southwestern Indiana.

Evansville, at this moment, has all the right elements: a strong economy, friendly neighborhoods, four-season beauty, great schools and universities, safe streets, recreational opportunities, a vibrant cultural life, and a future of unlimited promise.

Time goes on, and history never stops. It certainly isn't stopping now for Evansville, Indiana. ▓

Cook's Brewery was once one of Evansville's largest breweries, producing one of the most popular beers in the area. (University of Southern Indiana/University Archives/Special Collections)

Above: Bosse High School cheerleaders in 1944, one of the years in which the school won the state basketball championship. (University of Southern Indiana/University Archives/ Special Collections)

Left: Named after Evansville steel manufacturer and philanthropist George Mesker, Mesker Amphitheatre has been home to concerts and other entertainment events for years. (University of Southern Indiana/University Archives/Special Collections)

Above: Central Library has long served the area's reading needs with branches conveniently located throughout the city. Left: Prior to the age of personal computers, business machines such as those sold by IBM were state-of-the-art office equipment in the early fifties. (University of Southern Indiana/University Archives/Special Collections)

Downtown Evansville in the mid-forties. (University of Southern Indiana/University Archives/Special Collections)

LABOR IS THE GREAT
WHICH NEARLY ALL IF
COMFORTS AND NECESSITIES
HIEVE AND
NG PEACE
LL NATIONS
INDIANA
1816

2

CHAPTER TWO
FACES

Leaders, Legends, Movers & Shakers

Evansville and the state of Indiana have a long history of leadership.
Photo by L. Kent Whitehead.

Evansville is, and always will be, a city of pioneers, visionary leaders, heroes, the famous as well as the infamous, and citizens from all walks of life whose silent accomplishments mold its character and reflect its merit.

It is a city that thrives because its people have cared enough to invest their lives here. So many people, in fact, have kept the city flourishing from decade to decade that it is impossible to name them all. Nonetheless, here are some of those people, who have stamped their indelible mark on this place called Evansville.

Evansville's story would not be complete without the adventures of Isaac Knight, for whom Knight Township in Vanderburgh County is named. His exploits are a reminder of how treacherous pioneer life could be when the lands—and its inhabitants—were still wild and unsettled.

The year was 1793. On the riverbank, five boys from Red Banks (now Henderson, Kentucky) were cutting wild cane to feed their cattle. They were 17-year-old Peter Sprinkle and his younger brother George; John and 7-year-old Jacob Upp; and 13-year-old Isaac Knight.

Suddenly, Isaac and his friends were ambushed by Indians. In the melee that followed, Peter and Jacob were murdered and scalped. Isaac and the two others were captured and abducted to an Indian village up north. Later, the Indians took Isaac to a village in Illinois, where he was cared for by the mother of the warrior who had kidnapped him.

Prior to his capture, Isaac had been exposed to smallpox. He had become gravely ill by the time he reached the Indian village in Illinois.

Built in 1871, the Reitz Home is Indiana's only Victorian house museum. It sits in the heart of the city's Historic Preservation District. Photo by L. Kent Whitehead.

Smallpox spread through the village, and many Indians died. Realizing that Isaac had brought the disease into their camp, the chief and his council sentenced the boy to be burned at the stake. But Isaac narrowly escaped death when an Indian fur trader purchased him as a present for his childless wife.

For several years, young Isaac lived among the Indians, practicing their ways. But later, he daringly escaped from his foster parents while staying at a trading post on the Island of Mackinac in Michigan. He hid aboard a sailing ship en route to Detroit. From there, he fled to Cincinnati by wagon train, to Louisville by boat, and finally to Red Banks on foot where he was, at long last, reunited with his family.

The Knight family moved from Red Banks to Vanderburgh County. In 1815 and 1817, Isaac Knight bought large tracts of land on the east side of Green River Road from what is now the Lloyd Expressway to Lincoln Avenue. Where Lawndale Shopping Center now sits is a section of the land he once owned. Knight became a prominent man in the community and is listed as a voter in the Vanderburgh County election held in Hugh McGary's cabin on February 16, 1818. A stone marking his original gravesite has been placed near the corner of Lincoln Avenue and Green River Road.

An influential figure in the early growth of Evansville was Willard Carpenter, who moved to town from Troy, New York in 1836. With his two brothers, he started a dry goods business and built a hotel near the riverfront.

Carpenter devoted most of his life to building and bettering Evansville. He solicited funds to complete the Wabash and Erie Canal, invested in railroads, and helped runaway slaves flee from bondage.

Carpenter, though, had a reputation for Scrooge-like behavior, spending most of his time making and saving money. People familiar with his penny-pinching ways said he would scavenge cigar butts from the streets to smoke later. At age 57, however, Carpenter had an equally Scrooge-like conversion, partly the work of a traveling evangelist. During a prayer meeting in 1870, Carpenter confessed that he had worked thirty years to build up the city of Evansville, but had done little to build the Kingdom of the Lord. From then on, he focused his financial attention on giving to religious and civic causes. His financial benevolence helped construct the Christian Home for Girls and fund the magnificent Willard Library.

Another important entrepreneur and philanthropist was John Augustus Reitz, who emigrated to America from Germany and eventually moved to Evansville in 1838. With his sons, he established a sawmill in 1845, which became one of the largest and most successful in the city. He embarked on ventures in banking and manufacturing, and in the process, built a substantial fortune.

The magnanimity of his heart was surely greater than all his worldly possessions. During his time, Reitz and his family built the Little Sisters of the Poor and Sacred Heart Church, constructed Reitz High School, and helped finance Reitz Memorial High School. All tolled, the family donated more than $3 million to community projects.

Another notable business and civic leader of the past was Herman Fendrich, whose cigar factory in the 1800s was one of the most modern of the day. The factory could produce 100,000 cigars a day, most of them hand-rolled by women, and contributed enormously to Evansville's budding economy.

German émigré William Heilman established a successful foundry and machine shop business in Evansville in the 1800s. Heilman was active in local politics, serving several terms on the city council, and was elected to Congress in 1878.

Other successful politicians of the past include Conrad Baker, who served in the Civil War and was elected governor of Indiana in 1868; John W. Foster, an Evansville attorney who held several high diplomatic posts and served as Secretary of State under President Benjamin Harris in 1892 (his grandson was John Foster Dulles, secretary of state under Dwight D. Eisenhower); and Charles Denby, who was named Minister to China in 1881 and served in many other diplomatic posts. Born a slave in 1855, Dr. George Washington Buckner—noted educator and physician—was appointed Minister to Liberia by President Woodrow Wilson.

More recently, Richard Folz served as Lieutenant Governor from 1969 to 1973, and Robert D. Orr, who became governor in 1981, was the second person from Evansville to be elected to the state's highest office.

A president of National City Bank, C.B. Enlow (1879-1963) was a noted financier and community leader. One of the projects he championed was school construction. He directed a huge program that included the construction of Bosse High School, the purchase of land for Reitz Bowl, the construction of Lincoln High School, and the additions of gymnasiums or auditoriums to numerous public schools. Enlow Field is named in his honor.

Another noted financier was William H. McCurdy (1853-1930), a former president of both Old National Bank and the old Evansville Morris Plan. In 1903 McCurdy founded the Hercules Buggy Company and later brought Servel Refrigerator Manufacturing Company to Evansville. He made substantial endowment gifts to Evansville College (now the

Employees at Hermann Fendrich's cigar factory were mostly women, who could hand-roll as many as 100,000 cigars a day. (Elikofer Collection, Special Collections, Willard Library)

University of Evansville), where he served on the board of trustees. Two buildings have been named after him: UE's McCurdy Student Union and the old McCurdy Hotel (now the McCurdy Healthcare Center).

Industrialist Roderic Malcolm Koch (1904-1981) is known as one of the Evansville Museum's most generous benefactors and a developer of the world's first theme park, Santa Claus Land (now Holiday World).

Richard Meier (1897-1981), president of Interstate Finance Corporation (now American General Finance), provided key leadership to the city through an organization called Evansville's Future, a group of 100 businessmen formed to remedy the city's economic slump in the fifties. In addition, Meier worked diligently to break down racial barriers in the community and served on the Mayor's Human Relations Commission.

One of the first school leaders with a doctorate, Charles E. Rochelle (1895-1993) made it his life's work to improve educational opportunities for African-American children. He was a major champion of black high-school athletes and served on the Indiana Board of Education under six governors.

In 1998, Evansville lost two of its most influential movers and shakers—Norman P. Wagner and D.W. Vaughn, both former CEOs of Southern Indiana Gas and Electric (SIGECO), who were involved in practically every important community project. Wagner was a major force in attracting new business to the area and served as a director on numerous boards. Vaughn headed drives that raised hundreds of thousands of dollars for the United Way, Evansville Museum of Arts and Sciences, Evansville Philharmonic, and the University of Evansville, to name just a few. Of Vaughn, the *Evansville Courier & Press* editorialized just after his death: "In this time of time-consuming business commitments and out-of-town ownership of local business and industry, it becomes ever more difficult to find people such as Vaughn who will step up."

Willard Carpenter was a businessman and philanthropist who assisted runaway slaves on their way to freedom. (Special Collections, Willard Library)

Left: Noted educator and physician Dr. George Washington Buckner was appointed Minister to Liberia by President Woodrow Wilson. (Karl Kae Knecht Collection, Special Collections, Willard Library)
Center: C.B. Enlow was a noted financier and community leader who championed numerous community projects. (Karl Kae Knect, Special Collections, Willard Library)
Right: Robert D. Orr became Indiana's governor in 1981. He was the second person from Evansville to be elected to the state's highest office. (University of Southern Indiana/University Archives/Special Collections)

Among the most influential activists in the community have been women. Prior to 1920, women did not have the right to vote. Across the United States, and indeed the world, women responded with militancy, from suffragette marches in major U.S. cities to threatened guerrilla warfare on Parliament in Great Britain.

But militancy was not the tactic used by Evansville's first suffragettes, who feared that marching through the streets would hurt the cause.

Instead, their tact was more sedate, not at all radical. They organized a tearoom in the front lobby of a photographic studio on Main Street. It would be the gathering place of the Evansville chapter of the national Woman's Equal Franchise League. Its local organizers were president Dr. Frances Cantrell Hankins, one of the first female physicians in the area; and doctors' wives, Lelia Baughman, Maggie McCool, and Mary Cosby. They launched the local suffrage movement in 1913.

After just a year, the organization grew to 100 members. Other early suffragettes were among Evansville's most prominent women: Mrs. W.A. Carson, Emily Orr Clifford, Mrs. William Ehrich, Mrs. Edward Fehn, and Mrs. Louis Graf. Also involved was Miss Ethel McCollough, who became head librarian of Evansville's Public Library System in the 1920s and focused her attention on improving local libraries. (McCollough Branch Library is named for her.)

Indiana, however, was slow to adopt women's rights. The League accelerated its work, organizing suffrage leagues in nearby towns and setting up training classes for suffrage speakers. In 1917 Irene Erlbacher, then president of the local League, stated that the only hope for full suffrage in Indiana would be through an amendment to the federal Constitution.

Which is exactly what happened. Women across America won the right to vote on August 26, 1920 when the 19th Amendment went into effect.

In addition to pushing for women's rights, Evansville women have championed numerous other causes. Albion Fellows Bacon (1865-1933) was a nationally known reformer who worked tirelessly to abolish

tenements and other substandard housing over a 40-year period in Evansville and across the state. She organized the Vanderburgh Tuberculosis Association and helped found the old Boehne Camp Hospital for TB victims. In addition, she wrote Indiana's first housing law. The Albion Bacon Fellows Center, a domestic violence shelter for women and children, is named for her.

Countess Anneta Bentiboglia (1834-1905) left her native Italy to found the Monastery of St. Clare in Evansville. The countess has been beatified by the Roman Catholic Church—a step toward sainthood.

Sallie Wyatt Stewart (1881-1951), a former dean of girls at the old Lincoln High School, founded the Colored Federation of Women's Club in Evansville, a day nursery, and a boarding home for African-American girls. Stewart tried to bar in 1915 the showing of the *The Birth of a Nation*, a racist silent film produced by D.W. Griffith. In addition, she was charter member of the Interracial Commission in Evansville.

Called the "mother" of the University of Evansville, Emily Orr Clifford (1886-1955) spearheaded the effort to bring Moore's Hill College (the forerunner of UE) to town. She was also instrumental in the founding of the Evansville Museum and donated the land on which the YWCA was built.

Then there were the city's mayors. One of the most influential was Benjamin Bosse, a wealthy businessman who navigated Evansville through a period of great growth after he was elected to his first term in 1913. Under Bosse's administration, schools were built and improved, banks were constructed, a new police station was erected, and Bosse Field—dubbed by the mayor as the "biggest minor league park in the world"—was built.

Bosse is also credited with construction of the Cherry Branch Library, the first library north of the Ohio River established for African-Americans. He was among those who helped raise a half-a-million dollars to transfer a college in Moore's Hill, Indiana to Evansville, in

1919. The school would become the University of Evansville. Bosse served three terms—from 1913 to his death in 1922 at age 47 from pneumonia and a heart ailment.

Another three-term mayor was William H. Dress, who was responsible for bringing defense industries to Evansville during World War II. In office from 1935 to 1943, Dress was the moving force behind the effort to improve the airport so that it would be more attractive to the aircraft manufacturing industry during the war. Dress Plaza on the riverfront is named in his honor.

Vance Hartke was Evansville's mayor from 1957 to 1959, when he was elected to the U.S. Senate. During his mayoral campaign, Hartke vowed to build swimming pools in the city. He kept his promise and built four city pools, one of which still bears his name. Hartke served three terms as senator.

Another to make a lasting mark was Frank McDonald, Sr., a former sheriff and the most powerful mayor the city had ever known. He came to office during Evansville's most troubled period—just after more than 20,000 manufacturing jobs had been lost in the mid-fifties.

But under his twelve-year administration (1960-1971), revitalization swept the city. New industries were enticed to town. Urban renewal replaced crumbling slums. The Civic Center was constructed. Wesselman Park was established. City utilities were expanded.

Among his many other enduring legacies is what has become the University of Southern Indiana (USI). Almost single-handedly, McDonald made Evansville the site of an Indiana State University branch campus—which today is USI, the fastest growing university in the state.

Mayor Russell Lloyd was elected in 1971 and served two terms. Lloyd was a popular, charismatic leader who was responsible for improvements in city utility services and for winning federal money for the construction of the Lloyd Expressway. Just two months after retiring from office, Lloyd was gunned down at his Washington Avenue home by a 35-year-old Evansville woman who had a grievance against a city employee. She was sentenced to 40 years in prison.

Frank McDonald's son, Frank F. McDonald II, served as mayor from 1987 to 1999. He filled the unexpired term of Michael Vandeveer, who left office to enter business. McDonald was one of several leaders who pressed for the creation of the Evansville Economic Development Corporations, also known as Vision 2000. It has been a catalyst to attract new business and industry to the city and the region.

McDonald also concentrated on improving the city's infrastructure while reducing the cost of government. In addition, he oversaw the development of the first complete renovation plan for the city's Dress Plaza.

Though most people don't realize it, two Evansville attorneys—James D. Lopp Sr. (1915-1999) and Ted Lockyear Jr.—made legal history on June 5, 1961 when they convinced the United States Supreme Court that Leslie "Mad Dog" Irwin, an accused serial killer, did not receive a fair trial because of intense pretrial publicity in and around Evansville. In a historic decision, the Supreme Court overturned Irwin's first conviction and death sentence, and ordered a new trial. The Supreme Court wrote new rules guaranteeing a citizen's right to a trial free of "so huge a wave public passion created by media coverage." This marked the first time the high court had overturned a conviction due to pretrial publicity.

One of the first school leaders with a doctorate, Charles E. Rochelle (1895-1993) improved educational opportunities for African-American children and was a major champion of black high school atheletes. (University of Southern Indiana/ University Archives/Special Collections)

Albion Fellows Bacon was a nationally known social reformer who wrote Indiana's first housing law. (Karl Kae Knecht Collection, Special Collections, Willard Library)

Evansville has nurtured its share of celebrities and stars. One of the first to find fame was a silent film star named Jack Jacobi, the son of Dr. S.F. Jacobi who lived at 434 Chandler Avenue. As a young boy, Jacobi performed in local theater and eventually went to New York to appear in the new entertainment medium of moving pictures. He starred in three films before following the movie industry to California. There, he starred in at least two more films, *Marse Covington* and *Concealed Truth*.

Born in 1898 to Edwin and Ada Reynolds of Second Street and Chandler Avenue was a lovely, golden-haired child named Mary Ellen. She grew up to be Ziegfield Follies star and stage actress Marilyn Miller. Miller starred in the shows *Rosalie*, followed by *Smiles*, and *As Thousands Cheer*. Her films included *Sally*, *Sunny*, and *Her Majesty Love*.

At the peak of her popularity, she was stricken with a severe sinus infection that took her life suddenly on April 7, 1936. She was only 37.

Although Miller was enormously successful in her film and stage career, her private life was sometimes turbulent. She was married three times. Her first husband was killed in an automobile accident less than a year after their marriage. She wed Mary Pickford's brother Jack, but was divorced five years later. At the time of her death, she was married to a chorus man who had worked in one of her plays.

A contemporary of Miller's was the famed actress Louise Dresser, born Lula Josephine Kerlin in 1879 at 713 Locust Street in Evansville, the daughter of Mr. and Mrs. William Kerlin. Young Lula, who showed a talent for singing early on, had always admired soon-to-be-famous composer Paul Dresser, once the star comedian at the Apollo Theater in Evansville. Dresser was the older brother of the famous novelist, Theodore Dreiser. The two brothers had moved to Evansville in 1874 and lived in the 200 block of East Franklin Street.

Dresser helped Lula break into show business by arranging an audition for her in Chicago. She performed "My Gal Sal," which Paul had written in memory of his old girlfriend Sallie Walker, the madam of Evansville's fanciest brothels. Paul introduced Lula as his kid sister, so she said her name was Louise Dresser. She was a hit—and so was the song.

Louise Dresser's career blossomed. Once described as the most popular singer in America, she starred in numerous stage shows and silent pictures. Dresser retired to the Motion Picture Academy Country Home, where she died in 1965 at 86.

Among the more recent crop of Evansville actors to gain fame is Ron Glass, a graduate of the University of Evansville. Glass played detective Harris on the television series *Barney Miller* and starred in the NBC sitcom *Mr. Rhodes*. In a strange, tragic turn of events, his mother Lethia was found strangled to death in 1977 in her Fulton Avenue apartment. Her assailant was tried and convicted and is serving time in prison.

A 1946 gathering of Evansville mayors: Charles G. Covert, John W. Boehne, William H. Elmendorf, Herbert Males, Frank W. Griese, William H. Dress, and Manson Reichert. (University of Southern Indiana/University Archives/Special Collections)

Another Evansville native who has become a major artistic force in television is producer Matt Williams, a 1973 graduate of the University of Evansville. He wrote and produced such hit shows as *The Cosby Show*, *Home Improvement*, and *Roseanne*. His co-creator is David McFadzean, also from Evansville.

Internationally known saxophone player Boots Randolph lived in Evansville for a time before becoming famous. His hit, "Yakety Sax," put him on the charts. Among countless musical achievements, Randolph was the first musician ever to play sax on recordings with Elvis Presley and recorded soundtracks for eight of his movies.

Famed fashion designer Halston grew up in Evansville. He was best known for the pillbox hat, made fashionable by Jacqueline Kennedy; Ultrasuede; and body-conscious jerseys. Simplicity was his trademark, and he was fond of saying, "Less is more." Halston designed clothes for Elizabeth Taylor, Liza Minnelli, and other stars.

It would be hard to find a city this size in America that has produced more sports heroes than Evansville, Indiana. Quite probably the first of the city's crop of professional athletes was bicycling hall-of-famer Frank Kramer, an 18-time national sprint bicycling champion at the turn of the century.

Then came pros such as Bob Coleman, signed in 1910 by the Pittsburgh Pirates as a catcher; Sara Mae Turber, once ranked second in the world in women's lawn tennis; Charles Hornbostel, a track star and two-time member of the United States Olympic team in 1932 and 1936; and Bob Hamilton, a top professional golfer in the forties.

In professional football, the list of pros grows longer by the year. Among the former well-known players are: Ray Bawell, a defensive halfback for the Philadelphia Eagles; Don Hansen, a linebacker for the numerous professional teams, including the Green Bay Packers; Bob Griese, a star quarterback for the Miami Dolphins; and Scott Studwell, a middle linebacker for the Minnesota Vikings. Kevin Hardy, a graduate of Harrison High School, is a linebacker for the Jacksonville Jaguars.

Numerous baseball players from Evansville have earned fame on the professional playing field, too. Evansville native Pete Fox, an outfielder for the Detroit Tigers, is best remembered for setting a World Series record against St. Louis in 1938 by hitting six doubles in a seven-game series.

Evansville's Don Mattingly enjoyed a brilliant career with the New York Yankees, becoming the 11th Yankee to hit his 100th career home run. Mattingly retired from the Yankees in 1995 after thirteen years, and the Yankees retired his number, 23.

Pitcher Andy Benes, a graduate of the University Evansville, has played for the San Diego Padres, Seattle Mariners, St. Louis Cardinals, and most recently, the Arizona Diamondbacks. In 1994, he led the National League with 189 strikeouts.

Above: Evansville-born actress Louise Dresser was once described as the most popular singer in America and starred in numerous stage shows and silent pictures. She is pictured here in 1909 with Jack Gardner and Jack Lait. (University of Southern Indiana/University Archives/Special Collections) Left: Internationally known saxophone player Boots Randolph was a former resident of Evansville. (Celebrity Photo Collections, Willard Library)

One of the more recent, best-known professional athletes from Evansville is Calbert Cheaney, a 6-foot-7, 215-pound guard for the NBA's Washington Wizards. Another NBA player from Evansville is Walter McCarty, who plays for the Boston Celtics.

Evansville's famous athletes are admired not only for their skills on the playing fields and courts but also for their generosity of spirit to the community. They frequently return to their hometown to participate in various charity events or contribute funds to worthy causes. Through a personal donation, Cheaney, for example, made possible the construction of a church-affiliated education and recreation center in town.

On December 13, 1977, Evansville and the entire country were shocked when a plane carrying the University of Evansville basketball team crashed just after takeoff. All 29 people on board were killed, including 14 first-string players, coach Bobby Watson, officials of the university's athletic department, some fans, and popular Evansville radio sportscaster Marv Bates.

Through triumphs and tragedies, the character of Evansville has been revealed not in its outward cityscape of monuments and buildings, but rather in the inner striving of men and women who pushed back barriers of their own personal limitations to leave a legacy never to be forgotten. ▓

CHAPTER THREE
THE GOOD LIFE

The Charm of Small Town Living

Combined with a Big City Feeling

The bending, tranquil Ohio River borders some of Evansville's most historic neighborhoods. Photo by L. Kent Whitehead.

Lakeridge Crossing is an example of a total village community, with homes in many sizes, prices, and styles.
Photo by L. Kent Whitehead.

These lovely townhomes in nearby picturesque Newburgh are designed for those who prefer a leisurely lifestyle.
Photo by L. Kent Whitehead.

From a cluster of log cabins in 1818, only yards from the river-bank, Evansville's neighborhoods have fanned out over the decades, and in all directions. Today, these neighborhoods are as diverse as the population, with subdivisions of attractively landscaped homes; apartment or condominium complexes with all the amenities of a country club; century-old, museum-piece homes that have been scrupulously preserved; newer mini-mansions on rolling lots just outside the city; and resort-like retirement communities geared to older residents.

Drawn by short commutes to work and a cost of living that is well below the national average, people relocating to Evansville have at their doorsteps not only a variety of housing choices, but choices that are remarkably affordable—truly a steal, in fact. Consider that the average cost of a home nationally is about $130,000—much higher than Vanderburgh County's average of $96,500 in 1998. Further, appreciation is excellent too. In 1998, for example, the average sale price per home in Vanderburgh, Warrick, Posey, and Gibson counties ballooned by more than $10,000.

Besides its wide variety of pocketbook-friendly housing, Evansville is simply a wonderful place to raise a family. Neighborhoods have a friendliness and quality of life one might think is possible only in Andy Griffith's Mayberry. These are places where people really care about each other and newcomers feel like they've lived here all their lives.

Those who prefer real-city living adore downtown Evansville. Near the city's beginnings is the historic district, a crazy-quilt melange of residents representing nearly every segment of Evansville's population. The great homes found here were built in the mid-1800s, during the city's first big growth surge. Wealthy families who had made vast fortunes indulged their own tastes in styles traditionally symbolic of prestige and respectability, such as Victorian, Greek Revival, American Italianate, Federal, Queen Anne, French Second Empire, Neo-Classical, and variations thereon.

This part of downtown showcases many elegant mansions that hold their own special place in Evansville history. Built in 1900, the Elizabeth Hartmetz House at 220 S.E. Riverside Drive, along with the home next to it, stands on lots 1 and 2 of Hugh McGary's (founder of Evansville) original plat of Evansville. Down the street is the Charles Viele House, completed in 1856. Its third story features a lavish ballroom papered in gold leaf and capable of seating 60 people for dinner. The notorious showman P.T. Barnum once danced in the ballroom, and the Swedish nightingale Jenny Lind sang in the Viele's drawing room.

Modeled after an English manor house of the Tudor period, the Samuel Orr House at 603 S.E. First Street is the boyhood home of former Indiana Governor Robert D. Orr. A few blocks away at 310 S.E. First Street is the Watkins F. Nisbet Home, a Victorian mansion reputed to be the largest ever built in the city. In addition, it was the first home in Evansville to have a telephone, installed in 1882.

Close by is an Evansville neighborhood known as the Culver District. It includes portions of Southeast Second, Madison Avenue, Howard Street, and Parrett Street. Originally, it was a farm owned by Reverend Robert Parrett of England, who established the first permanent Methodist congregation in Evansville in 1825.

Lakeside cabins are the perfect get-away any time of the year. Photo by L. Kent Whitehead.

This is a charming neighborhood where one can feel the texture of the past. Architecturally intriguing, its silent surviving examples include Queen Anne, bungalow, prairie, Tudor, Italianate, and Colonial Revival.

A landmark in the neighborhood is the Rathbone Retirement Apartments at 1320 S.E. Second Street. It opened in 1915 as a nonde-nominational residential facility for elderly women of limited income.

Among the many homes of note is the Louis Daus House at 1403 S.E. Second Street. It was once the residence of the founder of Anchor Industries. By the early eighties, the home was so dilapidated that it was nearly razed, until grandson John Daus Jr. renovated it in 1981 and sold it to Randall T. Shepard, now chief justice of the Indiana Supreme Court, who finished the restoration. This home, and others like it, is a testament to what loving, thoughtful preservation can achieve.

The King Shotgun House at 20 Madison Avenue stands in fascinating contrast to the larger homes in the district. It features a lovely Venetian window in its gable peak. Built in the late 1800s, "shotgun homes" housed the city's working class citizens. The homes were constructed so that the front and back doorways were perfectly aligned. Someone once observed that if a shotgun were fired through the front door, the charge presumably would go through the house and out the back door without hitting anything—hence, the name "shotgun." Shotgun houses can be found throughout the city. Many have been carefully remodeled and turned into lovely residences or rental homes.

Downtown riverfront apartments afford the opportunity to enjoy the scenic Ohio River. Photo by L. Kent Whitehead.

DOWN ON THE FARM
BAKERY
Mayse Farm Market
Mayflower
FRESH FRUITS
AND VEGETABLES

The great growth of the mid-1800s spilled over to Evansville's West Side, where other stylish residences were built. On Wabash Avenue, a number of large homes were erected for some of the city's business and civic leaders, with an architectural flamboyance that had been previously found only in downtown neighborhoods.

Further east of the city is the Bayard Park neighborhood, an early twentieth-century residential area in which commercial development was barred. Visitors who stroll through the tree-canopied neighborhood, with its cottages, bungalows, duplexes, and two-story homes, will be transported back in time for a nostalgic glimpse into how the middle-class of Evansville lived during this period.

These are just a few of the many historic city neighborhoods that began to mushroom at the turn of the century and beyond. Fortunately, numerous older homes throughout Evansville's historic neighborhoods have been faithfully remodeled. Artistically painted and refurbished, they are fashionable residences of people who take considerable pride in their homes.

Whatever their age, these historic dwellings and neighborhoods have one thing in common—they are permeated with the flavor of Evansville. Living here, you are close to the history and heartbeat of the city.

Home building in Evansville was slack during the Great Depression, but picked up considerably afterwards. The famous flood of 1937 devastated the city and those who remembered it made an exodus to higher ground. As a result, there was a burst of new construction on the East Side, and around Stringtown, McCutchanville, and Newburgh. The result was the construction of many attractive subdivisions outside the city.

During World War II, the city's population soared with the inflow of workers hired by Evansville's flourishing wartime industries, which included the production of LSTs, fighter planes, and ammunition. After the war, there was a huge construction boom as well. Veterans returned from war, got married, became fathers—and needed homes for their growing families. As a result, sprawling subdivisions sprouted all over the city and in its suburbs. One of the greatest markets lay in the masses of returning GIs who wanted homes of their own but for very low downpayments. One solution was prefabricated homes pioneered in the area by Guthrie May and Company, which built entire subdivisions of these homes throughout the city. Other fancier, higher-priced homes were constructed, too.

Today, the city and its suburbs are experiencing a home construction boom not seen since the forties—a result of the influx of new industry being attracted to Evansville and the surrounding area.

Numerous residential developments have been springing up on the East Side, North Side, and in Newburgh. Found in rolling, wooded, and pastoral settings, these developments are master-planned communities featuring distinct neighborhoods, with the choice of estate-sized homes, family homes, starter homes, and empty-nester homes within the same community. Many of the neighborhoods feature elaborately landscaped boulevards, pristine lakes, clubhouses, swimming pool, and tennis courts.

This page: Visitors and residents alike can step back in time in numerous antique stores found everywhere in the city and its surrounding neighborhoods. Photo by L. Kent Whitehead. Opposite page: The Farmer's Municipal Market near downtown is a lively gathering place for people all over the area. Photo by L. Kent Whitehead.

Evansville families flock to Burdette Park for summertime fun.
Photos by L. Kent Whitehead.

A much sought-after area is McCutchanville near the Vanderburgh-Gibson County line. This upscale area is known not only for its spectacular older homes, many on huge, graceful lots, but also for its developing subdivisions built on gently rolling hills with a peaceful privacy found only in country living.

The fastest-growing neighborhoods are the new residential developments found in northeastern Vanderburgh County—close to the city comforts of Evansville, yet within a short commute to Toyota Motor Manufacturing complex in Gibson County. The trend is toward "total village communities," with estate homes, single-family homes, condos, and patio homes, all gathered around recreational facilities such as golf courses. Homes in communities like these, and other area subdivisions, come in many sizes, prices, and styles.

There is certainly no shortage of apartments or condos in the area, either. In Vanderburgh County in 1999, construction began on 362 apartment buildings—probably the highest number of new apartments ever built in the county's history. Anyone desiring the convenience and affordability of apartment dwelling should have no trouble finding a place to call home.

Downtown riverfront apartments, for example, give city-dwellers the opportunity to gaze out the window and watch the last moments of a brilliant sunset on the western reach of the Ohio River. Likewise, from

Evansville has idyllic settings for anyone who loves to fish, young or old. Photo by L. Kent Whitehead.

a townhouse or condo near the riverfront in Newburgh, residents can look up from their morning newspapers and see a barge being tugged through the sun-spangled waters of the Ohio.

In Evansville's central city, a sense of community mission has breathed new life into neighborhoods. One of the most dynamic examples of this spirit is the development of Lincoln Estates, a private, $8.1-million, 22-building project on Lincoln Avenue between Garvin and Governor Streets. Designed like a traditional neighborhood with distinct architectural features, the development provides town-houses for central city residents at very affordable rents. Lincoln Estates replaces the historic Lincoln Gardens, a housing project built in the 1930s by the Public Works Administration. Saved from the wrecking ball, one of the old Lincoln Gardens apartments has been converted into an African-American museum.

Rather than pulling up stakes to go south or west, many Evansville retirees prefer to stay put. One reason is the availability of resort-like retirement communities around the city. An example is Solarbron Pointe, one of Indiana's finest retirement communities. Hugged by rolling hills and natural woodlands, the community is nestled in a serene residential neighborhood on the far west side of Evansville near the University of Southern Indiana. Each private apartment home has a beautiful view of the lake, woods, or the garden courtyard. There are amenities galore, including a fitness and wellness center, an all-faiths chapel, library, hair salon, barbershop, chef-prepared dining, year-round activities, and much more.

Another one of the finest senior adult living communities in the region is Holiday Village, which provides independent and assisted living for elderly residents. This expanding community features private apartments, a physician and diagnostic center, and activities designed to help seniors live life to the fullest. Many other adult living centers do the same and are found in and around the Evansville community, making the area a much-loved haven for retirees.

Lovingly landscaped gardens are everywhere too, thanks in large part to the effort of Operation City Beautiful, Inc., an organization whose mission is area-wide beautification. But neighborhood associations share in the credit too, and are often formally recognized throughout the year for their many landscaping and improvement projects.

As important as specific neighborhoods and housing opportunities is the spirit of the people who live in those neighborhoods and homes. An integral part of the heritage here is the attachment to houses of worship, where people find affirmation of their deepest convictions and values. When new families and individuals move here, they are likely to find a house of worship that will fulfill their spiritual needs.

There are many major denominational churches, as well as non-denominational churches, throughout the city and its environs, providing a spiritual anchor to the neighborhoods they serve and offering services to the community as a whole. The Adath B'nai Israel Temple on Washington Avenue is the major synagogue serving Evansville's Jewish community. The temple offers special events and classes for the public too. Near the University of Evansville on Lincoln Avenue is the Islamic Center of Evansville, the mosque where the city's Muslims worship. There is also a contingent of the Baha'i faith, a religion that advocates world peace and the abolition of prejudice.

In Evansville, followers of different faiths often unite at the Four Freedoms monument to celebrate the National Day of Prayer, declared by the Continental Congress in 1775 but later not observed. Congress established a day of prayer in 1952, and in 1988, the first Thursday of May was officially designated the National Day of Prayer.

In a further show of religious unity, a group called the Evansville Interfaith Council is dedicated to breaking down the barriers of misunderstanding among different faith groups in the area. Religious leaders feel that the council has been a wonderful way for Evansville to develop as a whole community.

In Evansville, the people have hearts as big as their community. Nowhere is this stronger than in the spirit of volunteerism that permeates the entire city. Neighborhoods are known for their "pitch-in" attitudes, and citizen action has molded the character of the city. Neighborhood associations visit the elderly to assist with domestic duties, offer after-school activities for children, and remain deeply committed to development projects. In short, people here know that if they are not helping out, they are standing in the way.

In addition, Habitat for Humanity is active throughout the region, making the American dream of owning a home come true for countless citizens. Further, the United Way of Southwestern Indiana regularly raises record amounts of contributions from citizens and businesses alike and disperses them to various United Way agencies for the good of the community.

Across Evansville and in the surrounding communities, projects involving youth, the elderly, housing rehabilitation, hospice care, leadership training, marriage-building, health care, and much more are a deeply ingrained way of life. Nothing contributes more to Evansville's character than the neighborly, community-minded people who call it home. ▨

This page: Operation City Beautiful, Inc. is an organization dedicated to area-wide beautification. Photo by L. Kent Whitehead. Opposite page: Burdette Park is a 200-acre paradise, offering countless recreational activities. Photo by L. Kent Whitehead.

The Evansville community embodies a diveristy of faiths, evidenced by the number of churches, synagogues, and other places of worship throughout the city.
Photos by L. Kent Whitehead.

Choir members are the "ornaments" in the Living Christmas Tree, presented annually by Bethel Temple, a local Christian church. Photo by L. Kent Whitehead.

Boating is a favorite pursuit among Evansville residents.
Photo by L. Kent Whitehead.

Helfrich Golf Course is one of several world-class golf courses in the area. Photo by L. Kent Whitehead.

Photo by L. Kent Whitehead.

Photo by L. Kent Whitehead.

Photo by L. Kent Whitehead.

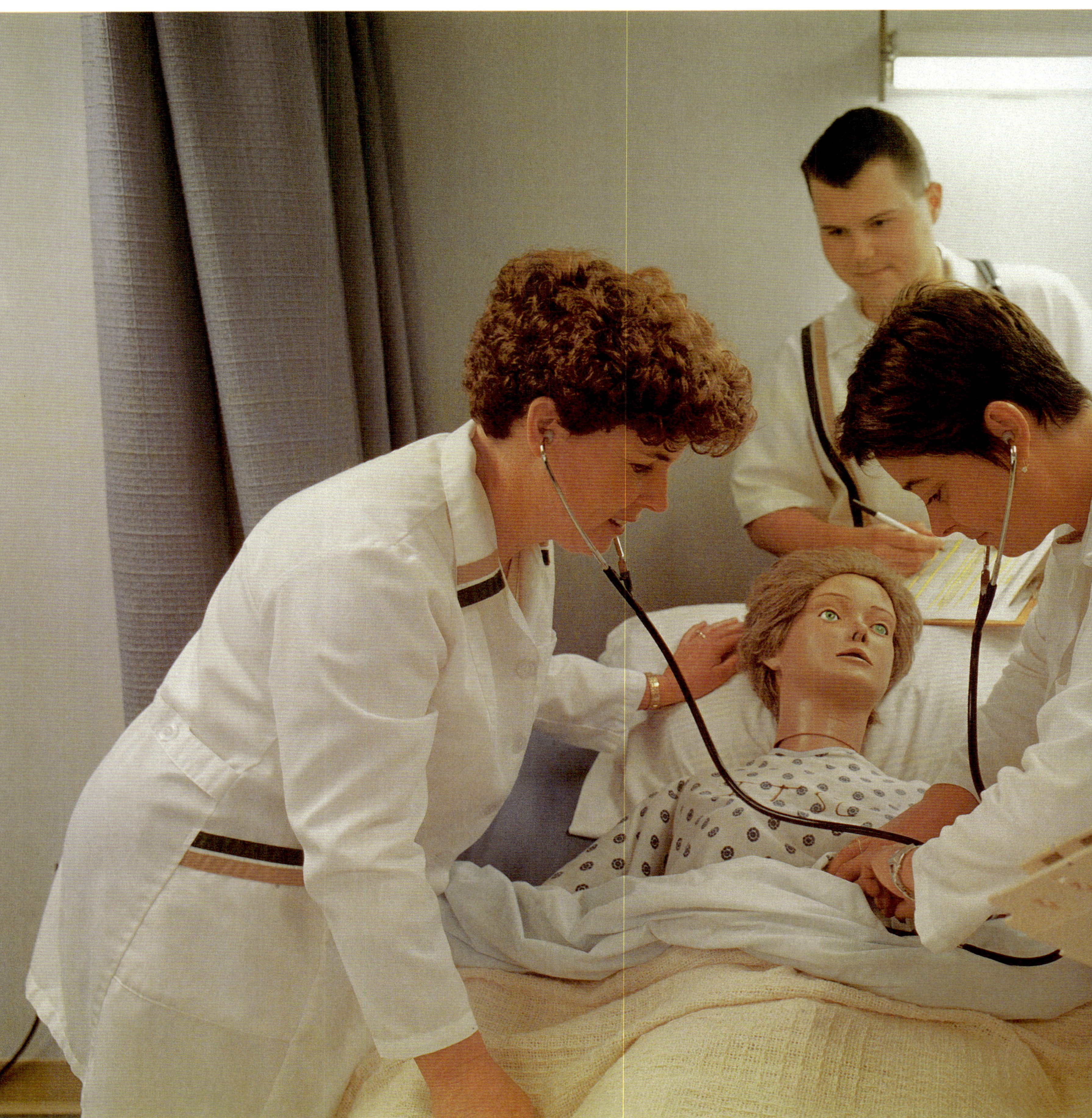

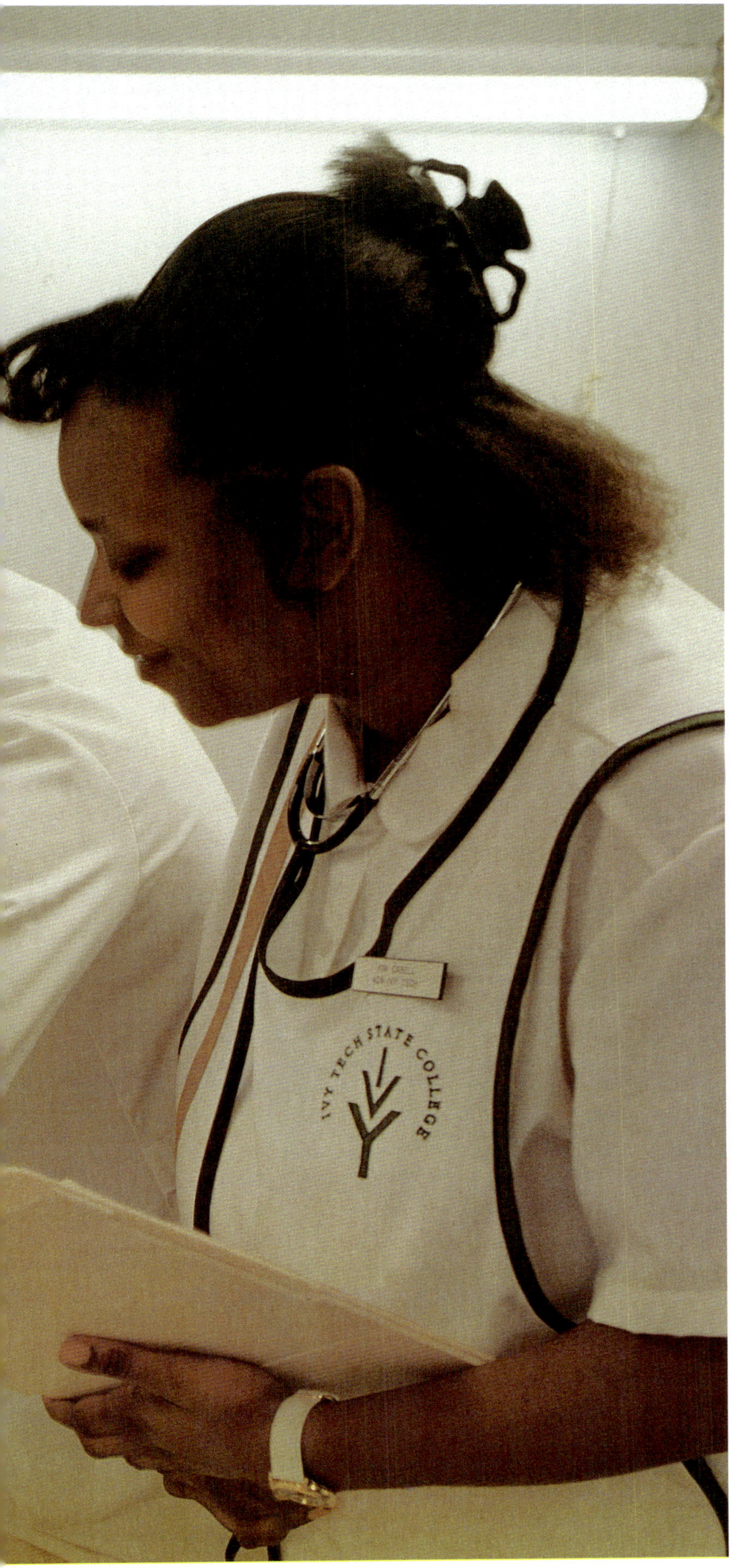

4

CHAPTER FOUR

HEALTH CARE

A Medical Community Dedicated to Making a

Difference in the Lives and Health of People

Health care professionals in Evansville are thoroughly trained in their respective fields. Photo by L. Kent Whitehead.

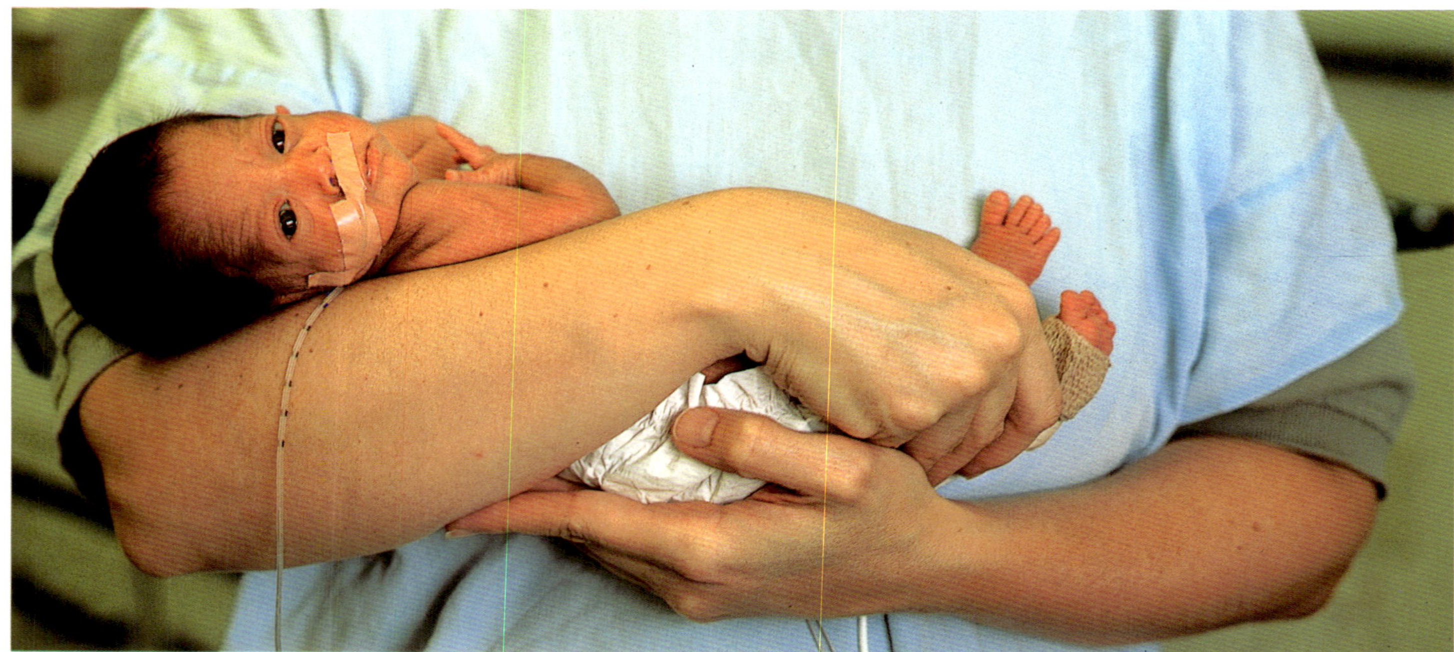

Step into any hospital, clinic, physician's office, or other medical facility in the Evansville region, and you'll notice the things you'd expect to see in a modern health care setting. The latest equipment, the finest facilities, efficiency in full swing. But look a little closer, and you'll sense an atmosphere of compassion and concern that can come only from a community of medical professionals with a special spirit of caring.

And that's exactly what the Evansville region offers—a community of thousands of health care professionals dedicated to healing and to providing the highest standards of care available anywhere.

It's no wonder, then, that a number of Evansville's health care providers have been recognized nationally as among the best in the United States. The region's health care institutions offer the latest in treatments and technologies—advances that are always on the leading edge of medical science. Annually, the area's two major hospitals operate approximately 1,000 beds in their facilities and deliver over 4,500 babies. More than 500 doctors and health care specialists and more than 100 dentists, orthodontists, and oral surgeons practice in the area.

Outpatient clinics, community health centers, behavioral health centers, home health agencies, free-standing surgery centers, and wellness and fitness centers also serve community health care needs. The city is also home to more than 35 nursing homes and other health care institutions dedicated to proving services to seniors and physically challenged individuals. Supplementing local health care services, the Evansville-Vanderburgh County Health Department provides routine immunizations, flu shots, and a variety of health screening tests at no charge.

In a nation where runaway health care expenditures have been the norm, Evansville is an exception. Health care costs in the area are just 90 percent of the national average, according to a survey by the American Chamber of Commerce Researchers Association.

Across today's ever-changing health care landscape, health provider networks have burgeoned, answering the call of the public and business alike for broad-coverage benefit plans and demonstrable quality that

St. Mary's Medical Center is a recognized leader and innovator in pediatric and neonatal care. Photo by L. Kent Whitehead.

leads to reduced costs. In Evansville there are numerous provider organizations, offering a variety of excellent health plan options. Providers include Anthem-Blue Cross and Blue Shield, the Sagamore Health Network, HealthLink, M-Plan, and Welborn Health Plans.

Locally owned Welborn Health Plans is one of the top-performing Health Maintenance Organizations (HMOs) in the United States. In fact, a leading news magazine gave the plan a five-star ranking and a score that put it second to what the magazine considered the best HMO in the nation. Another national magazine has rated the Welborn plan among the top HMOs in the country for three years in a row.

Many local businesses have established workplace wellness programs that help employees identify risk factors for disease, such as high blood pressure and obesity, and help them take steps to improve their health. In addition, Evansville's health care institutions regularly promote good health through community education and lifestyle programs which help individuals make choices that maximize their health and quality of life.

Evansville and its surrounding area have two large health care systems: Deaconess Hospital and St. Mary's Health Care Services. Both have been ranked among the nation's best for the quality of care they provide.

Deaconess Hospital

Established in 1892 by a group of Protestant laymen and ministers, Deaconess Hospital was modeled after the Deaconess hospitals of Europe, which employed consecrated nurses to heal patients' bodies while also nourishing the spirit. The hospital was initially housed in a large frame house at the corner of Mary and Iowa Streets, also the site at which Clara Barton, the honored founder of the Red Cross, had directed her work of aiding Ohio River flood victims in 1884. After decades of prodigious expansion and modernization, Deaconess Hospital has grown to cover more than 20 city blocks at its 600 Mary Street location. It is today one of the most respected medical centers in the United States, with a reputation for advanced technology, highly skilled physicians, a professional, dedicated staff, and compassionate care. The hospital serves the people of southern Indiana, southeastern Illinois, and western Kentucky.

The hospital's many areas of excellence include cardiac care, cancer care, emergency medicine, pulmonary medicine, and ortho-neuro care. Other major services include hospital-based home care, hospice care, outpatient surgery, family-centered maternity care, comprehensive rehabilitation, women's services, a pediatric unit, and medical, surgical, and cardiac intensive care units. Deaconess is also a leader in geriatric medicine, particularly with its Medwise Centers, which deliver comprehensive primary care services exclusively to people 65 and older.

Deaconess has been named among the "Top 100" hospitals in the United States. In its 10th annual "America's Best Hospitals" ranking in 1999, U.S. *News & World Report* named Deaconess Hospital as 34th best in the nation for the treatment of hormonal disorders. Treated by endocrinologists, these include thyroid and pituitary gland disorders and hormonal/glandular disorders that can produce such conditions as diabetes. The magazine based its rankings on quality of care measures such as technology, nursing care, and reputation among physicians.

One of the hospital's prime concerns is helping people with heart disease or other heart-related problems. Toward that end, Deaconess has a comprehensive cardiac program with a full range of advanced cardiac services, including prevention and wellness, chest pain management, diagnostic testing, acute treatment, and rehabilitation. The hospital has a long tradition of leadership in cardiac care. It pioneered the area's first cardiac catheterization lab in 1972 and first open heart surgery program in 1974.

Numerous home health agencies serve and support the community's medical needs. Photo by L. Kent Whitehead.

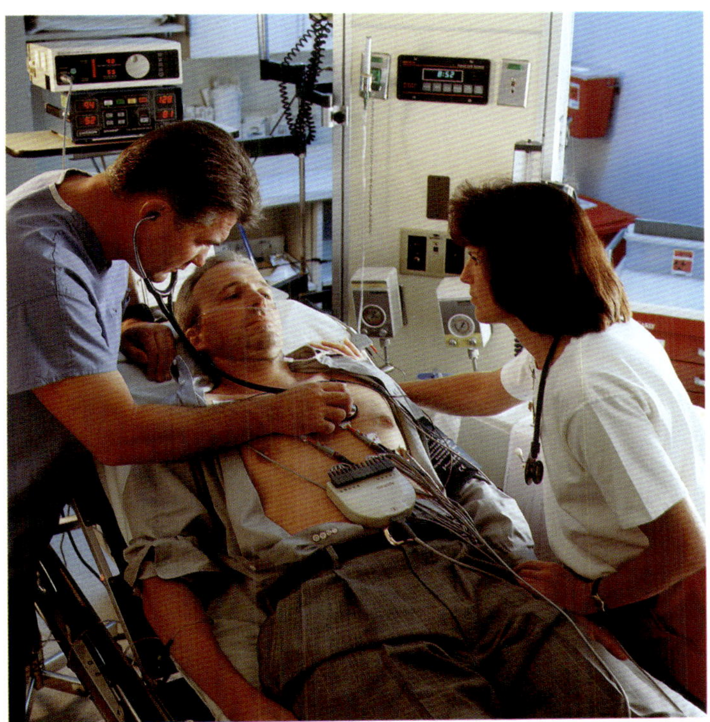

Deaconess Hospital has been ranked among the top 100 hospitals nationwide for its quality of care. Photo courtesy of Deaconess Hospital.

Deaconess Hospital's Heart Care Services received the 1999 National Consumer Choice Award. This recognition was based on a syndicated study of nearly 170,000 households that selected Deaconess as the most preferred facility for Heart Care Services in this metropolitan area. A leader in emergency care, Deaconess Hospital is the only emergency facility in Evansville with a board-certified emergency physician on duty 24 hours a day, seven days a week. Nearly 50,000 patients receive care each year at the hospital's Emergency Center. Further, Deaconess is notable for its Regional Emergency Services program, a network of community hospitals and emergency medical service providers throughout the tri-state area. The program staffs hospital emergency departments, develops emergency response protocols, and conducts education programs for emergency room staffs and other emergency medical providers.

Deaconess Hospital has long distinguished itself as one of the most progressive institutions in the nation for the treatment of cancer. The Deaconess Cancer Center is the only facility in Evansville with accreditation from the American College of Surgeons. Today, the hospital is

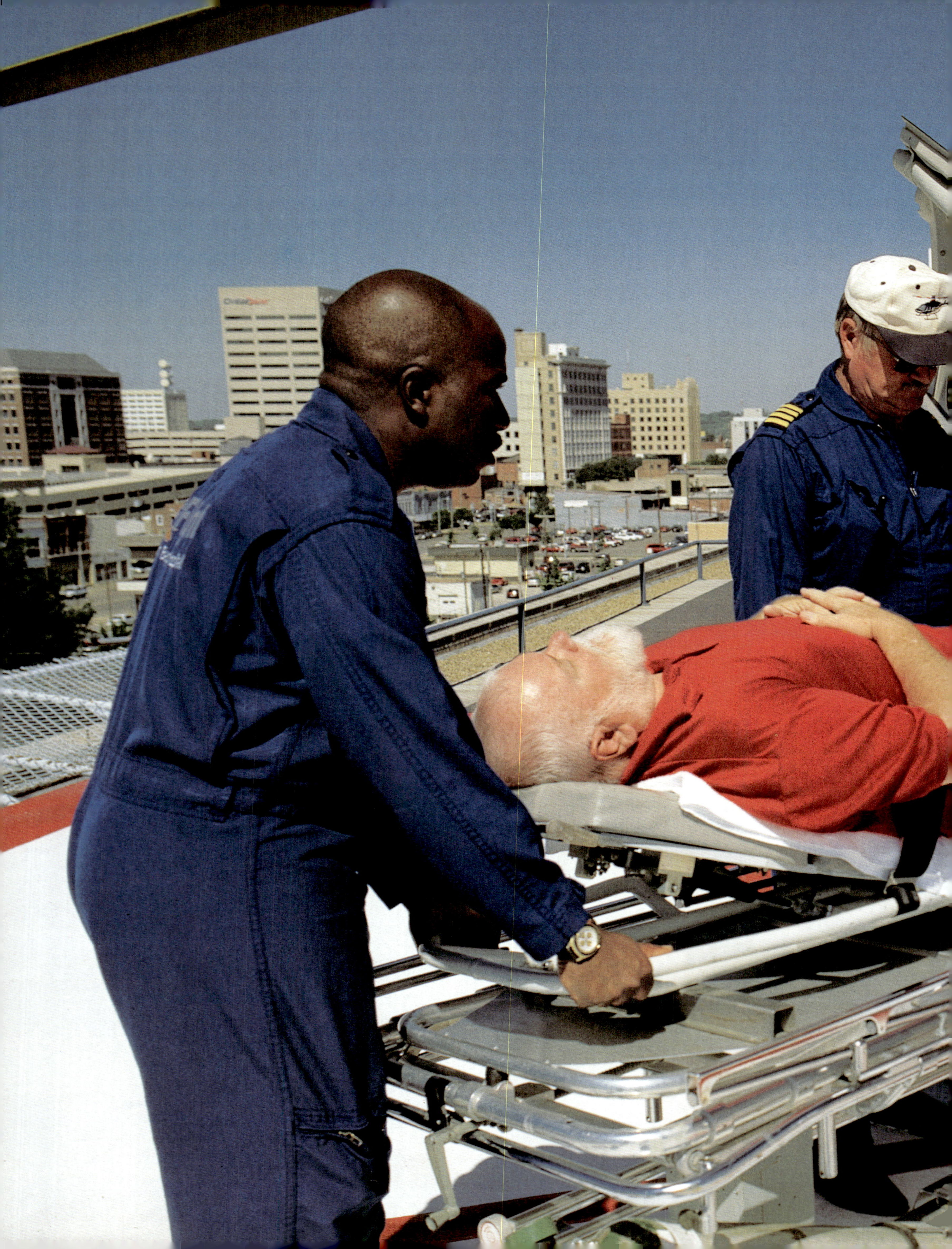

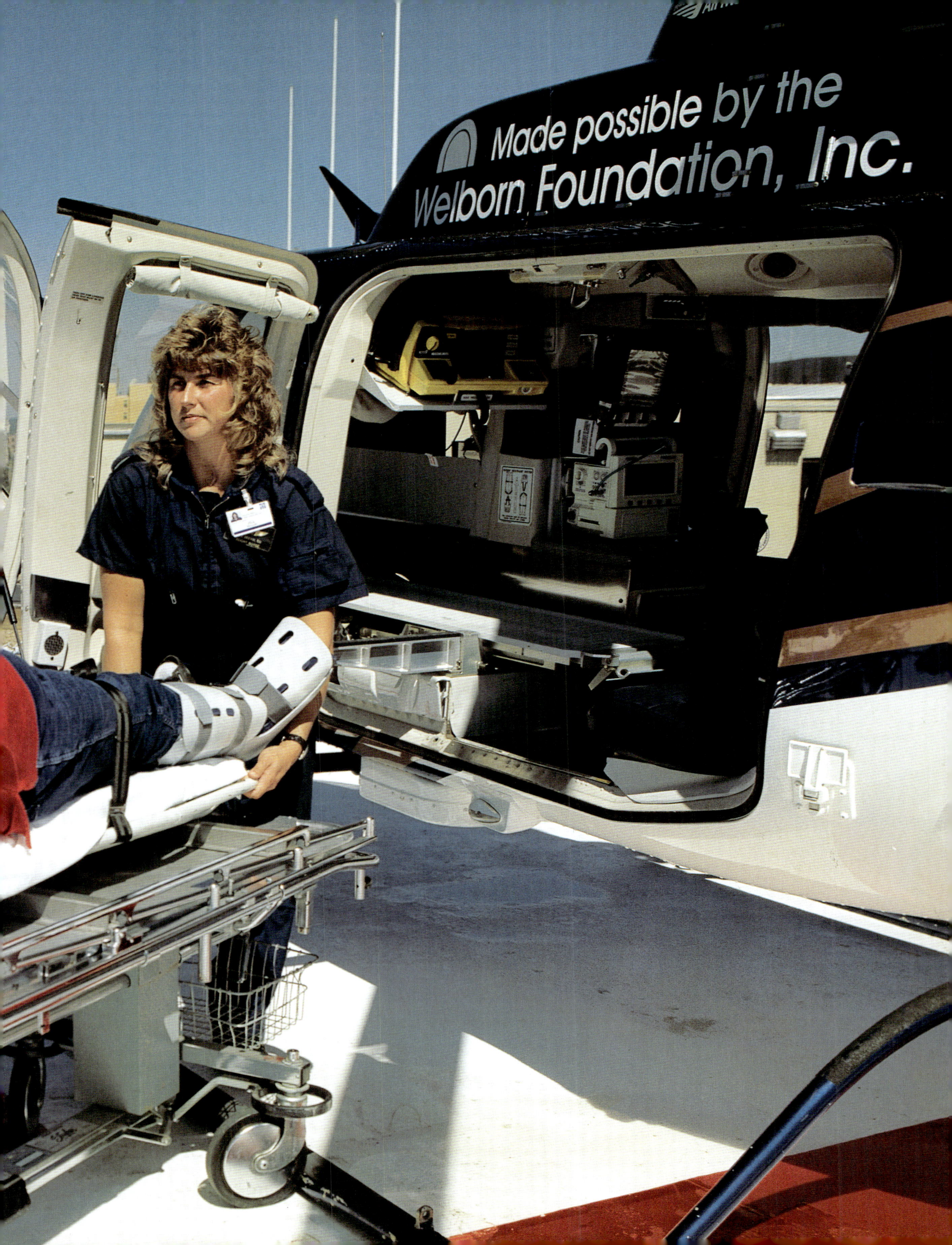

Made possible by the
Welborn Foundation, Inc.

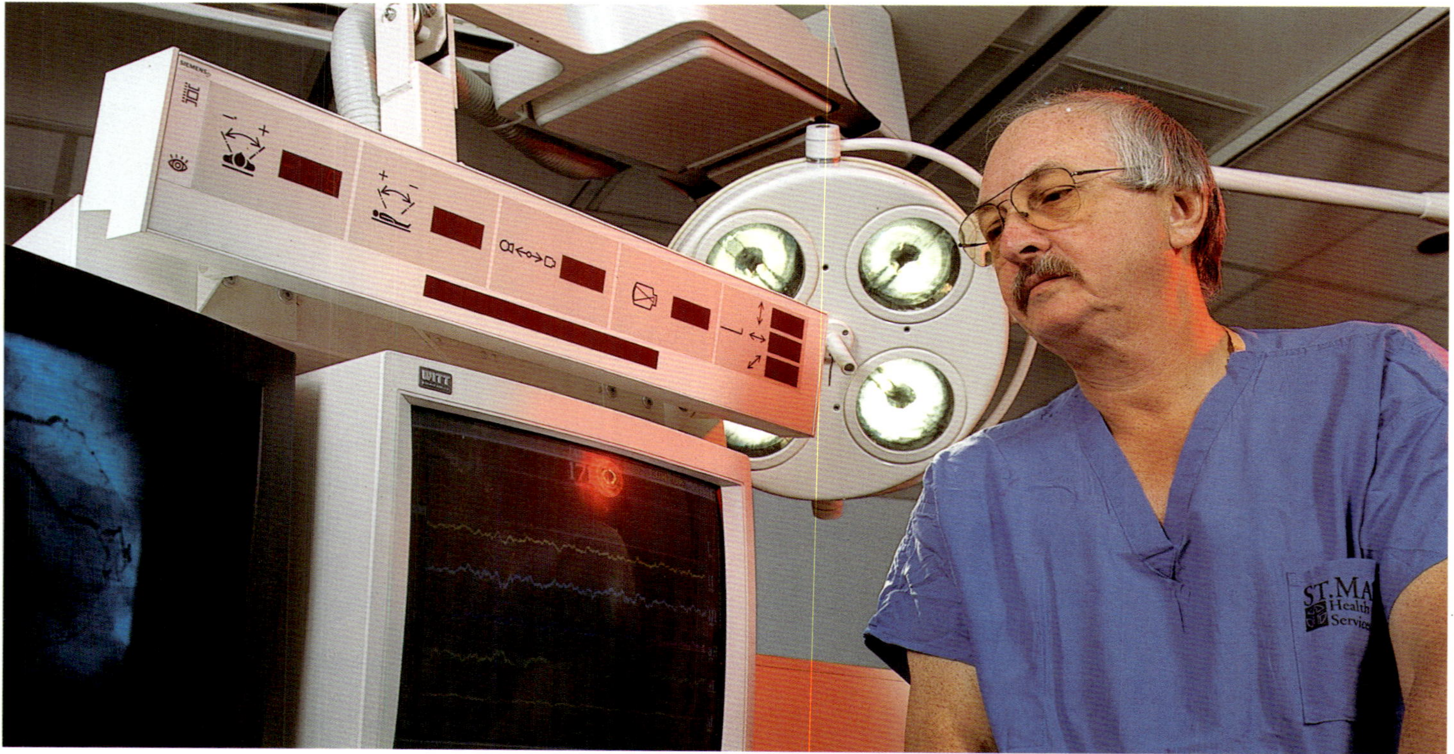

expanding and modernizing its cancer care facilities, originally established in 1974. In partnership with Welborn Clinic, the hospital is constructing a free-standing cancer care center on the Deaconess campus that will serve the entire region. It will offer a full range of diagnostic and outpatient therapy services.

Now more than ever, Americans are turning to alternative medicine for disease prevention and treatment. A recent national study reported that four out of every ten Americans are using alternative therapies. What's more, approximately sixty percent of households view alternative medicine as complementary to traditional medicine.

With such intense public interest in alternative medicine, Deaconess Hospital several years ago formed a task force of health care professionals and community representatives to investigate the feasibility of incorporating alternative care into traditional health care. The hospital determined that alternative medicine, also called holistic medicine, could complement and enhance traditional therapies. As a result, the hospital added holistic resources to its Resource Center for Healthy Living, which offers a variety of prevention and wellness services. Holistic Resources provides people with tools to heal the body, mind, and spirit; manages a lending library of more than a thousand books, tapes, and videos; and conducts ongoing holistic health classes for the community.

In 1998 Deaconess Hospital purchased the private Charter Behavioral Health Systems hospital on the east side of Evansville. Renamed Deaconess Crosse Pointe, the 60-bed hospital provides a full array of inpatient and outpatient psychiatric and chemical dependency programs for children and adults. In addition, the staff is specially trained in geriatric psychiatry.

Deaconess also serves as a community teaching hospital, with programs for residents and medical students in family practice, obstetrics and gynecology, internal medicine, surgery, and other specialties.

After more than a century of care to the tri-state, Deaconess Hospital upholds the convictions upon which it was built—compassionate care, quality caregivers, and commitment to delivering the highest technology available by medical science.

St. Mary's Health Care Services

Evansville's first community hospital was St. Mary's, established in 1872. It was housed initially in a government building originally intended to be a marine hospital for treating ailing river men. The facility, however, remained empty most of the time until some forward-thinking business leaders purchased the building and approached the Daughters of Charity about operating it. The hospital grew in response to demands for medical care, relocating to a new facility at First Avenue and Columbia in 1854. As the number of patients grew steadily, St. Mary's moved to the city's eastside and began building on an 80-acre tract between Lincoln and Washington Avenues, where it is now located.

The hospital is today St. Mary's Medical Center, named as one of the nation's "Top 100" hospitals three years in a row. It is the area's largest employer, making it a major contributor to the local economy. The medical center is a respected leader in numerous areas of health care, with hundreds of physicians and other health care providers dedicated to making a difference in people's lives.

St. Mary's, for example, has an outstanding reputation for excellence in areas of women's health, maternity care, and pediatrics. At St. Mary's Breast Center, a woman can have a mammogram and receive results in the very same visit. In the 1950s, the hospital was the first in the nation to allow fathers into birthing rooms—one of the many innovations in maternity care that continues to this day. St. Mary's has also expanded its women's services, including a one-stop women's health resource center.

St. Mary's has the only Pediatric Intensive Care Unit in the region. It is a specialized facility offering leading-edge capabilities, with specialists in pediatric cardiology, neurology, oncology, and other care areas available to meet young patients' unique needs.

In addition, St. Mary's has the only Level III neonatal intensive care unity in the area. Staffed by experienced caregivers in neonatology, St. Mary's Newborn Intensive Care Unit provides state-of-the-art technology in a fully equipped facility.

St. Mary's is also recognized as a top provider of cardiac care in the region and is home to the St. Mary's Heart Institute. The Heart Institute has led the way in providing life-saving care, leading edge diagnostic technology, and a wide variety of sophisticated treatment options. Open heart surgery, implantable defibrillators, and balloon angioplasty are part of the hospital's cardiac care program. To reduce the risk of future problems, cardiac rehabilitation begins almost immediately and continues after discharge. Further, community education and screenings emphasize the value of prevention.

Housed inside the hospital's Emergency Department, the Chest Pain Emergency Unit is the only such unit in the city. It is staffed with professionals who can effectively evaluate chest pain cases and respond quickly if a cardiac problem is detected.

St. Mary's has greatly expanded its cardiac treatment services with the formation of the Cardiac Emergency Network. The first treatment program of its kind in the tri-state, the network establishes an important relationship between hospitals in surrounding communities and St. Mary's Medical Center, opening up lines of communication and continuity of care. Further, the Network allows a systematic team approach in caring for heart attack victims, therefore reducing the time between the onset of heart attack symptoms and advanced medical treatment.

St. Mary's Cancer Center was the first in the area to bring together cancer care services such as surgery, radiation, and chemotherapy in one location. With the adjacent hospital and St. Mary's Breast Center nearby, all cancer services are available within a 500-yard radius.

The Cancer Center features state-of-the-art diagnostic equipment, too, and includes a patient resource center for the community. Computers linked to cancer information sites on the Internet, a library of books and videos on cancer, and a staff that will connect patients and their families to appropriate community resources are all available

Introduced in the summer of 1997, St. Mary's Mobile Outreach Clinic is a medical office on wheels. It travels to neighborhoods and shelters, serving those who otherwise might not have access to important medical services, such as general medical care, health screenings, and immunizations.

St. Mary's is an innovator in geriatrics. Its Senior Health Center is an outpatient facility for seniors and is staffed by four geriatricians. The only one of its kind in the area, the Center provides primary care

St. Mary's Medical Center has been named as one of the nation's "Top 100" hospitals three years in a row. Photo by L. Kent Whitehead.

geriatric services and conducts comprehensive geriatric assessments for patients referred by their doctors. The assessment addresses a patient's health condition, plus mental and social status.

St. Mary's Regina Continuing Care Center cares for the elderly and convalescing in a large, modern facility located on the St. Mary's campus. The 137-bed center is fully accredited by the Joint Commission on Accreditation of Healthcare Organizations. To achieve a home-like setting, Regina has implemented the "Eden Alternative" by adding plants and animals to the daily lives of residents. Pet therapy helps residents become caregivers as well as receivers, and can have a beneficial effect on health and mental outlook.

In 1999, St. Mary's Health Care Services purchased Welborn Baptist Hospital, located in downtown Evansville. Established in 1894, Welborn has a long tradition of bringing innovative, quality health care to the community. These accomplishments have included LifeFlight, the first and only operating air ambulance in the city; leadership in maternal and neonatal care, rehabilitation, psychiatric care, and occupational health; and the introduction of Magnetic Resource Imaging (MRI) and other new technologies to the Evansville healthcare scene.

Emergency medical services such as LifeFlight help ensure that people in need get the very best care, quickly.
Photo by L. Kent Whitehead.

Facilities such as the YMCA offer exercise and preventive health programs designed to promote wellness.
Photo by L. Kent Whitehead.

As a result of this acquisition, a parent company was formed—Mission Health System, Inc. Mission Health includes St. Mary's Medical Center, Welborn Baptist Hospital, St. Mary's Warrick, Mission Health Medical Group (a practice management organization), and the Harrisburg (Illinois) Medical Center, as well as specialty care centers for a range of health and medical needs.

The acquisition of Welborn expanded St. Mary's services in several important areas. One of these is rehabilitation. Located on the Welborn campus, St. Mary's Rehabilitation Institute is the largest rehabilitation facility in the city. Designed to help people recover as quickly and completely as possible, the institute provides comprehensive medical rehabilitation for stroke, orthopedic disabilities, pulmonary disease, multiple trauma, brain injury or spinal cord injury, neurological, and neuromuscular conditions.

In downtown Evansville, St. Mary's operates Mulberry Center, the largest local psychiatric unit. Formerly a part of Welborn Baptist Hospital, it is a 68-bed inpatient psychiatric unit and offers an array of outpatient counseling and mental health services. These include a 10-bed mental health unit for the elderly.

St. Mary's Health Care Services is operated by the Daughters of Charity National Health System, the largest not-for-profit health system in the United States. Its mission is to make a positive difference in the lives and health status of individuals and the community. At St. Mary's, this mission of bringing improved health to the entire community has continued, unbroken, for more than 125 years.

Women's Health Initiatives

Evansville's health care providers are deeply committed to women's health. St. Mary's is building a women's center on its grounds. The center connects to the medical center for immediate access to emergency and tertiary services. It will include a new labor, delivery, and postpartum recovery area for childbirths as well as a resource center for education, information, and outreach. Obstetricians and gynecologists will have private offices at the center, too.

Deaconess broke ground for its Women's Hospital in 1999. The new hospital, which is the only one of its kind in the region, offers comprehensive health care services for women. These include obstetrics, nursery (including facilities for high-risk infants), surgery, breast center, urodynamics, infertility services, diagnostic services, preventive health care, and educational services. Tri-State Obstetrics & Gynecology and Evansville Obstetrical & Gynecological Associates, Inc. collaborated with Deaconess on the project.

A Spectrum of Care

The Evansville community has a diverse and extensive network of primary care physicians and facilities. St. Mary's, for example, has developed relationships with many family practice physicians, so that families can find doctors convenient to their homes and workplace. In addition, Deaconess Hospital has primary-care facilities located in virtually every corner of the tri-state. Both hospitals operate free-standing facilities for minor emergency care and many routine procedures.

Founded in 1947, Welborn Clinic is a physician-owned and physician-directed group of doctors, with nearly 100 physicians covering 26 fields of medicine. Welborn Clinic has multiple facilities throughout the tri-state, conveniently located to where people live and work.

In addition to St. Mary's Mulberry Center, there are two other psychiatric hospitals in the area - the Evansville Psychiatric Children's Center and the Evansville State Hospital. Both provide services on an inpatient or outpatient basis.

Birmingham, Alabama-based HealthSouth Corporation, the nation's largest provider of outpatient surgery and rehabilitative services, has a for-profit rehabilitation hospital in Evansville. The hospital provides occupational and physical therapy, stroke rehabilitation, head injury rehabilitation, speech language pathology, and other rehabilitative services—all in a state-of-the-art facility located on Evansville's southeast side.

A Caring Community

In the caring spirit that is so characteristic of the area, Evansville has a number of organizations that provide inexpensive, or free, health care to those in need. The Community Health Center of Evansville, for example, is a not-for-profit agency that provides such care, and does so in an atmosphere that fosters and promotes the most positive regard for human worth and dignity. The mission of Impact Christian Health Center is to minister to the physical, emotional, and spiritual needs of local residents. The organization provides medical and dental care to people of all ages, regardless of their ability to pay, as well as offering preventive health and wellness programs.

Evansville's health care institutions and professionals are committed to doing what is best for the people they serve, with progressive, vital health care services that improve well-being. For those who call Evansville home, it is comforting to know that leading-edge health care, delivered by the best-possible medical experts, is available right here. ▓

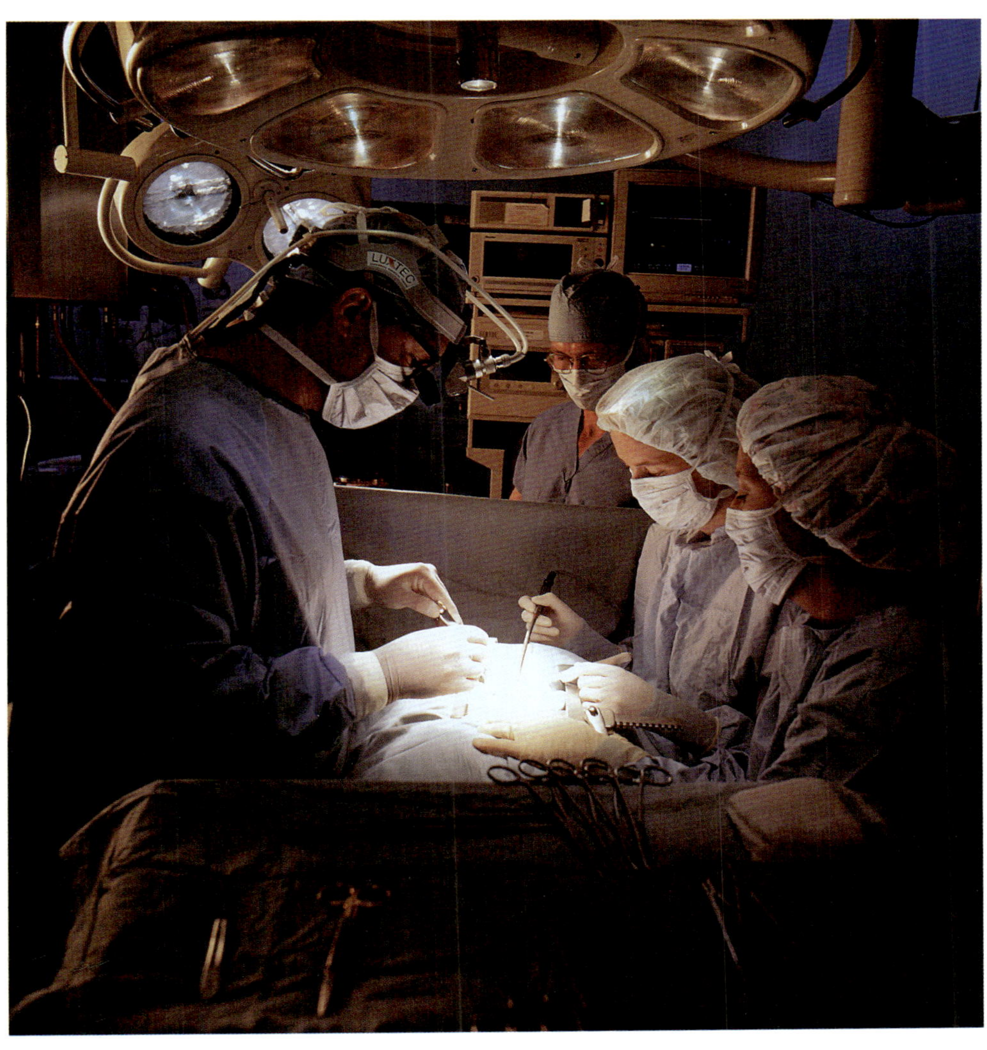

Deaconess Hospital's reputation for advanced technology and highly skilled physicians assures patients receive the finest care. Photo courtesy of Deaconess Hospital.

5

C H A P T E R   F I V E
EDUCATION

Opportunities as Dynamic and Challenging as

the World Awaiting Our Children

Students are equipped with technological expertise and well-educated in the basics. Photo by L. Kent Whitehead.

Well-organized sports programs round out a child's education. Photo by L. Kent Whitehead.

Here, as in every part of the country, Evansville-area schools and colleges grapple with the enormous challenges involved in educating students for the world that awaits them. As high-technology revolutionizes nearly every instructional area, educators know they must equip students with the technological expertise to compete in the ever-accelerating information age, yet ingrain in them the mastery of basic skills.

From school classrooms to college campuses, this challenge is being met successfully in the Evansville area. As a result, there is a growing number of students with impressive scholastic performance and the training necessary for competitive success. The vast educational opportunities available here are molding today's student into tomorrow's successful professional.

Few communities the size of Evansville offer the quality, diversity, and choice of educational opportunities as this area does: a progressive, superior public school system; outstanding private and parochial education opportunities; technical and vocational education for learners of all ages; and two major universities that are producing graduates with the talent to surpass world-class standards in all fields.

Education has a long history of excellence in Evansville. The city's first settlers came from middle-class and Scotch-Irish families; they believed strongly in education and, in the absence of schools, taught their children at home. The first actual school in Evansville was held in a primitive log cabin. There were very few books, so students had to memorize their lessons.

In 1822, the first schoolhouse was erected in Vanderburgh County at Third and Main streets. It was a "subscription" school, meaning that a teacher was hired to teach for a small amount of money paid by parents. The public school system was established in 1854.

Today, the public schools are operated by the Evansville-Vanderburgh School Corporation, the fourth largest public school system in Indiana and one of the 150 largest in the nation. The student population numbers approximately 23,000, with 6 high schools, 22 middle schools, and 20 elementary schools. To foster learning and provide individual attention, the student-to-teacher ratio is an impressive 16 to 1.

The Evansville-Vanderburgh School Corporation has the largest vocational education program in Indiana, plus it offers adult education classes for various needs, including continuing education, high school credit, and basic education for adults needing help in reading, math, and English skills. Respective schools within the school corporation have been recognized for positive achievements by local, state, and national media.

The Evansville-Vanderburgh School Corporation offers a complete range of services and individualized curricula for special students, designed to help them achieve academic success. Because there are 32 different languages represented by the student population, the school corporation provides a variety of English language services.

When students enter the 11th grade, they are required to select either a College Prep or a Tech Prep program. The College Prep program is designed for students who plan to attend college after high school graduation; Tech Prep, for those who plan to enter the job market or pursue post-secondary education after graduation. Approximately 72 percent of Evansville's public school graduates go on to college, universities, and technical schools immediately after graduating - an attendance rate that is higher than the Indiana average.

Educational quality scores consistently well in Evansville. High school students, for example, fare better on SAT tests than students do elsewhere in Indiana. On other standardized tests, Evansville public school students have scored above the national average in basic skills and above all Indiana urban school corporations on proficiency tests.

In addition, the city's public schools have graduated more students earning an Indiana Academic Honors Diploma than any other school corporation in the state. Clearly, Evansville's public school students are among the most successful in the state and nation.

The same level of academic performance is found in school districts surrounding Evansville. The Warrick County School Corporation is the 20th largest in the state and has a student enrollment of more than 9,000. The county is served by two senior high schools, one junior-senior high school, two junior high schools, and 10 elementary schools. The school corporation promotes the concept that it is essentially an "educational family" in constant pursuit of scholastic excellence. Students in Warrick County are educated through a sound basic skills curriculum supported by a variety of courses that fulfill and satisfy the needs and interest of students and enhanced by a diverse offering of extra and co-curricular activities. Sixty-eight percent of the school corporation's graduates go on to college.

In the Mt. Vernon community, just west of Evansville, there are four elementary schools, one junior high school, and one high school, serving approximately 2,700 students. Scores on standardized tests are above the Indiana average there too, and 64 percent of all students go to college immediately after graduating.

As an alternative to public education, two private schools, six parochial schools, and a system of Catholic schools administered by the Catholic Diocese of Evansville challenge students academically while preparing them for their professional future.

The Evansville Day School is an independent college preparatory school that offers a comprehensive core curriculum and a balanced program of extra activities that round out a child's development. With a student-faculty ratio of 9 to 1, the learning environment encourages and rewards individual effort. Known for its scholastic excellence, Evansville Day School has a Lower School (pre k - 4), a Middle School (grades 5 - 8), and an Upper School (grades 9 - 12). It is in the Upper School that students begin concentrated preparation for college. All Evansville Day School graduates attend the four-year college of their choice following graduation.

Recreational opportunities are an important part of a child's development. Photo by L. Kent Whitehead.

**Known for its scholastic excellence, Evansville Day School
is an independent college preparatory school.
Photos by L. Kent Whitehead.**

There is also a Montessori Academy in Evansville, based on the
innovative instructional methods of Italian physician-educator Dr.
Maria Montessori. The Montessori approach emphasizes early learning
of reading and writing and teaches children the lifelong joys of investi-
gation and the value of self-discipline.

Schools such as Evansville Christian School (pre k-8), Faith Heritage
School (k-12), and various denomination-based schools stress strong
values, parental involvement, academic challenge, and religious tradition. Rather unique among parochial schools is the Joshua Academy, a
central city private school established by the Nazarene Baptist Church
in 1998 with the help of St. Mary's Foundation. The academy is based
on the program of the West Side Preparatory School in Chicago started
by Marva Collins and stresses moral values, phonics, and memorization.
The Joshua Academy is a year-round school with 226 days of school,
compared to the 180 days most schools offer.

The Catholic Diocese of Evansville operates 18 elementary schools
and two high schools. Academically, students in Evansville's Catholic
high schools rank among the highest in Indiana. On standardized tests,
including SATs, they consistently score above Indiana and national
averages for math and English. Further, 80 percent of all Catholic high
school graduates go on to college.

The pursuit of higher education takes many forms in the Evansville
area. The city is home to the University of Evansville, located on an
80-acre campus in a historic east side neighborhood. For six years in
a row, the university has been ranked by U.S. *News & World Report* as
one of the top universities in the Midwest. Established in 1854, the
university offers more than 90 academic majors in liberal arts, fine arts,
education, engineering, business, medicine, and others. It also provides

Built in the 1920s, Bosse High School continues to serve students with the highest of educational standards. Photo by L. Kent Whitehead.

the opportunity to study abroad at Harlaxton College in England. More than 3,000 day and evening students from over 40 states and 42 foreign countries come to study at the university.

Students at the University of Evansville learn in a small, personalized setting: The student/faculty ratio is 13:1, and most classes have fewer than 20 students. By combining traditional classroom instruction with off-campus internship and research experience, students have all the resources they need to gain a competitive edge. How students live is just as important as their classroom experience—which is why there are more than 130 campus clubs and organizations in which students can become involved.

Indiana's fastest growing university is the University of Southern Indiana (USI), located on 300 acres of rolling hills in western Vanderburgh County. USI was first established as a regional campus of Indiana State University in 1965, but became a separate state university by act of the 1985 Indiana General Assembly. It opened its doors in 1965 with a freshman class of 412 students and two full-time faculty members. Today, the university has grown to an enrollment of more than 9,000 students, with 420 full-time faculty and administrators.

Students study toward associate and baccalaureate degrees in more than 60 majors and toward master's degrees in seven fields. Adapting to the complex needs of today's college students, USI offers off-campus classes, as well as televised and Internet courses designed to accommodate the lives of busy people. Because learning is a lifelong process, USI provides a continuing education program open to everyone in the community. USI also houses the Indiana School of Medicine Evansville Center. In 1998, a phenomenal 90 percent of all USI graduates found employment in their respective fields of study.

At both universities is the presence of nontraditional students. These include parents who have raised and educated their children, retirees who want to enrich their lives, and people who have worked in business or served in the military and want to switch careers or enhance their employability.

Area technical colleges are playing an ever-increasing role in educating students for successful careers. Ivy Tech State College, for example, is a public, statewide technical college with 22 campuses throughout Indiana. The Evansville campus is headquartered at 3501 First Avenue, with satellite facilities at 601 East Illinois Street and at 1034 31st Street in Tell City, Indiana.

Established by the Indiana General Assembly in 1963, Ivy Tech's mission is to enable individuals to develop to their fullest potential and to support the economic development of Indiana. Across the state, Ivy Tech offers 21 programs of study in more than 500 classes in business, visual communications, applied science, and health, with three degree options: Associate of Science, Associate in Applied Science, and technical certificates. Upon graduating from Ivy Tech with an Associate of Science degree, students can enroll at Indiana State University in Terre Haute. Credits from Ivy Tech also transfer to other colleges and universities. In addition to traditional classroom courses, Internet-based courses are offered as well to meet the needs of Ivy Tech's diverse student population. For lifelong learners, continuing education courses round out the college's curriculum.

Indiana Business College, which offers both a diploma program and a two-year Associate of Applied Science degree, has an Evansville campus located on the northeastern side of the city. Students can earn degrees in accounting, business administration, health claims examiner, medical assistant, medical records technology, and other business or

Through dedication to science and other fields of endeavor, students are well-prepared for the world that awaits them. Photos by L. Kent Whitehead.

The spirit of volunteerism so prevalent in the community is evident in the city's youth. Photos by L. Kent Whitehead.

medical-related fields. The college's Career Services department assists students, alumni, and employers in all aspects of the job search process.

ITT Technical Institutes have an Evansville-area campus too - located in nearby Newburgh. Curriculum offerings, leading primarily to associate's and bachelor's degrees, are designed to ready students for career opportunities in technology-related fields. The Newburgh branch of ITT offers programs of study in automated manufacturing technology and electronics engineering technology. The programs continue year-round so that students can complete their education and enter the work force as soon as possible.

On all counts, the lesson is clear: The educational institutions in the Evansville area provide superior instruction. The result is individuals who are educated not only to make a living, but also to make a life.

For six years in a row, the University of Evansville has been ranked by *U.S. News & World Report* as one of the top universities in the Midwest. All photos by L. Kent Whitehead.

Ivy Tech State College is a public, statewide technical college with 22 campuses throughout Indiana, including one in Evansville. Photo by L. Kent Whitehead.

Located in western Vanderburgh County, the Universtiy of Southern Indiana is the state's fastest growing university. Photo courtesy of USI.

Photo courtesy of USI.

6

CHAPTER SIX
THE ARTS

Cultural Vibrancy Is a Vital Element of

Evansville's Character

Shanklin Theater on the campus of the University of Evansville
hosts a wide range of performances, from local theater productions
to international dance companies. Photo by L. Kent Whitehead.

Evansville has always been a community that cultivates to a high degree the fine arts and graces of living. Its very locale is one that stimulates creativity, with soft Ohio River breezes that are a continual source of mental vigor. From the presence of the waterfront to the continually lovely view of terrain on the far shore, Evansville is saturated with inspiration—an atmosphere where the arts are encouraged and enjoyed—a true symphony of sights and sounds.

It is a city that compels the artist, writer, poet, dramatist, or musician to veer off on new tangents of creative activity. Ultimately, their visions materialize on canvas, paper, on stage, or in music, to be savored by the city's many art lovers, concert fans, theatergoers, and other patrons.

The respect for the arts here is traditional—traceable back nearly a century and a half ago when the city's first real theater, Apollo Hall, was constructed downtown and opened in 1852. Around 1868, Evansville's first opera house was built and was the scene of many productions, starring some of the nation's most famous actors and actresses until it burned to the ground in 1891. Since its earliest days, Evansville has always been an artful community.

Today, the Arts Council of Southwestern Indiana has seen to it that this tradition continues, by serving as a cornerstone for promoting the arts and distributing valuable information regarding performance schedules, special programs, classes, and hours of operation of various art-related attractions.

Enormously popular among young and old, longtime residents and visitors alike, is the Evansville Museum of Arts and Sciences, spectacularly situated on the riverfront. The largest museum in the United States to be funded entirely by voluntary contributions, it houses a comprehensive collection in art, history, anthropology, and science. Visitors can enjoy paintings from the 16th century to the present, stroll back in time on the street of 19th century Rivertown U.S.A., interact with hands-on exhibits in the Science Center, and stargaze in the Koch Planetarium in the evening. Changing exhibits keep the museum an ever-appealing attraction throughout the year. The museum also provides stimulating programs of tours and lectures, and sponsors workshops and classes.

For art lovers, the museum is only part of the art scene in Evansville. There are many smaller galleries throughout the city and in its outskirts, where the work of Evansville's many exceptionally gifted artists are exhibited and sold. The practical arts are well represented here too, with photographers, weavers, leatherworkers, ceramists, potters, crafts makers, and other artisans displaying their works in the city's many galleries and shops, and at its numerous arts and crafts festivals.

The Thrall Opera House in historic New Harmony is an architectural jewel. Photo by L. Kent Whitehead.

Outdoor art graces the cityscape too. Among the most notable is the Four Freedoms Monument situated between Sunset Park and Dress Plaza. The Ionic limestone pillars that make up the monument originally stood at the entrance to the old Chicago & Eastern Illinois railroad station at Eighth and Main Streets, a building that later became the Evansville Community Center. After it was torn down to make way for the Civic Center, the pillars were salvaged, but for years lay dirty and stained outside the Waterworks garage. In 1975, the Downtown Civitan Club raised money to use them in a display overlooking the Ohio River. The pillars stand for our nation's four freedoms - freedom of religion, freedom of speech, freedom from fear, and freedom from oppression. They are encircled by 50 stone tablets, symbolizing each U.S. state. With its American flag flying proudly around the clock, the monument is reached by climbing 13 steps that represent America's original 13 colonies.

Close by is the Korean War memorial, depicting two soldiers helping a wounded comrade. It was erected and dedicated in 1992. Near the Civic Center is the Desert Storm monument, erected in 1993. It displays a woman and man in combat gear. Both memorials were created from welded copper by the late sculptor Steve Shields of Hopkinsville, Kentucky.

At First and Main Streets is the large outdoor sculpture "The Bend in the River," created by Evansville artist Amy Musia and erected in 1993. It is a stone-and-steel tribute to city founders Hugh McGary and Colonel Robert Evans.

Another indication of Evansville's vibrancy as a cultural center is its love of music. Thousands of people, on average, attend the Evansville Philharmonic Orchestra every week of the September-through-May season. Founded in 1929, the orchestra began with a group of talented musicians who dreamed of forming a symphony. Their dream materialized, and the Philharmonic is today an 80-member symphony orchestra of renowned stature and unexcelled musical merit.

Each season, the Philharmonic offers Classics, Pops, family concerts, and special events, as well as performances by its Youth Orchestra, Chorus, Children's Chorus, and String Quartet. In 1999, the Philharmonic moved into the splendidly restored, 1920's-era Victory Theater, recognized throughout the city as an architectural jewel with precision acoustics.

Other popular forms of musical entertainment include the Evansville Symphonic Band, organized in 1947 and still going strong today. It presents its annual series of Old Fashioned Concerts during June. The band also plays at special events held year round.

The leading music-telling ensemble in the nation for children and families, Tales & Scales, is a performing troupe of classically trained musicians who entertain at numerous events and outreach activities, plus offer a full range of workshops. Their innovative blend of theater, storytelling, and music has earned recognition from the Indiana Arts Commission.

The exotic-looking Alhambra Theater was built in 1913 as a movie house. Photo by L. Kent Whitehead.

This page: The Korean War memorial was erected and dedicated in 1992. Photo by L. Kent Whitehead.
Opposite page: The city's most famous outdoor art is the Four Freedoms Monument, commemorating our nation's four freedoms—freedom of religion, freedom of speech, freedom from fear, and freedom from oppression.
Photo by L. Kent Whitehead.

For lovers of popular music, Evansville is a concertgoer's delight. Big names in rock, folk, and country such as Rod Stewart, Garth Brooks, Bob Dylan, The Beach Boys, and other entertainers have performed at the expansive Roberts Stadium, a popular entertainment and convention complex that seats up to 13,000 patrons. The stadium has also featured such events as Walt Disney on Ice, the Harlem Globetrotters, and the Hadi Shrine Circus.

In addition, local and national acts perform frequently at the historic Coliseum at 400 Court Street, a handsome building designed in the 20th Century Greek Revival style and constructed in 1916 as a memorial to war veterans. At Casino Aztar on the riverfront, nationally known entertainers are booked year round.

Outdoor entertainment thrives in the summertime at Mesker Amphitheatre, where a concert evening is truly a night under the stars. In a beautiful setting on the city's west side, crowds fill the seats and lawn to hear the sounds of top acts touring the country today, as well as enjoy locally performing orchestras.

Evansville also possesses ballet companies such as the Evansville Dance Theater, which annually performs the beloved Christmastime ballet, *The Nutcracker*, in concert with the Evansville Philharmonic Orchestra. The Evansville Dance Theater also provides dance instruction to dancers of all ages.

The Children's Dance Theatre of the Tri-State is a not-for-profit organization that gives area children the opportunity to learn classical ballet through weekly dance instruction, outreach performances in schools and other public places, professional dance exposure, and scholarships.

The dramatic arts are popular as well. There are numerous theater companies in the city, many of them presenting productions of local playwrights, as well as performances of recognized classics in drama and comedy. The Evansville Civic Theater, established in 1925, features local performers in all of its productions, which include musicals and plays. The Repertory People of Evansville is the city's version of Off-Broadway. The company has been producing professional quality theater since 1975 and is run entirely by volunteers, most of whom have professional theater experience. Also popular are the Evansville Children's Theatre, which brings professional touring productions to the city and has been recognized by the Indiana Arts Commission; and Totally New Theatre, with its contemporary musical productions for children and adults.

Evansville's newest theater company, River's Bend Playhouse, stages comedies and dramas in an historic part of the city. The theater group's Center for Lifelong Learning offers classes for children and adults. Scholarships are available too. In addition, the group has spearheaded efforts to resurrect and restore one of the city's oldest neighborhood theaters, the Alhambra Theater at 304 Adams Street, as a performance hall and activities center. Built in 1913, the Alhambra was designed to resemble an exotic Spanish castle for which it was named.

Downtown's newly renovated Evansville Auditorium and Convention Centre is host to many touring productions of Broadway musicals throughout the year. A few blocks away, the magnificent Victory Theater is a popular spot that draws the nation's top comedians, singers, and actors and actresses for show-stopping performances.

There are two theater centers in the city—at the University of Evansville and at the University of Southern Indiana. Each season, the nationally acclaimed University of Evansville produces new works, as well as classic plays. These run the gamut from full-length dramatic and musical plays to one-acts and works-in-progress. Performances are held at the University's Shanklin Theatre and the May Studio Theatre.

The new 125-seat Helen Mallette Studio Theater on the campus of the University of Southern Indiana is an intimate setting for stage and student-directed productions throughout the year. During the summer, the university produces The New Harmony Theatre, featuring well-loved musicals and dramas. In addition to local professionally trained thespians, famous-name stars often headline these productions.

Also under the auspices of the university is *Young Abe Lincoln*, a musical outdoor drama depicting the life and times of young Abraham Lincoln as he grew to manhood in southern Indiana. Through the deaths of his mother and sister, as well as his first experience with slavery, theatergoers see how Lincoln's youth shaped him into one of our nation's greatest presidents. The production is staged every summer at the covered Lincoln Amphitheatre in Lincoln State Park in nearby Spencer County.

Over the decades, Evansville has produced or attracted writers who later became well known: famed novelist Theodore Dreiser, who wrote of Evansville in his 1916 book *Hoosier Holiday*; the late children's author and storyteller, Vardine Russell Moore; and novelist Marilyn Durham, who penned *The Man Who Loves Cat Dancing*. Today, Evansville is home to many other successful published writers, expressing themselves in fiction, romance, inspirational, and how-to books. Each year, aspiring writers can match talents with award-winning writers of fiction, nonfiction, and poetry at the RopeWalk Writers Retreat, sponsored by the University of Southern Indiana and held in the solitude of historic New Harmony.

This page: Evansville is home to many gifted artists, such as Larry Hortenbury. Photo by L. Kent Whitehead.
Opposite page: Local artist John McNaughton with one of his fine works. Photo by L. Kent Whitehead.

The Victory Theatre Lobby. Photo by L. Kent Whitehead.

Expect to find local bards reading their own works at pubs and coffee houses, on lawns and college campuses, at fairs and festivals—wherever poets and poetry lovers congregate. The city's poetry scene is alive—and lively—due not only to the inspired poets who live here, but also to the enthusiastic crowds they draw. In fact, poet Walt Whitman could have been describing Evansville when he mused, "To have great poetry there must be great audiences too." Accordingly, the well-attended poetry readings held throughout the year give area poets opportunities to find a hearing.

Some of the city's liveliest show of appreciation for the arts centers on cultural events. The city's African-American cultural heritage, for example, is vibrantly celebrated throughout February with Black History Month, which features concerts, exhibitions, dramas, and films depicting various aspects of history and culture. For seven days after Christmas, many African-Americans celebrate their heritage with Kwanzaa, modeled after African celebrations. The festivities include ballet dancers, gospel singers, and carolers, and are staged to be shared with the community at large.

Evansville, then, is a city where the arts flourish. Vital, creative, and popular, they are certainly accepted as an important part of life in the area, expressing the essence and identity of this city at the river's bend.

The magnificent Victory Theater is an elegant setting for
concerts, plays, and other forms of entertainment.
Photo by L. Kent Whitehead.

Riverfest in the summertime means non-stop entertainment. Photos by L. Kent Whitehead.

STOP
ONE WAY

Above: Outdoor entertainment at Mesker Amphitheater is the place to enjoy top local and national acts during the summer. Photo by L. Kent Whitehead.

Left: The Evansville Civic Theater features local performers in all of its productions, which include musicals and plays. Photo by L. Kent Whitehead.

Above: Madame Butterfly is among the operas that have been performed in Evansville. Photo by L. Kent Whitehead.
Below: An authentic Japanese performance at Shanklin Theater. Photo by L. Kent Whitehead.

Evansville possesses several ballet companies, including the
Evansville Dance Theater. Photo by L. Kent Whitehead.

The local perfomance of an orchestra from Tochigi, Japan.
Photo by L. Kent Whitehead.
Next page: Changing exhibits, such as these giant puppets,
keep Evansville Museum of Arts and Sciences an ever-appealing
attraction throughout the year. Photo by L. Kent Whitehead.

EXPO WHEEL

7

C H A P T E R   S E V E N

CITY SIGHTS

Year-Round Attractions Make Evansville the Place

To Have the Time of Your Life

A much-anticipated festival is the annual West Side Nut Club's
Fall Festival. Photo by L. Kent Whitehead.

Evansville and its surrounding area possess untold surprises—from historical treasures to modern-day wonders. There is certainly no shortage of things to see and do, in and around this unique city bordering the mighty Ohio River.

Not far from the riverbank is the city's historic downtown district, which can be toured on foot, by trolley, or in a car. With its palatial old homes, the district is a showplace of architecture, where the atmosphere of earlier eras lingers on and history buffs can relive the city's past.

The crown jewel of the district is the Reitz Home and Museum, built in 1871 by John Augustus Reitz, who had amassed a huge fortune in lumber. This magnificent Victorian home features ornate plasterwork, exquisite parquet floors, Moorish arches, and handpainted ceilings. A visit to the Reitz home is an enchanting step back in time. Guided tours are available Tuesday through Saturday.

Nearby is one of the city's most active restoration areas—Goosetown. Its showpiece is the exotic-looking Alhambra Theater, built in 1913 as a movie house.

The historic old post office and customs house is today a business and retail center and home to the Metropolitan Evansville Chamber of Commerce. Photo by L. Kent Whitehead.

The Old Vanderburgh County Courthouse is an outstanding example of 19th century German Baroque architecture.
Photo by L. Kent Whitehead.

The Greyhound Bus Terminal is among the most outstanding examples of Art Deco design found in the nation. Photo by L. Kent Whitehead.

The Old Vanderburgh County Sheriff's residence and jail was erected in 1890 and modeled after a castle. Photo by L. Kent Whitehead.

Beyond downtown are other historical neighborhoods that reflect the lifestyle, taste, and fashion of an earlier time. Their homes have been lovingly preserved and stand as stately reminders of a bygone era. Walking tours of these neighborhoods are often conducted at various times during the year.

As enchanting as its historical residences are, the city's commercial buildings of yesteryear are also worth note. Among the most recognizable is the Old Vanderburgh County Courthouse, which occupies an entire city block in downtown Evansville. Completed in 1891, the building is an outstanding example of 19th century German Baroque architecture. It features a commanding central dome that rises to 216 feet and ornamental stonework that was sculpted on site. The courthouse is constructed of Bedford Stone, a limestone native to Indiana. The interiors are just as magnificent, with their wainscoting, oak woodwork, and brass hand rails. Courthouse business was conducted here until 1969, when these activities relocated to more modern facilities. Today, the courthouse rents space to businesses, meetings, and catered functions. Guided tours are available.

Other historical standouts in the downtown area include the Old Vanderburgh County Sheriff's residence and jail, erected in 1890 and modeled after a castle; the Old Post Office and Customshouse, built in 1875-1879 to house the U.S. Post Office, Federal Court, and Custom's Office; and the Greyhound Bus Terminal, one of the most outstanding examples of Art Deco design to be found anywhere.

An important stopping-off point downtown is The Pagoda at Sunset Park. Built in Japanese style in 1912, it once served as a venue for bands, a refreshment stand, and a river outlook. It was renovated in 1995 to 1996 and today serves as the headquarters for the Evansville Convention and Tourist Bureau.

On the outskirts of downtown is the magnificent Willard Library, the oldest public library in Indiana. Built in 1885 and designed by the architects of the Hotel del Coronado in San Diego, the Victorian Gothic building features an exquisite tower, mansard roofs, cornice turrets, and elegant dormer windows. The library houses an extensive collection of genealogical materials and more than 60,000 volumes by the world's greatest authors.

Settled in the late 1800s by German immigrants, Evansville's West Side is one of the city's most enduring sections, with a history and character all its own. Its main artery—Franklin Street—runs east and west and is lined with a mix of new and old commercial buildings reflecting an unparalleled blend of late nineteenth and early-twentieth century architecture. The finest example of turn-of-the-century commercial architecture can be found in the famous Rosenburger Building at 2100 West Franklin Street. Built in 1890, the mammoth structure is detailed with fine plate glass, fluted cast iron pilasters, and brick surfaces overlaid with ornamental sheet metal.

Bordering Franklin Street are residential neighborhoods dotted with picturesque mansions constructed in the late 1800s. Visitors who take a walking tour of the historic West Franklin district will appreciate its rich architectural heritage.

Surrounding Evansville are some amazing historical sights not to be missed. On the outskirts of Evansville is the Angel Mounds State Historical Site, one of the best preserved prehistoric Native American settlements in the United States. It thrived from the 11th through the 15th centuries. This attraction features one of the largest burial mounds

Built in 1885, the magnificent Willard Library is the oldest public library in Indiana. Photo by L. Kent Whitehead.

The quaint town of Newburgh is an antique lover's delight. Photo by L. Kent Whitehead.

found in the eastern U.S., an interpretive center housing exhibits and Native American culture, and a depiction of an archeological dig. Every September, the Site holds Native American Days to raise money for its programs.

Just east of Angel Mounds is historic Newburgh, founded in 1803 and the oldest settled town on the Ohio River. Its quaint shops and antique stores make the town a must-visit place, especially on leisurely weekends. The Historic Newburgh Bed & Breakfast is housed in one of the town's many historic homes. There are period antiques everywhere you look, and each room has a fireplace and private bath. Self-guided walking tours and guided group tours of the town can be arranged.

Northwest of Evansville is New Harmony, the site of two attempts at communal living in the early 19th century. In 1814, the charismatic George Rapp and a group of Lutheran dissenters settled there and created a self-sufficient, religious-based community with thriving industries. In 1824, they sold the town to Robert Owen, a Scottish industrialist. Although his utopian community lasted only two years, it was a haven for international scientists, scholars, and educators who sought equality in communal living. One of New Harmony's most enduring legacies is that it was the site of the first public school system open to boys and girls alike.

Today, visitors can tour the remaining structures of these two societies. Tours start at the Atheneum, a modern visitor's center. Also on the tour is the Labyrinth, a restored maze of hedges, and the Roofless Church. There are elegant bed and breakfast accommodations, as well as an inn with lofts and fireplaces located in New Harmony, too.

To the northeast of Evansville is the Lincoln Boyhood National Memorial. At seven years of age, young Abraham Lincoln moved with his family to Indiana in 1816, the year Indiana became the 19th state. He spent fourteen formative years near Lincoln City, where today tourists can see the site of the log cabin where he grew up, as well as visit the gravesite of his mother, Nancy Hanks Lincoln.

Just a short distance to the east is the town of Santa Claus, home of the world's first theme park. Santa Claus Land, which opened in 1946, is today called Holiday World® Theme Park. It is Indiana's largest water park, with a variety of family-styled thrills for people of all ages. A wavepool, water slides, an action river, beaches, and two children's activity pools are all part of the fun.

Evansville has its own water park too—Burdette Park. Located on the city's West Side, the park has a huge Olympic-sized swimming pool (among the largest in the Midwest), four water slide rides, and a kid's swimming area. There is more: covering roughly 200 acres, Burdette Park has chalets and cottages for rent, campgrounds, a fishing lake, tennis courts, party houses, softball diamonds, a miniature golf course, and a BMX racing track, used for regional and national meets.

Throughout the year, residents and visitors alike can enjoy Evansville's many public parks. All totaled, the city's park system has 56 parks and 23 recreational facilities, each managed by the Department of Parks and Recreation.

New Harmony was the site of two attempts at communal living in the early 19th century. Many structures of both societies have been lovingly preserved. Photo by L. Kent Whitehead.

Included in this system is the impressive Wesselman Woods Nature preserve, a National Natural Landmark and a State Natural Preserve with more than 200 acres of lush forestland preserved to look like it did 300 years ago. Anyone in pursuit of tranquility will enjoy this natural refuge, with its wildlife observation areas and wooded paths. It is a natural museum where young and old alike can experience living, breathing, wild nature. Year-round activities include Maple Sugarbush Weekend in early March, Pioneer Days in early May, concerts, outdoor movies, night hikes, and fall color programs.

Also part of the park system is Indiana's largest zoo— Mesker Zoo and Botanic Garden, graced with 70 acres, a collection of more than 700 animals, and hundreds of botanical species. A walk through the zoo takes visitors from the savannas of Africa to the Asian plains to the North American Forest. A petting zoo, train, paddleboat, and a seasonal butterfly exhibit round out the fun for zoo-goers of all ages.

The Department of Parks and Recreation offers many other facilities and activities too, including public pools, summer playgrounds, a rollerdome, and community centers.

Encircling Evansville is the Pigeon Creek Greenway, a park and trail system in various stages of development. The Greenway has expanded the amount of recreational space available in Vanderburgh County, providing pedestrian and bike trails, picnic spots, and related natural vistas.

It is difficult to choose where to begin when describing Evansville's other recreational opportunities. Throughout the city and skirting its limits are world-class golf courses and tennis courts. For golfers of all

Tours of New Harmony begin at the Atheneum, a modern visitor's center. Photo by L. Kent Whitehead.

Wesselman Woods Nature Preserve is a natural museum with wildlife observation areas, wooded paths, and activities geared to nature lovers. Photo by L. Kent Whitehead.
Next page: The region is blessed with a variety of parks, such as Lincoln State Park. Photo by L. Kent Whitehead.

Mesker Zoo boasts a collection of more than 700 animals, including lemurs. Photo by L. Kent Whitehead.

skill levels, the city has three 18-hole golf courses—Fendrich, Helfrich Hills, and McDonald's—as well as par three courses at Howell and Wesselman parks. There are also numerous other public and private courses in Evansville and the surrounding area. These courses are among the finest in the Midwest, with excellent design and rolling terrain to provide maximum challenge and enjoyment.

Tennis enthusiasts can enjoy their favorite sport at numerous spots around town. The city maintains several tennis courts, and there are private facilities as well.

For fast water fun, the Ohio River is a favorite place for boaters, water-skiers, and jet-skiers.

Scattered among a three-state area that includes Indiana, Kentucky, and Illinois are forested wildernesses, parks veined with wide, deep streams—the ideal setting for canoeing and fishing—and ancient caves for sightseers or serious spelunkers.

Sparkling lakes, breathtaking waterfalls, verdant state parks, ranges where elk and bison roam and ancient rock formations all lie within the range of a day trip. These are the perfect destinations for camping, picnicking, hiking, horseback riding, mountain biking, hunting, and beautiful scenic drives.

For winter pursuits, even snow skiing at Paoli Peaks is so close and convenient that many Evansville ski enthusiasts consider it practically an in-town activity. Open December through March, Paoli Peaks offers plenty of winter excitement and does so around the clock, seven days a week, with giant moguls jumps, snow ramps, and more.

Sports lovers with a penchant for spectator sports find themselves in athletic heaven in Evansville. Since 1995, the city has been home to the Evansville Otters, a Class A Frontier League professional baseball team. The Otters play their home games at Bosse Field, which was built in 1915 and used in the movie *A League of Their Own*. Total yearly attendance at games averages 84,000 fans a season.

Wildly popular are college sports. The University of Evansville Aces bring Division I basketball to crowds exceeding 11,000 a game in the city's newly remodeled Roberts Stadium. What's more, the university's soccer team annually ranks among the NCAA Division I Top Ten. The university also has men's and women's teams in baseball, swimming, volleyball, and other sports.

The University of Southern Indiana's Screaming Eagles are NCAA Division II members, bringing additional basketball excitement to sports fans throughout the city. Women's basketball, soccer, and baseball teams carry a strong following too.

Legend has it that the game of blackjack was invented in Evansville. In 1995, the game returned to town when the *City of Evansville*, a 310-foot long replica of the side wheel racing steamboat *Robert E. Lee* docked at the riverfront, bringing riverboat casino gambling to the city. As a part of the Casino Aztar complex, the riverboat features more than 1200 slots, 50 blackjack tables, craps, roulette, and other gaming excitement. Billed as the Midwest's Premier Entertainment destination, Casino Aztar also boasts five outstanding restaurants, two sports lounges, a magnificent adjacent hotel, and concerts by the nation's top recording artists.

While many play a hand or two of cards at Casino Aztar, others play the ponies at nearby Ellis Park Race Course. Nestled between Evansville and Henderson, Kentucky, Ellis Park features the finest in thoroughbred racing. Live racing runs from late June through Labor Day, and there is also racing via satellite from race tracks across the country.

Festivals characterize cities as much as other activities do. In Evansville, one of the main festivals is the annual Thunder Festival, which is, in fact, the largest Fourth of July celebration in the nation. Beginning in late June, this two-week extravaganza celebrates Evansville for what it is: a dynamic town that loves where it is—on the banks of a beautiful river.

Mesker Zoo and Botanic Garden is the largest zoo in Indiana. A walk through the zoo takes visitors on a safari-like tour. Photo by L. Kent Whitehead.

Mesker Zoo is home to exotic animals from all over the world.
Photos by L. Kent Whitehead.

The Thunder Festival showcases the spectacular Thunder on the Ohio, in which the world's fastest racing boats hydroplane across the river at speeds up to 200 mph. Other exciting festival events include an oldies sock hop, an extraordinary fireworks display, hot-air balloon races, a golf outing, a chili cook-off, shows with live entertainment, and a Fourth of July parade.

The Thunder Festival is not the only peculiar-to-Evansville event. A much-anticipated festival is the annual West Side Nut Club's Fall Festival, held every October on West Franklin Street. People from around the city flock to the festival to enjoy a variety of food and revel in its fun-charged atmosphere. Proceeds from this well-attended event are donated to benefit schools, non-profit organizations, and other worthy causes.

All tolled, there are nine or ten major events going on in and around the city most months of the year: an alcohol-free New Year's Eve event called The First-Night Celebration, the family-oriented Newburgh Summerfest in June, Downtown After Sundown in June and August, the Casino Aztar Riverfest in July, the Vanderburgh County Fair in July, the ever-popular Germania Maennerchor Volkfest in August, the Evansville Iron Street Rod Frog Follies in August, the Newburgh Fiddler Fest in September, the Shrine Circus in November, and the Fantasy of Lights in November and December.

The spectacular Thunder on the Ohio showcases the world's fastest hydroplane racing boats. Photo by L. Kent Whitehead.

The saying "shop 'til you drop" knows no bounds in Evansville. Shoppers hunting for antiques, looking for one-of-a-kind gifts, or scouring the racks for the latest fashions will not be disappointed. The city is a shopper's paradise, with its ultra modern shopping malls, as well as the many quaint boutiques located in downtown Evansville, the Franklin Street area, in a special neighborhood called Olde Town, or in historic Newburgh.

Eastland Mall, located on the city's East Side, houses 164 businesses, including three major department stores and a recently expanded and renovated food court. Across the street is Eastland Place, home to 40 stores and restaurants. Evansville's downtown has more than 40 shops and restaurants, too.

Other favorite shopping places include the East Side's Washington Square Mall, which holds the distinction of being Indiana's very first indoor mall. It opened in 1963 and today boasts 40 businesses, including two major department stores. Washington Square Mall also houses Hands On Discovery, an interactive children's museum for kids, ages 2 to 12. Next door to the mall is Lawndale Shopping Center, filled with stores for every retail shopping experience.

The Thunder Festival is family entertainment.
Photo by L. Kent Whitehead.

These boats race across the river at speeds up to 200 mph.
Photo by L. Kent Whitehead.

North Park Shopping Center features 30 restaurants and stores, and Northbrook Shopping Center houses 19 stores and restaurants. Town Center Mall has 13 stores on the south side of the city and 10 stores conveniently located on the city's north side.

The expanding west side is home to two shopping complexes: Franklin Street Shopping Center with its 62 stores and restaurants and University Square Shopping Center with more than 25 stores and restaurants. The newest west side shopping complex, Eagle Plaza, is home to an ultra-modern, 16-screen movie theatre with stadium-style seating throughout and wall-to-ceiling-to-floor screens.

With the city's boom in tourism has come unprecedented growth in hotels and new restaurants. Accommodations for every taste and need dot the cityscape: riverfront hotels with breathtaking views, convenient interstate stopovers, nostalgic bed and breakfasts, and intimate country inns. In Evansville, diners can also enjoy some of the Midwest's finest foods, including gourmet, barbecue, ethnic, home cooking, and more. Hospitality is the city's specialty.

More than 188 years after its founding, Evansville continues to draw visitors and inspire its residents. Those who quest after history, natural wonders, adventure, shopping, and pure fun will have the time of their lives in Indiana's premier river city. ▓

The city is home to the Evansville Otters, a Class A Frontier League professional baseball team. Photo by L. Kent Whitehead.

Fendrich Golf Course is among the city's 18-hole courses.
Photo by L. Kent Whitehead.

Ellis Park features the finest in thoroughbred racing.
Photo by L. Kent Whitehead.

The annual Thunder Festival is the largest Fourth of July celebration in the nation. Photo by L. Kent Whitehead.

The Evansville Museum of Arts and Sciences is the largest museum in the United States to be funded entirely by voluntary contributions. Photo by L. Kent Whitehead.

The museum's train is a popular fixture in Evansville. Photo by L. Kent Whitehead.

The ever-popular Burdette Park features four water slides. Photo by Brad Whitehead.

Few sights are more spectacular than a sunset on the Ohio River. Photo by L. Kent Whitehead.

CASIN

Burdette Park is a haven for wildlife.
Photo by L. Kent Whitehead.

Casino Aztar lives up to its billing as the Midwest's Premier Entertainment destination. Photo by L. Kent Whitehead.

Evansville residents flock to the Vanderburgh County Fair in July. Photo by L. Kent Whitehead.

The West Side Nut Club Fall Festival is held annually in October. Photo by L. Kent Whitehead.

Riverfest entertainment goes on all day.
Photo by L. Kent Whitehead.

Riverfest in July is a fun-for-the-whole-family event.
Photo by L. Kent Whitehead.

No matter what's going on in Evansville, everyone catches the spirit. Photo by L. Kent Whitehead.

The Fantasy of Lights has become a dazzling holiday tradition.
Photo by L. Kent Whitehead.

Evansville residents look forward to the Fantasy of Lights every
November and December. Photo by L. Kent Whitehead.

Riverfest is a festival of fun. Photo by L. Kent Whitehead.

8

CHAPTER EIGHT
COMMERCE

A Community Where the American Dream

Comes True Every Day

Reitz Hill provides a panoramic view of Evansville.
Photo by L. Kent Whitehead.

The city has a future of unlimited promise.
Photo by L. Kent Whitehead.

Travel to any corner of the world, and you're not far away from Evansville - its products, that is. In just five years, exports from the Evansville metropolitan area have jumped by 32.5 percent, signaling a brisk demand for Evansville-made products around the globe. Mexico, Brazil, South Korea, and Canada are among the top market destinations for local products.

The Evansville region is known far and wide for the production of appliances, nutritional products, pharmaceuticals, aluminum sheet, auto glass, coal and oil, and plastics. The region is also recognized as an agricultural center for corn, soybeans, and wheat.

Instrumental in the region's economic health is the Metropolitan Evansville Chamber of Commerce. The chamber assists businesses in expansion, retention, and start-up efforts; lobbies at the state capitol in Indianapolis for local business concerns; markets the metropolitan community to businesses outside of Evansville; and provides many other services to its member businesses. The chamber's members include virtually all of the region's major employers, as well as many small-and medium-sized businesses.

Over the years, major national corporations have established regional operations here - primarily in response to the area's favorable tax rates, rich natural resources, diverse transportation routes, and productive workforce.

One of these companies is Whirlpool Corporation, whose Evansville Division manufactures high-efficiency refrigerators at its highway 41 plant just north of the city limits. The plant is one of the area's largest employers.

Near the heart of downtown is Mead Johnson Nutritionals, a Bristol-Myers Squibb company. Mead Johnson is a leader in world nutrition with products such as infant formulas, vitamins and disease-specific nutritionals. Among its most well-known products are Enfamil® infant formulas, Boost®, and Viactiv™ calcium supplements. The company conducts business in four regions worldwide—North America, Asia Pacific, Europe, and Latin America. Its parent company, Bristol-Myers Squibb Company, is a diversified worldwide health and personal care company whose principal businesses are pharmaceuticals, consumer medicines, beauty care, nutritionals, and medical devices.

Evansville is the corporate headquarters of one of the giants in the transportation industry - Atlas Van Lines. The moving company is the industry's fourth largest and the third largest mover of household goods. For the past 10 years, Atlas has been the fastest growing moving company in the industry.

Another well-known manufacturing company in the area is the Aluminum Company of America (ALCOA), which produces aluminum sheets for beverage cans at its Warrick County plant. The plant has experienced steady growth since 1960, after ALCOA helped pioneer the development of the easy open end, which featured a pull-tab opener that permitted quick opening of beverage cans without the use of a can opener. The invention represented a revolution in the can industry.

The Evansville area has also become a major center for companies involved directly or indirectly in the automotive industry. Toyota Motor Manufacturing Indiana, Inc., in Gibson County, produces approximately 100,000 Toyota Tundra pickup trucks annually. In November 1999, *Consumer Reports* magazine rated the Tundra as the best full-sized pickup on the market. Other accolades followed that same year, including *Motor Trend's* Truck of the Year Award and *4-Wheel & Off-Road Magazine's* Four-by-Four of the Year Award.

The plant also manufactures the Sequoia, a new sports utility vehicle, and plans to turn out 50,000 a year. At the end of 1999, Toyota announced an $800 million expansion at the Gibson County plant—an expansion designed to boost the plant's capacity by an additional 150,000 vehicles a year.

Located in nearby Spencer County, AK Steel's Rockport Works produces cold-rolled and coated steel products for Toyota and other

Photo by L. Kent Whitehead.

Evansville welcomes the new frontier of high-tech companies, from web page design firms to computer-related businesses.
Photo by L. Kent Whitehead.

automakers, as well as for other markets requiring finished steel products. Rockport Works is the most powerful cold rolling mill in the world, with the ability to process carbon steel at the rate of 545 tons per hour. The sheet it produces is as thin as a credit card.

Grown from a small company that began selling turpentine in 1903, Red Spot Paint & Varnish Co., Inc., is today recognized as a global leader in the development of ecologically sound, high-performance coatings for automotive plastics. Red Spot supplies all domestic automakers and many foreign manufacturers with interior and exterior coatings for plastic components.

Just northwest of Evansville is PPG Industries Inc., which manufactures automotive windshields and tempered glass. The plant is among PPG's 50 production facilities in the United States. PPG Industries is a leading global supplier of coatings, continuous-strand fiberglass, flat and fabricated glass, and chemicals.

Located on the city's east side, Guardian Automotive Trim produces plastic exterior trim components for automakers. The plant is owned by Guardian Industries, a privately owned company headquartered in Auburn Hills, Michigan.

George Koch Sons Inc. designs, manufactures, and installs automotive finishing systems for body assembly plants, flatline finishing systems, wood strand dryers, process heating systems, and general industrial paint and powder finishing systems. The company is a major subsidiary of Koch Enterprises Inc., a diversified, privately owned corporation that is listed in the *Forbes* Top 500 Private Companies in the United States.

The production of plastics in various forms continues to be a major industry in the region, with hundreds of extruders, fabricators, molders, finishers, and suppliers contributing to the economy. The giant among plastics producers in the region is GE Plastics, located in Mt. Vernon, Indiana.

The huge facility is a key center of LEXAN® resin production. LEXAN goes into the design of such products as eyewear, compact discs, kitchen containers, and business equipment. Other resins produced at the GE plant include ENDURAN®, manufactured for kitchen and bath applications, as well as for medical equipment; ULTEM®, used in electronic, aerospace, food service, automotive, and medical applications; VALOX®, found in computer keyboards, appliances, automotive components, electrical connectors, and industrial systems and control; and XENOY, for applications ranging from thin-wall automotive bumpers and body panels to housings for business equipment and cellular phones.

Founded in 1953, Rexam Closures manufactures proprietary and custom plastic closures for containers at modern plants in Evansville, and Princeton, Indiana. The company pioneered the development of child-resistant closures, which remain a significant portion of its product line.

Natural coal deposits are mined at Black Beauty Coal's Mine near Farmersburg. Photo by L. Kent Whitehead.

Robur produces gas-fired air conditioners.
Photo by L. Kent Whitehead.

Berry Plastics, which has 12 plants in the United States and one in Europe, is a leading U.S. manufacturer of injection-molded plastic packaging. The company manufactures a wide range of products in five major product lines: aerosol overcaps, open-top containers, drink cups, housewares and lawn and garden products, and custom molding. In fact, Berry Plastics is the world's largest manufacturer of aerosol overcaps, producing over two billion units annually.

Other plastics companies include Wabash Plastics, Inc., an injection molding operation that makes pans, crisper covers, butter doors, and control boxes for Whirlpool; and its sister plant, Crescent Plastics, one of the top profile extruders in the country. Crescent's other sister company is Cresline Plastic Pipe Company, one of the largest pipe manufacturers in the United States.

Evansville is also home to other notable businesses. Faultless Caster, for example, designs, manufactures, and markets casters and other mobility products worldwide. The company provides more than 10,000 different standard caster and wheel combinations to meet nearly every caster application.

Anchor Industries, founded in 1892 as a small riverboat supply house known as Anchor Supply Company, has developed into one of the world's largest custom fabric product manufacturers. Today, Anchor produces all kinds of tents and fabric structures as well as custom awnings, safety pool covers, canopies, and carnival tents.

Located in nearby Darmstadt, the Azteca Milling Company plant uses locally grown white corn to make a variety of Mexican-style food products, such as tortillas and taco shells. Many of these products are used by fast-food restaurants around the country. Annually, the plant purchases about five million bushels of corn, mostly white corn, from local farmers. Azteca was one of the companies attracted to Evansville through the efforts of Vision 2000, a local economic development group.

Big business isn't the only towering sight on Evansville's industrial landscape. Because of the entrepreneurial spirit that is so alive here, more small businesses are taking root in Evansville than ever before, and many are family owned. Evansville is a place where the American dream comes true again and again.

Not all of the city's centers of power are industrial and manufacturing concerns. Evansville is home to the *Evansville Courier & Press*, a Scripps-Howard company, 11 radio stations, four network-affiliated television stations; one Public Broadcasting System (PBS) television station; and 10 cable television stations. Service-related companies, such as engineering firms, advertising and marketing agencies, market research firms, insurance companies, printers, and construction companies, have experienced unprecedented growth, fueled by the economic boom in the area. Particularly significant in terms of the area's future is the growth in high-tech companies, from web page design firms to computer-related businesses.

One of several plastics companies in Evansville, Rexam Closures manufactures proprietary and custom plastic closures. Photo by L. Kent Whitehead.

For more than 166 years, Old National Bank has been one of the area's most respected banking institutions.
Photo by L. Kent Whitehead.

Vital to the success of any industry is easy access to energy. Evansville is cradled by land abundant in natural resources, with supplies of oil, natural gas, and coal all nearby. The largest coal producer in Indiana, Black Beauty Coal Company, is headquartered in Evansville. With eight mines in Indiana and three in Southern Illinois, Black Beauty markets a range of low, medium, and high sulfur coal products to electricity generators and industrial users. The company is partly owned by the Peabody Group, the world's largest coal company.

The major utility serving the region is Southern Indiana Gas and Electric Company (SIGECO). It reaches more than 120,000 retail electric customers and 104,000 natural gas customers in a ten-county area of southwest Indiana. Located in the heart of coal country, SIGECO's generating stations are designed to efficiently burn local coal with minimum environmental impact. SIGECO has long been known for maintaining low operating costs - which translates into low cost power. Its current retail electric rates are in the lowest 25 percent nationwide, and natural gas rates are in the lowest 10 percent nationwide. SIGECO is a subsidiary of Vectren, based in Evansville.

As crucial as abundant energy is, so too is the availability of good transportation. Geographically, Evansville's location on the banks of the Ohio River has always made it a strategic transportation route for goods and commodities. The Ohio River carries more freight tonnage than any inland body of water in the world, and provides economical and efficient access to national and international markets. Navigation is possible on a year-round basis because the river rarely freezes. The Evansville area is served by five barge lines: American Commercial Barge Lines, Ohio River Company, Union Barge Line, Valley Lines, Inc., and the Ohio Barge Line, Inc.

Evansville also has two barge terminals: Southwind Maritime Centre in Posey Country and Valley Terminal in Evansville. One of three State of Indiana ports, Southwind is comprised of approximately 745 acres, with two miles of riverfront access. The port offers a range of services including dry and liquid cargo handling, tug, towing, fleeting and switching services, heavy-lift capabilities, a complete range of material handling equipment, waste disposal, sanitation service, and sanitary/fire protection. The port is a designated Foreign Trade Zone, opening up foreign markets for area businesses. The Valley Terminal has complete modern mechanical facilities for the transfer of materials utilizing barge, rail, and truck. There is also space to provide warehouse and open storage facilities if necessary. The city is also a hub for several railways: CSX Transportation, Conrail, Norfolk Southern Corp., and Indiana Hi-Rail.

There are six major highway systems providing access for several industrial and commercial areas throughout the Evansville region. Interstate 64 provides east-west access to Louisville (I-65) and St. Louis. U.S. 41 provides a four-lane north and south access and connections with Interstate 64 and the Kentucky Parkway System. Interstate 164 connects I-64 and Indiana 57 with U.S. 41 south of Evansville. Indiana 62 and State Road 66 provide east-west access, and Indiana 57 provides access to the northeast.

Efficient interstate and intrastate shipping to and from the area is provided by more than 40 general commodity motor carriers, all of which maintain terminals in the area, and by over 12 express services.

The city's central location is advantageous not only for river, rail, and highway transportation but also for air travel. The Evansville Regional Airport is a modern terminal designed to comfortably and

The Petroleum Club is a popular dining establishment where business people often gather. Photo by L. Kent Whitehead.

efficiently serve all travelers. Six airlines (USAir, American Eagle, Comair, Atlantic Southeast, Northwest Airlines, and Trans World Express) service the airport, providing jet and commuter air service for over 48 flights a day. Each month, more than 25,000 passengers board planes at the airport.

Contributing to the stability and success of commercial life in the Evansville region are its area banks and savings & loan institutions. The major banks in the area are Old National Bank, National City Bank, and Fifth Third.

For more than 166 years, Old National Bank has been one of the area's most respected banking institutions. Its holding company, Old National Bank Corp, is the largest independent bank holding company headquartered in Indiana, with $7 billion in assets. Old National provides a full range of financial services, including retail and commercial banking, insurance, trust, and brokerage, through 137 banking centers throughout Indiana, Illinois, and Kentucky.

National City Bank has long been known as the premier business bank in the area it serves. The bank's history in the community dates back to 1850, when its forerunner, The Canal Bank, was founded. National City's holding company is National City Bancshares, a $2.1-billion multibank holding company with headquarters in Evansville. The holding company owns 12 banks that operate from 67 locations in Indiana, Illinois, Kentucky, and southwestern Ohio. It is the second-largest independent bank holding company based in Evansville.

In 1999 Cincinnati-based Fifth Third Bancorp acquired CNB Bancshares, the bank holding company for Civitas Bank. It is the largest banking holding company headquartered in Indiana, with assets exceeding $7.1 billion and operations in Indiana, Michigan, Kentucky, Illinois, and Tennessee. Civitas was formerly known as Citizens National Bank, which was established in Evansville in 1874. Citizens was the first bank in the area to offer 24-hour automated teller machines.

The Fifth Third transaction created the third largest bank in Indiana. At the time of the acquisition, CNB Bancshares operated 144 banking offices, a consumer finance company, a leasing company, a credit life insurance company, and a property casualty insurance agency. For eight years in a row, Fifth Third has been named the number one bank in America by Salomon Smith Barney in the Top 50 Bank Annual.

In addition, Union Planters Bank has two locations in Evansville. Headquartered in Memphis, Tennessee, Union Planters Corp. (the bank's holding company) has assets of $19 billion.

Numerous savings and loan institutions, as well as credit unions, serve Evansville customers as well. These institutions rank among the nation's strongest and safest financial institutions.

Evansville is a hub for several railways.
Photo by L. Kent Whitehead.

The Evansville Regional Airport is a modern terminal designed to comfortably and efficiently serve all travelers. Photo by L. Kent Whitehead.

A financial dynamo in the area is American General Finance. It is one of the largest consumer finance companies in the country, with more than $9 billion in assets. With its corporate headquarters in Evansville, American General operates offices in 41 states, Puerto Rico, and the U.S. Virgin Islands.

What makes all these companies run so successfully is human ingenuity. The people here are known for their hard-work ethics, productivity, and diverse talents. For businesses, this means the availability of workers with the professional integrity and world-class expertise necessary for competitive success in all fields of endeavor.

People with talent and ability; an attractive quality of life; a stable, thriving, and business-friendly environment. It is this perfect mix of resources that make Evansville a place where any business, large or small, can thrive. ▨

The Ohio River remains a significant factor in Evansville's economic development. Photo by L. Kent Whitehead.

The region is an agricultural center for soybeans. Photo by L. Kent Whitehead.

Among its many uses, locally grown white corn eventually
finds its way to Mexican food products.
Photos by L. Kent Whitehead.

Agriculture remains a significant industry in Evansville.
Photo by L. Kent Whitehead.

GOLD
NATIONAL
Citizens Bank
Citizens Bank

At dawn on the streets of Evansville, a vital Midwestern city begins to stir. Photo by L. Kent Whitehead.

OLD NATIONAL
OLD NATIONAL

Photo by L. Kent Whitehead.

9

CHAPTER NINE
NETWORKS

Photo by L. Kent Whitehead.

❋ SIGECO ❋

Generating Opportunities

At home or at work, in the factories or on the farms, Southern Indiana Gas and Electric Company has been the financially-sound, investor-owned utility in Southwest Indiana since 1912.

SIGECO was formed at a time when the typical household burned coal for heat and used ice to keep foods fresh. The arrival of gas and electric service provided superior replacements for these necessities and fueled the desire for additional household conveniences. Prosperity brought new businesses, additional residents, and growing demands for energy into the area, creating steady growth in the region and for SIGECO.

During the many changes in the business landscape since its founding, SIGECO has remained a low-cost energy provider. SIGECO is recognized as one of the lowest-cost producers of electricity in the U.S., with retail electric rates 32 percent below the national average. SIGECO's gas rates are among the lowest in the state of Indiana.

Low electric and gas rates provide a strong incentive to attract and retain businesses in SIGECO's Southwest Indiana service area. SIGECO's economic development office works with local and county governments, and with business leaders, to cultivate relationships that lead to new jobs and opportunities. As a result, growth in the region is outpacing the national rate

SIGECO is a visible member of the communities it serves, sponsoring efforts that enrich everyday life. Education is one example. For the classroom, SIGECO provides kindergarten, third grade, and fifth grade teachers with lesson materials about electric and gas safety, how energy is transformed and used, and ways to conserve energy.

A $100 million scrubber investment in 1995 reduced sulfur dioxide emissions over 95 percent, a level well within requirements of the Clean Air Act of 1990. Photo by Fred Reaves/ImageOne 1999.

Environmental Stewardship

SIGECO's efforts to meet environmental requirements are producing benefits beyond compliance with government standards. The flyash removed from SIGECO's Culley Generating Station is a key constituent of a relatively new building material—autoclaved aerated concrete block (AAC). While new to the United States, AAC is a widely-used building material around the world. AAC weighs about two-thirds less that concrete and has exceptional sound deadening and thermal qualities. It can be shaped with ordinary woodworking tools. AAC block will be used to construct the Habitat for Humanity's New Millennium Home being built in Evansville. Wallboard in the home will be made from gypsum created as a by-product of the scrubbing processes at the Culley Generating Station.

Operating alternatively-fueled vehicles is another of the ways SIGECO has demonstrated its commitment to the environment. Within SIGECO's fleet are a growing number of vehicles fueled by compressed natural gas (CNG). These and over 100 other CNG-fueled vehicles in the area can refuel at SIGECO's Eco-Fuel Compressed Natural Gas Station.

Programs to help endangered wildlife return to safe populations have also received attention. SIGECO supports efforts to increase awareness and promote the protection of the threatened North American Eastern Bluebird. Twenty nest boxes have been placed in the wooded area surrounding the A.B. Brown Generating Station. SIGECO has offered nest boxes to the public at a nominal price, hosted a day-long bluebird seminar, and provided special instructional programs for use with K-5 classes. SIGECO joined with the Department of Natural Resources in protecting and encouraging the preservation of the peregrine falcon by placing a nest site at the A.B. Brown Generating Station. Falcons today

When frigid weather strikes, SIGECO's gas storage fields help meet increased demand and reduce the need for gas purchases at peak prices. Photo by Fred Reaves/ImageOne 1999.

Coal procurements through SIGCORP Fuels have helped SIGECO reduce coal costs below those of any electric utility east of the Mississippi River. Photo by Fred Reaves/ImageOne 1999.

often choose power plant stacks for raising their young. The stacks resemble the sharply-defined bluffs that are the falcon's native nesting area and are usually near fresh water.

Structured For Growth

SIGECO was recently restructured into business units to better achieve competitive goals. Creating these business units is part of a growth plan to leverage strengths as competition draws near and to broaden the offering of services to SIGECO customers.

The Power Supply unit contains SIGECO's power production plants, with a generating capacity of 1,256 megawatts and among the lowest operating costs in the industry. A planned cogeneration plant will create additional generation capacity by the early 2000s using new clean coal technology. Power is marketed to municipalities, other utilities, and power resellers when it is not needed for retail customers.

The Energy Delivery unit provides gas and electric service to approximately 150,000 residential, commercial, and industrial customers in a 10-county area in Southwest Indiana. Support functions related to the Power Supply and Energy Delivery units will be organized into the Support Services unit.

Forming SIGCORP Capitalizes on Change

The regulatory environment that SIGECO operates within has changed in recent years. Natural gas production is deregulated, and transmission and marketing of natural gas has changed. New federal policies allow the operation of independent power plants, outside the regulatory realm of investor-owned utilities such as SIGECO, with mandatory open access to utility-owned transmission lines for transmitting electricity between producers and distributors. Many states have already introduced deregulation, giving energy customers a choice of providers and services.

To capture and maximize the opportunities deregulation offers, a holding company, SIGCORP, was formed in 1996. This step signaled dramatic change in the business in order to provide customer solutions in an evolving energy marketplace. This plan included creating a SIGCORP telecommunications presence, expanding SIGCORP's energy services businesses, and investing in other businesses or projects that offer higher returns than the regulated utility business.

While SIGECO is SIGCORP's flagship regulated utility subsidiary, the other subsidiaries contained in the growth plan are organized into three non-regulated operational groups—Telecom Group, Energy Services Group, and Complementary Ventures Group.

Telecom Group

SIGECOM is a partnership between SIGCORP and Utilicom Networks, a Massachusetts technology company. SIGECOM represents an $80-million investment to build a fiber-optic-based network with leading-edge telecommunication services for greater Evansville. The project's first phase, when complete, will have the potential for serving more than 80,000 homes and businesses.

SIGCORP COMMUNICATIONS builds high-speed fiber-optic communications networks for municipal utilities, enabling them to manage power loads more efficiently and offer communication services such as cable television and Internet access.

Cable TV, high speed Internet access, and telephone service are among the offerings from SIGECOM, a SIGCORP subsidiary, with capacity for over 80,000 homes and businesses. Photo by Fred Reaves/ImageOne 1999.

This boiler installation at Bristol-Myers Squibb is among the projects designed and installed by Energy Systems Group, with new branch offices in Indianapolis and Cincinnati. Photo by Fred Reaves/ImageOne 1999.

Energy Services Group

SIGCORP Energy Services markets wholesale natural gas to industrial and other large-volume customers throughout a seven-state region and offers customers a wide range of other energy management services.

Energy Systems Group, an affiliate owned jointly by SIGCORP, Indiana Energy, and Citizens Gas and Coke Utility, provides energy conservation savings to institutions, governmental units, and commercial entities through risk-free building improvements and equipment upgrades.

Air Quality Services, a joint venture firm, owned by SIGCORP and Environmental Management Consultants Inc., was created in 1998 to offer air quality monitoring and testing services for industry and utilities in the region.

Complementary Ventures Group

Southern Indiana Properties participates in structured finance and investment transactions, including leveraged leases of real estate and equipment, which have provided above-average returns to the company.

SIGCORP Fuels provides SIGECO's generating plants with a dependable, low-cost source of coal. It also markets coal to other utilities.

Southern Indiana Minerals processes power plant combustion by-products and markets these industrial minerals to the paint, coatings, and construction industries.

SIGCORP Capital provides financing and cash management services for SIGCORP's nonregulated subsidiaries.

Partnering for Progress

In June 1999, SIGCORP announced a merger with Indiana Energy, Inc. intended to result in a new holding company named Vectren. The merger combines two Indiana companies with strong balance sheets, low-cost operations, growing service areas, diversified product portfolios, and track records of delivering superior shareholder value. Through its utility subsidiaries, Vectren will offer gas and/or electricity to more than 650,000 customers in adjoining service areas that cover nearly two-thirds of Indiana. Vectren's non-utility subsidiaries will offer energy-related products and services, fiber-optic based telecommunication services, materials management, locating and trenching services, and energy marketing to customers throughout the surrounding region.

Andrew E. Goebel, SIGCORP's president and chief operating officer, said, "Simply put, this combination makes sense. It's a marriage of strengths. SIGCORP has the lowest average retail electric rate in the state and each company has among the lowest gas rates. Furthermore, over the last several years, our customer growth rates have exceeded the national average."

Energy Systems Group, a SIGCORP affiliate, offers improvements and upgrades for energy conservation, reflected by this de-aerator installation at Bristol-Myers Squibb. Photo by Fred Reaves/ImageOne 1999.

"We have known Indiana Energy for years and, in fact, are partners in Energy Systems Group, LLC, a joint venture formed in 1997 that provides energy-related performance contracting services. As one company, we will serve 650,000 Indiana customers, providing superior customer service and some of the most competitive energy prices in the country. This combination will enable us to cross-sell a greater array of products and services to our existing and future customer base and to make the necessary investment in technology to continue delivering first-class customer service and other business applications in an increasingly competitive environment. We believe that the combination of these two Indiana companies will strengthen our commitment to our communities and provide customer benefits that further enhance Indiana's economic development efforts. We intend to be a focused, high-quality, high-service regional player in our regulated businesses," Goebel concluded.

The merger is conditioned, among other things, upon the approvals of the shareholders of each company and customary regulatory approvals. The companies anticipate that the regulatory processes can be completed by March 31, 2000. ▓

Large-volume and industrial customers can purchase natural gas and management services from SIGCORP Energy Services. Photo by Fred Reaves/ImageOne 1999.

Low gas and electric rates, energy sevices, and telecommunications services from SIGCORP head the list of business incentives in southwest Indiana. Photo by Fred Reaves/ImageOne 1999.

❈ INSIGHT COMMUNICATIONS ❈

Customers of Insight Communications have come to expect a lot more than basic cable service from this provider. One of the nation's largest cable operators, Insight offers its million-plus customers a variety of state-of-the-art entertainment, educational, and information services in each of the many communities it serves. Headquartered in New York City, Insight has operations in Indiana—where it is the largest cable operator in the state—as well as in California, Illinois, Kentucky, Ohio, and Georgia.

The company's primary business is the distribution of information and entertainment programming. Its customers enjoy many channels of news, sports, movies, comedy, drama, and educational programming with the simplicity and reliability of cable's broadband, fiber-optic networks. Insight is also developing and providing the services that are becoming part of everyone's future: high speed Internet access, digital cable, and telephone service. In deploying such advanced services, Insight's joint venture with AT&T in most of its operating areas benefits customers on many levels; with Insight's expertise in cable television and AT&T's proven experience in telecommunications, the resources and capabilities are solidly in place as the industry continues to move forward.

When Insight took over the Evansville area's cable operations from the previous operator in 1998, customers noticed a quick improvement in services, followed by an enhanced variety of options. The infrastructure of Insight's cable system lets customers select from a large menu of services that will be continuously updated and advanced as improved technology becomes available. By implementing this cutting-edge, "future proof" system, Insight has protected its customers from hardware obsolescence; this enables the company to deploy new technologies more easily and uniformly with all of the latest advancements in entertainment and communication services. Furthermore, Insight's technology means that customers do not need a satellite dish or antenna for clear reception of local channels.

Insight offers customers a diverse array of channels with a variety of entertainment and information options. Basic Cable service provides clear reception of local broadcast and cable channels and connects customers to additional services. Classic Cable service offers the most popular cable networks available today, with a broad range of programming that provides something for every member of the family. Numerous premium movie channels are also available.

In 1999, Insight's Evansville system was rebuilt in an $11 million upgrade that increased bandwidth capacity to 750 megahertz. The resulting two-way fiber optic system delivers a clearer digital picture with fewer disruptions and doubles the channel capacity of the former channel line-up, both analog and digital. The upgrade also introduced two revolutionary products into the Insight family of services. The first is LocalSource(SM), which is an interactive community information and entertainment guide created exclusively for Evansville-area customers. They can use LocalSource(SM) to access local weather, sports, cinema listings, restaurant menus, school activities, and much more. The second new product is a video-on-demand service called On Set, which downloads current movies into the digital set-top box, so customers can watch any available movie at any time, with the ability to rewind, fast-forward, and pause.

This system upgrade also gives Insight customers the opportunity to enjoy high-speed access to the Internet through the same cable lines that provide their television service. Called Insight@Home, this service gives Insight customers a range of high-speed data services at speeds up to 100 times faster than normal dial-up phone lines—which means no more long waits for large digital files to download.

In mid-1999, plans were underway for Insight to join forces with AT&T to provide telephone services to Insight customers. Customers who choose this option will receive all of their cable television, Internet, and telephone services on the same cable line. Representative of the very latest in integrated technology, this project demonstrates Insight's commitment to providing the technological innovations customers will come to expect in the new millennium.

Insight employees are committed to top-notch customer service as a key priority.

Insight's recent multimillion dollar rebuild of Evansville's cable system is providing the most leading-edge services in the industry.

Yet all of this technology does not mean very much if customers do not quickly and courteously receive customer and technical support when they need it. Therefore, Insight makes customer service its highest priority. As friends and neighbors within Evansville-area communities, Insight's customer service representatives, installers, and technicians strive to deliver unparalleled service, program choices, and technical support. The customer service representatives are Insight's goodwill ambassadors; they offer front-line support to help customers choose programming packages and help them solve technical problems, often over the phone.

Among its customer service commitments, Insight joins the cable industry in its On-Time Guarantee initiative, which credits customer accounts if installers fail to arrive on time for a scheduled installation or service appointment. Insight also makes every effort to accommodate customer schedules for service and repair appointments whenever possible and is always committed to improving customer service in additional ways.

Insight Communications is an active member of the Evansville-area community. The company offers the use of its channels to local programs that provide heightened awareness and information about community events, issues, and activities. Through an industry-wide initiative called "Cable in the Classroom," Insight also provides free cable service to every elementary, junior, and senior high school in the communities it serves, allowing teachers to create new curricula and innovative learning environments by accessing cable programming. In addition, Insight employees regularly participate in community activities such as food drives, Red Cross blood drives, and Chamber of Commerce activities.

As Insight heads into the new millennium, it continues to grow while still holding the same high values that have brought it to this point. The company makes significant investments in its people, its operations, and its future to realize its vision: becoming a multifaceted communications business driven by quality customer service.

❖ EVANSVILLE COURIER & PRESS ❖

The Evansville Courier Company is best known as the publisher of *The Evansville Courier & Press*, a morning newspaper with a circulation of some 74,000 subscribers daily and 110,000 on Sundays. Readership is calculated at 170,000 daily and 253,000 on Sunday.

We've been publishing newspapers continuously in Evansville, Indiana, since 1865. Of course, there have been a few changes since then. What began as a one-employee/owner, 4-page weekly newspaper produced on a hand-fed press, has grown into a four-section daily newspaper employing 325 full-time and 100 part-time employees. It has become the dominant player in providing news and market information to Southern Indiana and contiguous regions in Kentucky and Illinois.

And we're not "just" a newspaper anymore. We're proud of our award-winning newspaper, one of the most colorful in the United States and one of the crown jewels of The E. W. Scripps Company. We're making a name for ourselves in other areas, too. *The Courier & Press* is establishing itself in commercial printing, in producing high-end, calendar-and-catalog-quality electronic pre-press and color separation work, and as an alternate delivery system capable of delivering product samples ranging from shampoo to fresh-cut flowers. The advertising department offers its customers an Internet presence, direct-mail capabilities to targeted zones, a total-marketing package to non-subscribers, and a wealth of specialty publications ranging from gardening to health.

The Courier & Press is housed in a modern, state-of-the-art facility that provides employees a comfortable, professional work environment. Ours is one of the most modern newspaper facilities in the United States. Our line of flexographic presses and color separation equipment gives us the capacity to produce one of the most vivid, colorful

newspapers in the world, and, indeed, we utilize the capacity. The quality of our production has won numerous awards both nationally and internationally, and in early 1999 *The Courier & Press* was inducted into the prestigious International Color Quality Club sponsored by NAA/IFRA at Lyons, France.

Flexographic printing uses water-based inks, which means the customer experiences no ink rub-off. The process is also the most environmentally friendly printing that can be done. *The Courier & Press* is deeply committed to community service and is a major sponsor of the United Way, the Evansville Philharmonic Orchestra, the Evansville Museum, and dozens of other non-profit initiatives.

Our most vital commitment to the community, however, is to fulfill the Scripps mission: "Give light and the people will find their own way." ❖

❈ EVANSVILLE REGIONAL AIRPORT ❈

Evansville Regional Airport has been renamed several times and has undergone many changes since its founding in 1928, but one thing hasn't changed — convenience. Having a quality regional airport located just a few minutes from anywhere in the city means that residents of Evansville and its environs can "fly easy" for business or pleasure.

Convenience is only one reason to fly out of Evansville Regional Airport. Another is the competitive fares, in all three major price classes — excursion, coach, and first class. A good combination of jet and turbo prop service makes it possible for travelers boarding at Evansville to make connections to anywhere in the world from eight major hub cities: Atlanta, Chicago, Cincinnati, Indianapolis, Detroit, Memphis, Pittsburgh, and St. Louis. A major expansion and modernization project in 1989 added a 140,000-square-foot passenger

terminal with 10 carrier gates, as well as 1,050 well-lit and secure parking spaces. Three years later, Business & Commercial Aviation declared that Evansville Regional Airport had the best air service of any U. S. city of comparable size.

In 1999, 50 airline departures took off daily from EVV's three runways. The carriers currently based there are American Eagle, Comair (Delta Connection), Atlantic Southeast Airlines (Delta Connection), Northwest Airlink, TransWorld Express, and US Airways Express. The number of passengers arriving and departing annually has continued to increase; in 1998, more than 500,000 passengers traveled through the airport.

Two fixed-base operators — Tri-State Aero Inc. and Million Air — provide fuel, storage, and maintenance for general aviation, corporate, and commercial aircraft.

EVV plays an important role in the economic success of Southwest Indiana. When Toyota and AK Steel decided to locate new facilities there in the mid-1990s, one major consideration was the presence of the airport. Thousands of business travelers fly in and out of EVV every year; many of them take advantage of the private conference room in the terminal where they can hold meetings at no charge. Warehouse facilities on the airport's 76-acre Foreign Trade Zone are under construction. The state legislature, working with the airport, has designated certain areas on and near the airport to be declared an Airport Development Zone. Such designations will allow the inventory of all businesses located there to be exempt from taxation.

Evansville Regional Airport is a self-supporting public agency operated by the Evansville-Vanderburgh Airport Authority District. An advisory team of local business leaders appointed in 1997 established a vision statement for the airport's future. It reads: "The Evansville Regional Airport of 2005 will provide service that meets the business and non-business air traveler needs and will be an effective economic engine and job producing catalyst for the community."

Whether flying for business or pleasure, the thousands of travelers coming through Evansville each year can be assured that high-quality service, convenience, and competitive fares will continue to be the top priorities of Evansville Regional Airport. ❈

10

CHAPTER TEN

MANUFACTURING & DISTRIBUTION

Photo by L. Kent Whitehead.

Ferro Corporation, Filled and Reinforced Plastics Division

Ferro Corporation, Filled and Reinforced Plastics Division, is a world-class manufacturer of custom-compounded, filled, and reinforced polypropylene resins.

- "Ferro Touches Your Life, Every Day,"® providing custom plastic compounds to processors who manufacture components for a wide array of automotive, major appliance, small appliance, pool and spa, lawn and garden, power tool, food packaging, and medical markets.
- QS-9000 and ISO-9001 Registered.
- The answer is, "Yes, we can!" Ferro has built its business on custom compound formulations, including those with end-uses requiring Underwriters Laboratory approval, National Sanitary Foundation, or FDA compliance. Chemists and master craftsmen create custom formulations, including color matching, and provide consistency batch after batch.
- The Division is a "full service" compounder, providing teams of experts available to assist in every aspect of a product's design and manufacture.
- The Filled and Reinforced Plastics Division prides itself on its ability to respond to customer needs or emergencies—On-a-dime.
- Environmentally Correct—Post-consumer, post-industrial, and internally recycled materials incorporated in Ferro compounds allow customers to share their vision of environmental responsibility.

Located at 5001 O'Hara Drive, in Evansville, Indiana, the Ferro Filled and Reinforced Plastics Division proudly flies the hard earned Indiana Quality and the QS-9000 flags beside the United States flag, the Indiana State flag, and Ferro's Corporate Flag. Photo by Bill Palmer, Action Photography, Ltd.

- Walking the Walk—An excellent safety record, over 3.5 million hours without a lost-time accident—and still counting—is a reflection of the Division's involved, pro-active management team and conscientious, dedicated employees.
- Cost Awareness—Ferro knows you have to consider the bottom line and continues to keep costs down through high-volume purchasing power, inventory control, and recycling/waste minimization efforts to keep their customers competitive in their businesses.

Ferro's Filled and Reinforced Plastics Division, located in Evansville, began in 1973 as Complas, with one plastics extruder and eight employees. In 1979, Ferro Corporation purchased Complas and in 1989 established the Filled and Reinforced Plastics Division. Today, the Division is one of the world's largest compounders of polyolefins with three plants, 240 employees, a 400,000-pound-per-day manufacturing capacity, and annual sales of $80 million.

Ferro's Filled and Reinforced Plastics Division has built its business one compound formulation and one customer at a time. Each customer is special and each compound is designed to fit a unique market application, meeting exacting specifications for physical properties, color, weatherability, durability, temperature extremes, appearance, and chemical resistance.

If you require an FDA or National Sanitary Foundation (NSF) compliant product, the Division has the technical expertise to help you meet your needs.

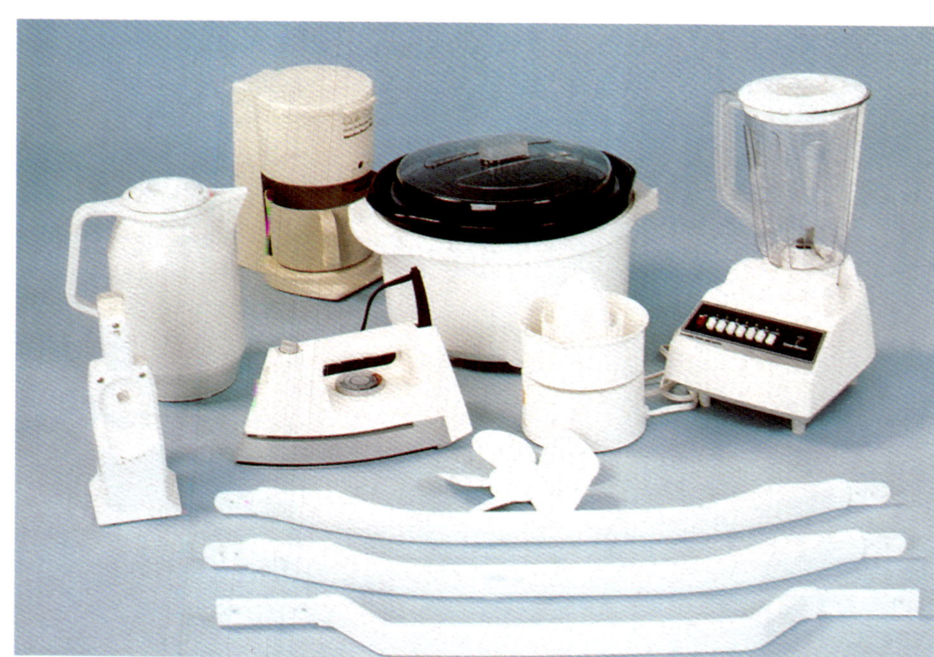

"Ferro Touches Your Life, Every Day,"® - supplying large and small appliance manufacturers with custom formulated and color matched raw materials to meet rigorous customer, UL, and FDA requirements. Photo by Don Hardesty Photography.

Ferro's Filled and Reinforced Plastics Division incorporates millions of pounds of recycled polypropylenes into custom compounds, many of which are intended for the automotive industry, because Ferro knows its customers share in their vision of environmental stewardship. Photo by Don Hardesty Photography.

Are you a manufacturer of disposable medical supplies? Polypropylene-based medical products could help you address environmental and public relations issues.

Ferro's Filled and Reinforced Plastics Division has assembled teams of experts to assist customers at every stage, from inception to full production, including Research and Development for new applications, mold design, compound formulation, color matching, and processing advice.

Ferro's QS-9000 and ISO-9001 registrations provide you with assurance that the product will continue to meet your specifications time after time after time.

The Path to QS-9000 and ISO-9001

QS-9000 and ISO-9001 registrations are not passing fads. They require a great deal of commitment, planning, and old-fashioned hard work. Ferro's efforts began in 1994, when management committed to attaining ISO-9001 registration. Employees at all levels reviewed and documented work procedures and, where necessary, modified work practices to comply with ISO requirements. The Division achieved ISO-9001 registration in early 1996. In 1997, Ferro began to work toward the QS-9000 registration, which it attained in early 1998. Maintaining these valuable registrations requires untiring diligence and undergoing a semi-annual external audit. Ferro also maintains a group of volunteer internal quality auditors to insure adherence to their adopted quality standards.

Quality gets recognized

Ferro's products have received numerous quality awards, year after year, including the Indiana Quality Award. Ferro values every customer, and its customers have demonstrated their appreciation by honoring Ferro with their long-term business and their coveted quality awards, including Ford Motor Company's Q-1 Supplier Award, Toledo Mold & Die Corporation's Distinguished Supplier Award, The Hoover Company's Quality Supplier Award, and Hamilton Beach/Proctor Silex, Royal Plastics, Sunbeam/Oster, and Calsonic Supplier Awards.

Success doesn't "just happen." At Ferro, much progress can be traced to a Total Quality Management (TQM) initiative begun in 1994, under the guidance of the Business Development Center at the University of Southern Indiana. The university aided Ferro in the creation of a unified strategy for long-term success, which included ISO-9001 registration. The TQM effort evolved into an informal Business Process Redesign (BPR), and throughout 1996 and 1997 it grew into a formal, structured program. Employees from all levels were involved in the BPR effort to critically review, improve, and document all business activities from order generation through order fulfillment.

TQM and BPR efforts have aided the Division in operating efficiently, providing excellent product quality, and responding to customers' needs. In 1997, 1998, and 1999, customer surveys conducted by an outside consultant scored Ferro's Filled and Reinforced Plastics Division consistently higher than its competitors in product quality, service, price, and value.

What are your needs? Ferro's teams of experts can help with every aspect of product design, including initial engineering, mold design, and custom formulations meeting UL, FDA, and NSF requirements and often provide cost savings over other thermoplastics. Photo by Don Hardesty Photography.

Ferro's QS-9000 registration assures every customer they'll receive quality and consistency batch after batch, shipment after shipment. Photo by Bill Palmer, Action Photography, Ltd.

Ferro knows that customers' requirements can change without warning. Computerized manufacturing and inventory control systems, a complete stock of color pigments, and purchasing leverage lets Ferro provide what you need, when you need it. From color matches and small quantity samples for prototyping to railcars of your product, Ferro prides itself on meeting your changing needs.

Integrated Recycling Programs

Ferro's Filled and Reinforced Plastics Division has been recognized as a model plastics recycler, receiving Honorable Mentions for the Southern Indiana Rural Development Project's 1998 Quality of Life— Corporate Leadership category, the 1998 Indiana Governor's Award for Excellence in Recycling, and the 1997 Senator Richard Lugar's Productivity Award. The prestigious environmental group Keep America Beautiful, Inc. has recognized Ferro as a major partner in developing recycled materials for use at Ford Motor Company.

This recognition is due to the long-term emphasis the Division has given to recycling and waste minimization. Long before recycling was fashionable, Ferro recognized that tracking and managing its waste

streams would minimize waste and reduce landfill costs. Since 1989, they have diverted 20 million pounds of waste (used oil, corrugated packaging, office paper, wooden pallets, and scrap metal) from the landfill to recyclers. In addition, Ferro incorporates post-industrial (PIR) and post-consumer (PCR) plastics into its products. Use of recycled plastics has increased from zero pounds in 1991 to 29 percent of total plastic resins used in 1998. To ensure a recycled polypropylene supply of consistent quality and quantity, Ferro—Evansville established an independent post-consumer recycling facility and partnered with another company that supplies the Division with PCR and PIR polypropylenes.

The Division recycles internally by reclaiming raw materials for use in production. Finely powdered mineral fillers captured by the dust collection system sometimes are reintroduced into the process. Scrap plastic from extruder start-ups and malfunctions is reground and re-used. Even leftover samples pulled by the Quality Assurance and Color departments for quality checks are reprocessed whenever possible.

The Division has found that recycling and waste minimization improves housekeeping and working conditions, protects the environment, and provides a significant economic benefit.

Working Hard, Having Fun, Being Safe

The Division knows its most important assets are its employees. From hard-working extruder operators to Research and Development chemists to managers to janitors, every person is an essential member of the Ferro team. Ferro does its best to provide secure employment, a competitive wage/benefit package, a chance for good times, and, most importantly, a safe place in which to work.

The last lost-time accident at Ferro—Evansville was on May 20, 1992. The approximately 240 employees have chalked up over 3.5 million work hours without a lost-time accident. Their OSHA recordable rate was nearly three times lower than the national average for plastics

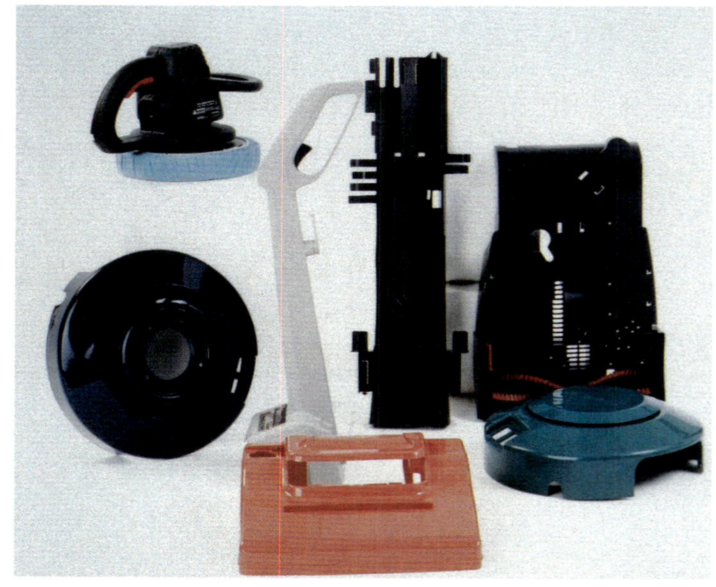

Durability, weatherability, and chemical resistance are important for outdoor products and lawn and garden equipment - Ferro can make it tough, attractive, and make it economically. Photo by Don Hardesty Photography.

compounders. The Division has earned the Ferro Corporation's President's Award for Safety and the Society for Plastics Industry's Safety awards for five consecutive years.

Ferro does not neglect the good times; everyone enjoys the company picnics and Christmas parties. Safety milestones are observed with prizes and catered dinners. During every shutdown, management takes a busload of employees on a trip to visit with key suppliers and customers. The annual Sales meeting is probably unique in the plastics industry, as Ferro assembles suppliers, customers, sales representatives, managers, and employees for several days of free-flowing discussion of technologies, opportunities, problems, and success stories. The strategy must be successful, since the Division enjoys long-term relationships with suppliers and world-class manufacturers such as Bissell, Calsonic, Daimler-Chrysler, Ford, Hoover, Maytag, Proctor-Silex/Hamilton Beach, and Whirlpool.

The pleasant environment and quality people at Ferro Corporation's Filled and Reinforced Plastics Division make working for and with Ferro something every person will enjoy. ▨

Begun in 1973 with eight employees, Ferro's Filled and Reinforced Plastics Division is now one of the world's largest custom compounders of polyolefins, utilizing state-of-the-art production technology, with a 400,000 pound-per-day capacity and over 240 employees. Photo by Don Hardesty Photography.

The Division is justifiably proud of their excellent Safety Record - over 3,500,000 hours worked without a Lost-Time Accident - and still counting! The Safety Program is indicative of their high caliber employees and conscientious management. Photo by Bill Palmer, Action Photography, Ltd.

❈ BERRY PLASTICS CORPORATION ❈

Berry Plastics, a leading manufacturer of injection-molded plastic packaging, is a fast-growing company headquartered in Evansville. Established in 1967 as Imperial Plastics, the company has grown to over $300 million in sales encompassing twelve facilities in the United States and one in the United Kingdom. Berry Plastics manufactures five major product lines: aerosol overcaps, open-top containers, drink cups, housewares, and custom molded products.

In most of its product lines, Berry has become the market leader. For example, the company is the world's largest producer of aerosol overcaps, producing more than 2 billion annually! The diversity of its products and wide variety of its customers (none of which represents more than 3 percent of sales) offer a cushion against adverse economic and environmental conditions.

Berry Plastics could not have achieved this continued success without its commitment to producing high-quality products. The work ethic and advanced teamwork capabilities of employees ensure efficiency in all phases of manufacturing, from product engineering through graphic design, maintenance, production, and on-time delivery. At the Evansville plant (the largest injection-molded packaging plant in the country), Berry operates 50 molding machines and more than 20 printers and silk screeners, thereby providing its customers with start-to-finish confidence.

As one of Evansville's premiere employers, Berry Plastics strives to keep a close-knit atmosphere in its near-Downtown facility (a portion of which is located in the historic building that once housed the Fendrich cigar factory).

Berry Plastics' eight hundred employees, many of whom live nearby, pride themselves on their ability to improve, earn, and grow. They are supported in these efforts by frequent on-the-job training. The company promotes primarily from within and offers five apprenticeship programs— building maintenance, machine maintenance, accessory equipment, tooling, and molding — by which employees can improve their advancement opportunities.

Aerial view of Berry Plastics.

The company takes great pride in its annual Earth Day school program. Volunteer employees visit area third grades each April to present programs on recycling and conservation. The third graders are then invited to tour the manufacturing facility for a first-hand look at how Berry minimizes waste in production. Each year, about 2000 students tour the plant, and, according to all accounts, employees enjoy it as much as the children!

Berry Plastics projects a healthy future as it continues to expand through acquisitions, as well as through the development and introduction of new products into its diversified markets. ❈

Evansville third graders tour the facility for Earth Day 1999.

❈ ALCOA WARRICK OPERATIONS ❈

One of the largest aluminum smelting and fabricating facilities in the world, Alcoa Warrick Operations is also a full partner in the life of Southwestern Indiana. Since it plays such a large role in the community, Warrick Operations takes very seriously its responsibility to provide a safe working environment where members of the community can find ongoing opportunities for career growth and development.

Two Alcoa business units—Primary Metals and Rigid Packaging—operate at Warrick Operations. The plant produces molten metal that is ultimately rolled into aluminum sheet for the beverage, food can, and building products markets. Warrick Operations is located along scenic Indiana Highway 66 and the Ohio River in Warrick County. The plant has 120 acres under roof and 300 acres within the fence. In total, Alcoa owns 9,000 acres in the area, many devoted to agriculture and recreational uses.

When construction of Warrick Operations began in 1956, the Tri-State was reeling from the closing or relocation of several major employers. The community welcomed Alcoa, which quickly became a cornerstone of the regional economy and one of the area's largest employers. For more than 40 years, Warrick Operations has based its continued success on Alcoa's fundamental values of integrity, respect, and demonstrated support of the community. These values take tangible form in three ways.

First is the health and safety of the thousands of men and women who work there. As Alcoa's top internal priority, health and safety are built into every production step and every area of the plant. In partnership with the United Steelworkers of America Local 104, which represents

Alcoa Warrick Operations, one of the largest aluminum smelting and fabricating facilities in the world, supplies aluminum sheet to the beverage and food can industries. The first aluminum was produced here in 1960, but the plant has been continually modernized to compete with facilities around the world.

hourly employees, all Alcoans are educated in how to create an injury-free workplace and how to play their role in achieving it.

Second is the obligation to protect the environment while maintaining financial strength. One sentence from its Environmental, Health, and Safety Policy demonstrates how Warrick Operations puts this belief into action: "We will work safely in a manner that promotes the health and well-being of the individuals and the environment." Therefore, along with health and safety, Warrick Operations incorporates sustainable development by integrating environmental considerations into all relevant business decisions. These efforts have led to Warrick Operations being recognized both within the Alcoa family and within Indiana for its innovative approach to environmental management.

Third is philanthropic support of the community. Through Alcoa Foundation grants, community service, and employee charitable giving, Warrick Operations has returned millions of dollars to the community that has helped it prosper over the decades.

Alcoa's values have served the company well and made Warrick Operations a dependable partner to the Tri-State community. ❈

Protecting the environment and the health and safety of all Alcoa employees is the top priority of everyone who works at Warrick Operations.

❈ MULZER CRUSHED STONE, INC. ❈

Some businesses start with a Grand Idea; some start with a simple necessity. Mulzer Crushed Stone, Inc. began with both. In the middle of the Depression, Arnold, Roland, and Edgar Mulzer started a company for one simple reason: They needed jobs. In the early days, the Mulzer brothers didn't even dig ditches—they finished up after the ditch diggers. By building the small "box culverts" that connect county roads and private drives to state highways, Arnold, Roland, and Edgar started building a reputation for quality work and on-time delivery that still form the successful core of Mulzer Crushed Stone, Inc.

Road construction after the Depression virtually ended when the United States entered World War II. While Edgar served in the Pacific, Arnold and Roland started mining coal to support the war effort. After the war, the brothers learned that Southern Indiana needed a good aggregate producer, so they purchased a limestone quarry in Eckerty, Indiana. Their original businesses led to the success of Mulzer Crushed Stone, Inc., but the heart of the Mulzer companies today is the production and distribution of crushed stone, sand, and gravel.

Mulzer Crushed Stone, Inc. delivers much of its products by truck throughout Southern Indiana, Northern Kentucky, and Eastern Illinois. However, the region's river system offers an excellent, low-cost transportation option, so the company began shipping on the Ohio River in the 1950s. Mulzer Crushed Stone, Inc.'s river distribution system lowers the shipping cost for all their customers, both big and small.

Mulzer Crushed Stone, Inc. can deliver aggregates to large projects throughout their market area. From highways like I-64 and I-164 to industrial sites like Toyota and Alcoa, they have helped build many large construction projects. They also supply aggregate to smaller jobs every day. Virtually every home and subdivision in the Evansville area is built on Mulzer stone. Mulzer Crushed Stone, Inc. supplies high-calcium limestone to electric utilities, which use it to reduce harmful acid emissions

Much of the stone for Evansville comes by river.

from high-sulfur coal. The company's leadership in the scrubber stone market is but one example of their custom products.

Mulzer Crushed Stone, Inc., currently in its third generation of family ownership, employs over 550 people throughout the Tri-State. It is not unusual for employees to remain with the company more than 35 years; many families have a second and even a third generation working there. What started out in 1935 as a family business continues today as a company with the friendliness of a family business and the resources of a large corporation. ❈

We need aggregates today as much as yesterday.

Photo by Mike Grandmaison.

11

C H A P T E R   E L E V E N
THE BUSINESS COMMUNITY

Photo by L. Kent Whitehead.

❈ FIFTH THIRD BANCORP ❈

From the very beginning, Evansville was a dynamic city. It grew rapidly from a tiny pioneer settlement to become a regional center of commerce and industry — a distinction it retains today. For more than a century and a half, the city has continued to evolve and reinvent itself while retaining at its core the same solid values of its early inhabitants. An on-the-move city like Evansville requires a financial institution that can not only respond well to change but anticipate it — one that also holds those same core values while successfully implementing innovative financial services and products its customers need. Such an institution is Fifth Third Bank, which recently purchased Evansville's CNB Bancshares, Inc.

Fifth Third freely admits to "being the bank with the funny name." The unusual moniker comes from its history. It began as the Bank of the Ohio Valley, which opened its doors in Cincinnati in 1858. In 1871, that bank was purchased by the Third National Bank. At the turn of the century, Third National merged with the Fifth National Bank, and eventually the organization came to be known as "Fifth Third Bank." In the ensuing years, Fifth Third has been distinguished not only by its unique name but also by being recognized by financial analysts as one of the strongest top-performing banks in the nation.

In 1999 Fifth Third Bancorp earned the number one spot in Salomon Smith Barney's Top 50 Bank Annual for an unprecedented eighth year in a row. The report ranks the country's top 50 banks according to profitability, operating growth, fee income, operating efficiency, capital strength, and asset quality. Over the last 25 years, Fifth Third has consistently increased its earnings at an average rate of 18.7 percent and risen to eighth among all public companies for its combined earnings and dividend growth consistency. During this time, Fifth Third outperformed the S&P 500 Index by 13-fold and posted nine stock splits while maintaining a high capital ratio and strong credit quality.

Completed in October 1999, the merger of Fifth Third and CNB Bancshares brought together two of the strongest and most well respected financial institutions in the Midwest. Both of them have a long, solid track record of delivering shareholder and customer value. At the time of the merger, CNB had assets of $7.2 billion. Included under its umbrella were a number of financial institutions in Indiana, Illinois, Kentucky, Tennessee, and Michigan. The largest of these institutions, with 145 locations, was Civitas Bank, formerly known as Citizens National Bank, which had been a financial mainstay of the Evansville community for more than 100 years.

Fifth Third Bancorp is a diversified financial services company headquartered in Cincinnati, Ohio. It entered Indiana in 1987. It operates 14 affiliate banks and other financial service subsidiaries principally in Ohio,

The Main Office of Fifth Third Bank in Downtown Evansville.

Kentucky, Indiana, Arizona, Florida, and Michigan. With $41 billion in assets and 644 full-service banking centers in those states as of October 1999, Fifth Third Bank is among the top-30 largest bank holding companies in the country and among the 15 largest in market capitalization.

The purchase of CNB vaulted Fifth Third to the third largest bank in Indiana. President and CEO George A. Schaefer, Jr., stated, "Indiana has one of the highest population growth rates of our market area, and teaming up with Civitas is a smart move for customers, shareholders, and employees. Civitas' customers can now take advantage of Fifth Third's size and financial strength, which allows us to offer highly competitive rates on banking and investment products. Civitas' franchise complements our geographic territory and gives us a presence in several new markets — which translates to a win for our customers with easy access to a greatly expanded network of full-service locations."

Former CNB President and CEO Jim Giancola, who is leading Fifth Third's Indiana banks, says, "Fifth Third and Civitas' partnership sets the stage for our continued expansion in Indiana. Civitas is proud to be part of this success story, as our new size and strength will enhance the types of products and level of convenience we can offer to our customers."

The Banking Center within the Toyota plant is also equipped with an ATM and a Virtual Bank, allowing Toyota Team Members access to bank services at all hours.

Customers, employees, and shareholders alike will benefit from the fact that both Fifth Third and Civitas espouse the values of aggressive sales, hard work, and teamwork. Both have an excellent track record of delivering shareholder value and are renowned for their operating discipline. And throughout their histories, both banks have offered unparalleled service through courteous personal transactions and technological conveniences, a broad line of innovative financial products and services, and outstanding citizenship and involvement in the communities they serve. By blending the qualities of both organizations, Fifth Third will continue to stand among the most respected financial institutions in the United States — and grow even stronger.

The two institutions conducted the task of product mapping in late 1999 and early 2000 to match the types of accounts and services they offer. Civitas' popular Totally Free Checking remains an element of the Fifth Third Bank product mix. Between the time this account was introduced in June 1998 and the end of 1999, Civitas opened more than 44,000 Totally Free accounts — most certainly a great tool for establishing key banking relationships with its new customers. Another CNB product that remained in place is the High Yield Money Market Account.

A Fifth Third product that was included in the product mix was its Club 53. This is an interest-bearing checking account available to customers age 50 and over. It requires a daily balance of only $100 to waive the $5 monthly fee. It features unlimited free check-writing, free Club 53 checks, and a 25 percent discount on other select check orders. Club 53 also offers a unique group travel program that allows members to travel to many exciting locations at substantial discounts.

Innovation Integral to Fifth Third

A financial institution will not thrive if it does not successfully anticipate the needs of its customers and create ways to meet those needs. Fifth Third and Civitas have frequently introduced new products and services to make banking more convenient and advantageous for customers.

For instance, Civitas was one of the first banks in the country to allow individual and small business customers to use the Internet to access their accounts online, while Fifth Third is a leader in e-commerce, processing more than 4 billion electronic transactions in 1999. From their homes and workplaces, customers can conduct banking transactions at any hour of the day in a secure electronic environment. They need no special software, just current versions of Microsoft Internet Explorer or Netscape Communications browsers, which contain the encryption mode that keeps online transactions private and safe.

Using online banking, Fifth Third customers can make account inquiries and enter transactions in online checking and savings registers, transfer funds, pay bills, maintain a personal financial statement, e-mail a customer service representative, open an account, and even take a loan self-test and apply for a loan.

Customer service innovation has also led to extra banking convenience for students at the University of Southern Indiana in Evansville and Indiana University in Bloomington, where virtual branches have been installed on campus.

From the time Toyota Motor Manufacturing, Indiana, first came to the Evansville area in the mid-1990s, it has had an excellent relationship with Fifth Third (then called Civitas). The bank suggested opening a full-service branch inside the plant, available to the more than 1000 Toyota team members — a proposal that TMMI wholeheartedly embraced. This gave Fifth Third the distinction of being the first bank ever selected to have a branch office in one of Toyota's North American facilities.

Toyota Motor Manufacturing, Indiana selected the former Civitas Bank for its corporate banking needs and incorporated a banking center inside its new truck manufacturing plant in Princeton, Indiana, just north of Evansville. Bank Associate Neely Pierce assists a Toyota member with his banking needs.

Fifth Third associate David Bunch responds to a customer's question. Fifth Third bank is committed to prompt and courteous service. The Evansville based Call Center has recently expanded in size to handle customer inquiries more efficiently.

Other Fifth Third Products and Services

Midwest Payment Systems (MPS) is the nation's oldest and now the largest third-party Electronic Funds Transfer processor, handling in excess of 220 million electronic transfers per month. As part of Fifth Third, MPS has the financial stability to invest in the technology necessary to provide high performance, customized processing solutions. For instance, BillPayer 2000® is the MPS-patented electronic bill payment service that pays varying bill amounts on varying dates automatically. Users of this service include customers of Cincinnati Bell, *The Cincinnati Enquirer*, Cinergy, and Time Warner Cable.

MPS provides the following services:
- Card issuance and authorization support for ATM and debit cards
- Terminal driving for virtually all ATM types, including support for dial and other communication ATMs
- Unbiased gateway access to all national and regional networks
- In-house card production services
- Online back office support tools, including card management and exception item processing
- Remote banking and bill payment products.

Retail Banking handles checking and savings accounts, direct installment loans, and auto lending and leasing. In fact, in 1999, Fifth Third delivered more loans, leases, and checking and savings accounts than at any other time in its history. In addition, Fifth Third provided convenient access for more than 3 million customers at banking centers, Bank Mart ® and Quick Source ™ locations inside grocery stores, and at nearly 1300 ATMs in Ohio, Kentucky, Indiana, Florida, and Arizona.

Retail Banking also handles a growing number of home mortgages. Fifth Third is now the number one home loan lender in portions of Ohio and Northern Kentucky.

- Fifth Third Online, the bank's Internet Personal Banking Service enables customers to access their checking, savings, credit card, CD, and loan accounts from their home computers, 24 hours a day, seven days a week. Customers have the freedom to tailor personalized banking

Regional Retail Manager Ted Sheppe presents an Evansville high school senior with a check for $1,000. The presentation is a part of the very popular Leadership Scholars program held in conjunction with WFIE-TV. In the first three years of the Leadership Scholars program, more than $170,000 worth of scholarships were awarded to high school seniors displaying strong leadership skills.

statements, check balances, determine whether checks have cleared or been deposited, and get up-to-date interest payment information. Most importantly, Fifth Third Online provides the flexibility and speed to pay bills, transfer funds, and apply for loans via the Internet in real time.

Commercial Banking builds and maintains solid business relationships while providing the highest quality service and commercial products to business customers. Truly the place for one-stop shopping for businesses, the Commercial Banking Group offers start-up financing, sophisticated cash management, leasing, venture capital, expansion and mortgage financing, international expertise, and initial public offering services.

• Fountain Square Commercial Funding Corporation, Fifth Third's off-balance-sheet facility for funding generally short-term, high-quality loans, finished 1999 with more than $1.1 billion loans outstanding, up from only $468 million two years earlier.

• Corporate Treasury Management, Fifth Third's corporate electronic banking service, is designed to increase business productivity by offering customers the freedom to perform many cash management functions, including balance reporting, account reconciliation, stop payments, wire transfers, and electronic data interchange functions, in a secure, user-friendly environment.

• Commercial Leasing handles small-ticket leasing to businesses, while Foreign Currency Trading offers letters of credit and other related services for customers doing business abroad. The Brussels and Hong Kong offices have made Fifth Third a dominant provider of banking services to foreign-based companies with operations in their markets.

• Investment Advisors Group builds wealth for individuals and families, institutions, and not-for-profit clients by building relationships, working to understand their needs, and offering the best investment and planning solutions available. Its investment and brokerage professionals have received the highest ratings for their overall performance, while the Fifth Third Equity Income Fund was recognized by the Wall Street Journal Mutual Fund Scorecard as the number one performing equity income fund for its one-year investment performance.

Fifth Third Bank, "Working Hard To Be The Only Bank You'll Ever Need." ▩

METROPOLITAN EVANSVILLE CHAMBER OF COMMERCE

In the late 1990s, the Evansville region began to experience an economic rebirth that was fueled by the influx of new corporations, bolstered by the rise of many smaller suppliers, and complimented by the expansion of numerous existing companies. This rapid growth provided a welcome boost to the area's economy, yet it also introduced a host of new challenges for the Southwestern Indiana business community. As the one organization specifically designed to support the local business community, the Metropolitan Evansville Chamber of Commerce took the lead in coordinating efforts to deal with these challenges.

"Southwestern Indiana and the Metropolitan Evansville Chamber of Commerce are ending the 1990s with unprecedented growth and opportunity," says MEVCC President and CEO Robert L. Quick. "As the decade concluded, the Chamber emerged as the leading voice of existing business, shaping those issues that have the greatest impact on their bottom line."

MEVCC was founded in 1915. Throughout the years, it has maintained one focus: to strengthen the Evansville community by striving to create a competitive business environment. At first, when the world's businesses were not as intricately connected as they are today, MEVCC dealt mainly with local and regional business concerns. But as the regional economic picture evolved to encompass ever-enlarging horizons, so did the Chamber.

For instance, as a way of keeping abreast of the rapid changes occurring at the time, MEVCC declared 1997-98 a time of introspection. It conducted a six-month study of the community in order to fully understand its business needs. Based on the results, MEVCC was able to refocus and strengthen its already-strong business expansion and retention efforts, to enhance its other programs, and to add new ones. Thus, at the dawn of the 21st century when the economy of Southwestern Indiana is intimately linked with the global marketplace, MEVCC continues to grow and expand to meet the increasing, quickly changing, and more complicated needs of the businesses it serves.

As a regional Chamber of Commerce, MEVCC offers services in 11 counties in Southwestern Indiana and the Tri-State region. It is a nationally accredited Chamber with an experienced, professional staff. Membership has been growing steadily, topping 1,400 by the year 2000, and retention of existing members has remained well above the national average.

A work of art! The Old Post Office built in 1879 takes us back to 19th Century architecture. This historical landmark houses the Metropolitan Evansville Chamber of Commerce.

The Chamber is involved in many issues that have a direct impact on its members and the community:
- Workforce Development—An available and skilled workforce is an issue that affects every existing and future business in their region for years to come. The Chamber has also secured the services of the Hudson Institute to devise a regional workforce strategic plan for worker recruitment and retention, worker skill improvement, and other strategies to address and plan for the future.
- Progress and Legislative Advocate—MEVCC endorses the completion of I-69, including a loop around Evansville, in addition to other local and regional infrastructure developments, such as Highway 41 and the Lloyd Expressway. MEVCC is the only Chamber in the region with a full-time lobbyist working for its members. In addition, the MEVCC maintains a strong government relations department that offers pro-business advocacy at all levels of government. Governmental relations specialists work to ensure that business concerns and needs are being addressed by city, county, and state officials. The MEVCC has three governmental committees: Environmental, Governmental Affairs, and Transportation.

MEVCC also offers programs that assist its members in a variety of ways:
- Retail/Service Assistance—The Southwestern Indiana Small Business Development Center (SBDC) includes on-site consulting for existing businesses; new business start-up assistance; seminars, conferences, and workshops on various business-related topics; a computer learning center where members can review current and new software programs; and expert volunteer consultants and staff who can assist members with technical issues.
- Business Expansion & Retention Assistance—MEVCC advocates for existing business development of all its members and researches methods for job creation, job retention, and workforce development. Among these services are assistance with tax abatement, location incentives, and facility layout; and a comprehensive resource database covering training,

The skyline of downtown Evansville overlooks the Ohio River and represents a city of growth and prosperity.

financing, real estate availability, incentive programs, employee recruiting, and utilities and infrastructure programs.
- Manufacturing Assistance—Indiana Business Modernization and Technology (BMT) offers hands-on business and technical assistance to help manufacturers increase their profitability by increasing sales, improving cash flow, reducing costs, and accessing various resources. Manufacturers can also receive high-impact assessments that provide a confidential, comprehensive evaluation of their operations.
- Government Marketing—The Government Marketing Assistance Group (GMAG) exists for one purpose—to help Indiana businesses market their products and services to federal, state, and local governments.

GMAG sponsors workshops and conferences on how to do business with governmental agencies, conducts counseling sessions, and otherwise assists members in receiving government contracts.
- Disaster Preparedness Programs—Partnering with the Southwestern Indiana Disaster Recovery Business Alliance, MEVCC offers programs to help businesses prepare for the unexpected, including earthquakes, tornadoes, ice storms, etc.
- Business Referrals and Networking Opportunities—Chamber members are referred as potential sources when the MEVCC receives inquiries regarding products and services. MEVCC events, such as luncheons,

Business thrives on connections. Through Chamber activities, thousands of these connections are made possible.

seminars, and networking gatherings, provide an opportunity for members to exchange ideas to grow their businesses.
- Publication Listings—The Impact newsletter and Membership Directory connect and market members' businesses to more than 2,400 community leaders on the constantly growing membership list.
- Web Site and Free Hot Links—The MEVCC Web site, which receives an average of 43,000 hits a month, has been recognized by the American Chamber of Commerce Executives as one of the Top Eight Chamber Web sites in the country along with being rated as one of the top 10 Chambers out of hundreds of Chambers in the country! Members receive free advertising on the Web site and a free hot link to their company home pages.

The new century and the rapidly changing economy offer many challenges for Evansville companies. As a progressive force in the local business community, the MEVCC will continue to review, expand, and improve its programs and services so that its members—and the entire community—can ride the wave of success for many years to come.

The Chamber has sixteen full-time employees collectively working to do what no one business can do alone.

❖ THE NATIONAL CITY BANK OF EVANSVILLE ❖

Originally named the Canal Bank in 1850, this was the first nationally chartered bank in Evansville to open its doors. It grew rapidly and, through countless relationships formed with the city's residents, came to play a large role in the city's history. The names of the directors and officers of National City Bank, in its 150 year history, would read like the Who's Who of Evansville. Some of the prominent names involved with the history of National City include Francis Joseph Reitz, C.B. Enlow, Wayne Worthington, and John Lippert. The accomplishments of these people in their civic and professional duties would fill many volumes. Many buildings and well-known places in Evansville are also named after previous officers and directors of National City. These include Wheeler School, Carpenter School, Willard Library, Bosse Field, Bosse High School, Reitz High School, Reitz Memorial High School, Enlow Field, Mesker Park, Mesker Amphitheater, and Garvin Park.

In 1914, the Bank built a grand building at the corner of Third and Main streets in downtown Evansville. With its Italian Renaissance design and exquisite features, it was one of the most notable bank buildings in the Midwest. In 1922, its name was changed to The National City Bank of Evansville. With a continued commitment to the Evansville community, in 1998, National City Bank constructed an elegant nine-story office tower adjacent to the 1914 building. Although more contemporary in style, it mirrors the design of the original building.

National City branches were remodeled during the last half of the 1990s to improve the environment for employees and customers alike. They all have the distinctive burgundy roof and white columns, not to mention the easily recognizable black and gold sign. The Eastland Banking Center was constructed as an Express Banking Center to offer retail and commercial customers convenience, speed, and accuracy.

National City's elegant nine-story office tower built in 1998 adjacent to the bank's 1914 building.

With video monitors, express teller booths, and automatic cash dispensers, transactions are nearly twice as fast. This is the first drive-up facility in Evansville that is specially equipped to handle heavy deposits of up to twenty-five pounds.

Solid Growth for National City Bank's Parent Company

The 1990s were a time of substantial growth for National City Bancshares, Inc. (NCBE). The multi-bank holding company made solid acquisitions to create a larger financial and geographical base. National City better positioned itself to meet the challenges of the financial industry, which were changing more rapidly than ever before as the world entered the new century.

A very public mark of NCBE's success came in 1997, when *US Banker* magazine ranked it 10th in the top 200 mid-sized banking companies listed, according to five areas of performance-driven criteria. NCBE had moved up from 11th the previous year.

Renovations Extend to Products and Services

The physical renovations of the facilities were accompanied by various improvements in National City's products and services.
- In 1995, National City Bank introduced its own MasterCard® credit card program. The program offers the standard MasterCard and Gold MasterCard with travel and gift rewards for using the card. National City's MasterCard is locally approved and serviced.
- In 1996, National City introduced its new Phone Bank service. This service allows customers to access their accounts by phone 24-hours a day. Phone Bank customers can check balances, see what checks have

In 1914, National City opened a bank that was considered the finest and best bank of its size in North America, which now houses its Trust Department and parent company, National City Bancshares, Inc.

cleared, transfer money between their accounts, and get loan information by using a touch-tone telephone.

- The National City Check Card was introduced in 1996. This new product offers customers a convenient way to make purchases or ATM transactions. The amount is deducted from the checking account each time it is used. It can be used everywhere MasterCard is accepted and also as an ATM card.

- Business customers gained more control over their accounts in 1997, with Direct Access. This software package allows them to download account information daily to review and reconcile accounts, execute internal account transfers, make stop payments, move funds with wire transfers, and perform ACH transactions, such as direct deposit, pre-authorized debits, and corporate payments.

- The National City Web page made its debut in 1997. The site offers information on National City's products and services, how to apply for certain services, locations of banks and ATMs, employment opportunities, news releases, stock information, and much more.

National City's spacious lobby, shown here in the early 1900's, reflects the ornamental detail used throughout the interior and exterior of the bank.

- Since 1998, home owners are able to take full advantage of their home's equity with Home Owners MasterCard Equity (HOME) Card, which combines the home equity line of credit with a Gold MasterCard. It offers a low variable rate, tax advantages, and can be used anywhere MasterCard is accepted. Furthermore, there are no closing costs, and customers can use up to 100 percent of their home's equity.

- Bank Anytime was introduced in August 1999. Using this service, National City's customers can view transactions, transfer funds between accounts, transfer funds between banks, and pay bills simply by using the Web, PC dial-up software, and/or a touch-tone phone. Bank Anytime allows customers to perform banking transactions and bill paying 24-hours a day.

Some Things Will Never Change

Over the last 150 years, National City Bank has introduced many new products and services. Yet one thing will never change: National City's commitment to extraordinary customer service and dedication to the communities it serves.

Understanding the importance of supporting the community that has helped it to prosper for so long, NCBE makes significant contributions of time and money to charities and other causes every year. Employees also donate significant amounts of their time to support many good causes within the community.

National City Bancshares, Inc.—Building for tomorrow in all we do today. ▨

National City's eastside Express Banking Center offers high technology with convenient, express service and a unique drive-up feature that allows business customers to make large, heavy deposits.

❖ OLD NATIONAL ❖

Evansville's Old National is coming full circle. Its original predecessor institution began in a one-room building near the corner of Main and Water (now Riverside) streets in 1834. Today, at the start of the 21st century, Evansville's oldest bank and oldest continuing corporation is returning to the riverfront, preparing to build a 20-story corporate office tower at Main and Riverside.

Based on a heritage of traditional community banking, Old National has created a strong financial presence in the Tri-State area. In 1999, *US Banker* magazine rated Old National Bancorp's performance 19th in the nation for banks with less than $25 billion in assets and 28th for overall financial performance out of all banks in the country. The magazine also declared that Old National's assets at the time—$6.2 billion—ranked it in 71st place out of the top 100 banks in asset size. All of Old National's rankings were up sharply from previous years.

Foresight leads to creation of Indiana's first bank holding company. By the early 1980s Old National Bank had assets of nearly $700 million and 10 branches throughout Vanderburgh County. In anticipation of changes in state and federal banking regulations that would allow banks to expand beyond their home county and state, the bank announced the creation of Old National Bancorp, Indiana's first bank holding company, in 1982. Old National was thus prepared to meet the demands of the new competitive financial environment when banking statutes did indeed change.

Old National declared 1999 to be the year of "One Bank, One Name, One Direction" and joined all 140-plus affiliate banks in Indiana, Illinois, and Kentucky into a single Old National organization. However, each banking center has kept its own board of directors, still decides how to support the local organizations of its choice, and maintains the ability to make its own loan approvals. In short, each banking center remained autonomous while becoming part of a larger corporate structure that allows better efficiency and improved customer services delivered by the same friendly, experienced employees as before.

Old National Products and Services

In addition to a variety of checking and savings accounts, Old National provides the following financial services:

- OLD NATIONAL TRUST provides trust and asset management services

Jim Risinger, President and CEO, Old National Bancorp.

offered by specialists in law, accounting, financial analysis, financial planning, investments, and taxes. Trust services are available to individuals and families, as well as businesses. The investment philosophy of Old National Trust Company is centered on three crucial issues: assuming a long-term perspective, balancing risk and perspective, and investing in high-quality instruments. All clients receive services tailored to their individual needs.

- Wealth Management Group is a unique service offered by Old National Trust. By combining the benefits of trust and brokerage, with all services delivered by a personal banking team, Wealth Management Group is a prime example of new approaches that appeal to customers who want both safety and growth.

- Old National Trust also offers corporate trust services. In this role, Old National Trust can serve as trustee, fund manager, paying agent, transfer agent, stock registrar, dividend-paying agent, and special purpose agent.

- ONB INSURANCE GROUP, an independent insurance agency, has been serving the Tri-State area since 1923. ONB Insurance agents draw from the services of many highly-regarded insurance providers to design a personalized program offering the best insurance coverage for clients' personal or business needs.

- TOUCHTONE BANKING is Old National's online banking system. With TouchTone Banking, customers can check account balances and histories; make loan payments; verify deposits and checks that have been paid; transfer funds between accounts; obtain currents interest rates on CDs, IRAs, Money Markets, and savings and checking accounts; order checks; leave a

The Evansville Municipal Market is just one of the many historical developments in Evansville that Old National has had the opportunity to help restore. Photo by L. Kent Whitehead.

A community bank—Old National is committed to strengthening Evansville's neighborhoods and businesses—the Lincoln Estates project is one example of this commitment. Photo by L. Kent Whitehead.

Old National has over 165 locations throughout Indiana, Kentucky, Illinois, and Tennessee.

message for the bank; and much more — all from the privacy of home or workplace. In addition, with TouchTone Banking with Bill Paying, customers can also pay bills from anywhere in the United States in just minutes.

- CORPORATE CASH MANAGEMENT allows businesses to spend more time being productive while Old National designs and provides financial services to help minimize costs and eliminate unnecessary steps in the production process. Corporate cash management services include collection services, disbursement services, and information services.

Old National in the Community

Not only do customers see Old National representatives behind the desk or the counter when they conduct their financial transactions, they also see them in the community as friends and neighbors, service club members, volunteers on boards—in the whole range of activities and events that bring a community together and make it strong.

Old National also takes an active role in the financial success of its communities. Supporter of the Chamber of Commerce and economic development organizations like Evansville's Vision 2000, Old National understands the importance of supporting existing businesses and paving the way for new ones to relocate or establish themselves.

The Future

Old National looks forward to the 21st century as it continues to expand its role as a financial leader. Jim Risinger, CEO of Old National, said, "Our aim is not just to be big, but to be better than big. We must utilize our size to provide the full range of financial services our customers deserve, but we must provide those services in the same personable, caring, community-oriented environment which has earned us our customers' trust. In that execution, we will claim a unique market niche which gives us the muscle of the big banks with the soul of a community bank—a market niche which positively separates us from both sets of competitors."

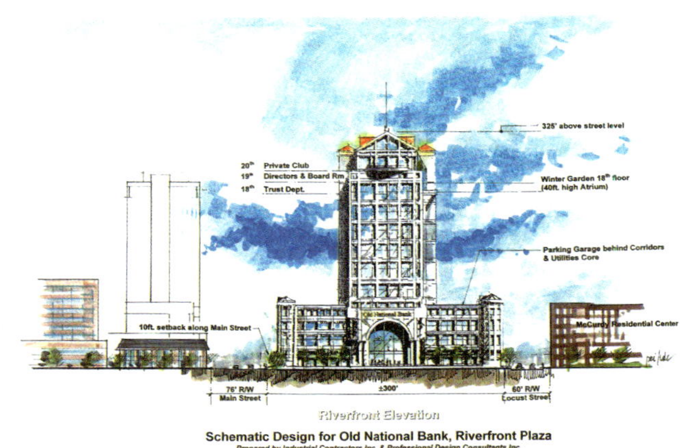

Schematic Design for Old National Bank, Riverfront Plaza
Prepared by Industrial Contractors Inc. & Professional Design Consultants Inc.

Looking toward the future—a sketch of the proposed Old National Bank, Riverfront Plaza.

Mike Hinton, president of Old National Bank, added, "Old National is Evansville's bank. As this city's oldest corporation, we recognize that Old National's fortunes are inextricably tied to the fortunes of our community. That recognition has produced a group of consistent, familiar, and caring bankers who are fully committed to helping our city grow and prosper."

Atlas Van Lines, Inc./ Shetler Moving & Storage, Inc.

Americans are always on the move, and they have made Atlas Van Lines one of the major players in this $8 billion industry. From its world headquarters in Evansville, Atlas oversees a marketing and operations network of more than 600 independent agents in the United States and Canada, plus 200 more overseas. The company has grown to become North America's fourth-largest van line and third-largest carrier of household goods, handling more than 128,000 such shipments in 1998 alone. Atlas also handles thousands of other moves each year, including office and industrial relocations, electronics equipment of all kinds, fine arts and trade show exhibits, and general commodities.

The foundation of Atlas' success is based upon its World-Class Commitment to quality service. An important aspect of that commitment is the use of innovative technology to make the moving process easier. For instance, when an early version of the WATS system was introduced in the early-fifties, Atlas made the new toll-free phone service available to its customers. That dedication to customer service technology continues today. In 1996, Atlas was the first van line with a Web site, giving customers 24-hour access to important information about Atlas and its agents. Since then, it has garnered much recognition, and the Web site was recently exemplified in the *New York Times* bestseller "HyperWars" as the "friendly expert" in making the relocation process smoother for its customers.

Yet when it comes to moving a family or a business across town or across the continent, technology alone means little. In a high-tech world, "high touch"—or a lot of friendly, personal service—means a great deal to customers and helps ensure their satisfaction. Moving is stressful for any family, so they appreciate a patient, experienced mover who cares about doing the job right—and cares about them.

Customers can depend on this kind of service thanks to Atlas' policy of self-haul, which means that Atlas agents manage and handle their jobs from start to finish. So, unlike many other movers, Atlas agents do not transfer responsibility to someone else for moving their customers' household goods. Knowing that their belongings have been entrusted to an Atlas agent for the entire trip provides customers with great peace of mind.

From accounting, to marketing, to web sites - America's third-largest carrier of household goods depends on its 500 Evansville employees at its world headquarters to provide the office and administrative support necessary to keep its 400 U.S. agent locations going strong. The fastest growing van line in the industry, Atlas has its Canadian headquarters in Oakville, Ontario and its international headquarters in Seattle, Washington.

Domestically, Atlas provides transportation services for household goods, electronic products, tradeshow exhibits, museum pieces, and freight. North of the border, Atlas has some 200 agents handling transportation throughout Canada and cross-border. And internationally, Atlas utilizes motor, rail, ocean, and air carriers to fulfill world transportation needs.

Atlas was founded in Chicago in 1948. Thirty-three agents created their own national interstate moving company based on agent ownership. That model proved extraordinarily successful, and the company grew rapidly. Headquarters was moved to Evansville in 1960. The company found out the hard way that agent ownership was the only way to maintain its success. Several years after its stock went public, Atlas was acquired by a "white knight" that saved it from a hostile takeover. But, as a small cog in a large corporate wheel—and minus agent ownership—Atlas lost momentum. Fortunately, 27 agents repurchased the company in 1988 and returned it to agent ownership. After a long haul, their company turned toward success once again. In 1994, shareholders voted to establish a new holding company, Atlas World Group, Inc., which included Atlas Van Lines and its seven subsidiaries. By 1999, the number of agent-owners stood at 70 and annual revenues had climbed past $500 million.

In 1999, Atlas began construction on a new headquarters building that will double the amount of office space—right next door to the existing one. This new building is a public demonstration of the company's dedication to the city that has contributed so greatly to its success.

All moving companies use cartons to pack customers' belongings and use trucks to haul them, so there is actually very little that distinguishes one from another—except for the quality of service. Therefore, Atlas implemented mandatory quality guidelines in 1992 for everyone in the network, from agents and drivers to headquarters personnel. Atlas now monitors its agents on 12 specific quality areas, and each year the bar is raised.

Shetler Moving & Storage, Inc.

The Atlas Van Lines agent in Evansville is Shetler Moving & Storage, Inc., family-owned and operated for more than 100 years.

A black and white photo in the Shetler conference room depicts company founder B. J. Shetler posing in 1899 with a horse-drawn wagon in Evansville. The side of the wagon proclaims, "Keep Moving is Our Motto. Moving, Packing, Storage, and Transfer."

B. J. Shetler Transfer & Storage began by hauling Murphy beds from Globe Bosse World Manufacturing, one of the world's largest furniture makers of the time, to the train depot. Shetler later began making extra income by helping families move, and eventually this turned into his full-time business. He upgraded to his first truck in 1916 and continued to expand.

The company remained under family ownership, and in 1948, Joseph B. Shetler was one of the 33 agents who started Atlas Van Lines. Since that time, Shetler Moving & Storage has been the sole

Evansville's own Shetler Moving & Storage was one of the 33 founding agents of Atlas Van Lines in 1948. At that time, Shetler had been in the business nearly 50 years - and had been part of the industry's transition from horse-drawn wagons to trucks, with Benjamin Joseph Shetler (at the wheel) retiring his horses and purchasing his first truck in the early 1900s. Today, Tom Shetler, Sr. and Bob Shetler, sons of Joseph Shetler (right), still run the family business from Evansville.

Atlas agent in Evansville. After beginning with one man and his two horse-drawn wagons, Shetler has developed into "the First Family of Moving." The largest moving company in the Tri-State, Shetler has about 75 employees, a branch office in Cincinnati, and annual revenues that reached $5 million in 1999.

Both Shetler and Atlas specialize in corporate relocations. They follow a number of guidelines to ensure a quality move. Every customer is assigned a personal move team that organizes, plans, and monitors the move from start to finish under the direction of a relocation coordinator. Shetler self-packs and self-hauls more than 95.2 percent of the moves they handle and offers full-value protection for all belongings. Even after the move is completed, they will return to pick up boxes and other debris left after unpacking—a service that customers appreciate.

With more than a century of service, Shetler Moving & Storage, Inc. offers experience, management involvement, flexibility, and the ability to respond—in short, an unprecedented commitment to service.

VANDERBURGH COUNTY BOARD OF COMMISSIONERS

The three-member Vanderburgh County Board of Commissioners is the county's executive and legislative body. Its responsibilities include road maintenance, dealing with development issues, and oversight of county facilities. Among those facilities are The Centre, Burdette Park, the Coliseum, and the Old Courthouse.

The Centre

The Centre, Evansville's new auditorium and convention center, opened in October 1999 to reveal a spectacular new facility that promises to boost the city into greater regional prominence. A two-year, $35 million renovation transformed the former Vanderburgh County Auditorium into the second-largest convention center in Indiana. According to Sandy Aaron, executive director of Ogden Management, the firm hired to manage The Centre, "With all the growth Evansville has seen recently, it has been missing out on a large meeting space. The Centre will become a hub for meetings and conventions."

With 40,000 square feet of convention space, 38,000 square feet of meeting rooms, and a 2,500-seat auditorium, The Centre holds up to 7,000 people when entirely booked, according to Aaron. Billed as "more than an auditorium," The Centre "is extremely versatile," she says. "It's truly multi-use and able to handle everything from conventions, Broadway shows, concerts, and retail trade shows to closed-circuit boxing, company functions, and athletic clinics."

Its versatility is demonstrated in several ways. Meeting rooms can be arranged to hold groups as small as 75 or as large as 1,500; the exhibit hall can hold up to 4,000. With its built-in flexibility for performance creativity, the auditorium is capable of handling both large-scale, Broadway productions, as well as smaller, more intimate performances.

Aaron believes The Centre is an added attraction for new businesses and industries investigating the Evansville area as a site for relocation or construction of a new facility. In addition, existing businesses find it to be an excellent venue for holding functions like annual meetings.

The Centre also gives Evansville the potential to expand events and activities already ongoing at other venues like Roberts Stadium or Downtown's newly refurbished Victory Theater. "The Centre allows us to sell an Evansville experience, instead of just one facility," says Aaron.

Major construction of the Centre. Photo by L. Kent Whitehead.

Burdette Park

For those seeking a "wonderful way to have a wonderful day," Burdette Park is the place to go for all kinds of outdoor recreation. Located on 135 acres of wooded, rolling hills on Evansville's west side, Burdette Park is open year-round. Admission to the park is free.

The park had its beginnings in 1921 as the Burdette American Legion Post. The legion opened it to the public as Burdette Park in 1928. In 1934, workers in the WPA began to develop the park's attractions by building lakes and some basic structures. Since that time, many other attractions have been added.

Southwest Indiana water lovers flock to Burdette Park, according to Steve Craig, park manager, who explains that the swimming pools are among the Midwest's biggest and best. There's even a large baby pool for toddlers and young children. The Aquatic Center has eight water slides—four for adults and four for children—that offer experiences ranging from leisurely river rafting to breathtaking rides down speed slides. A bumper boat pool for all ages rounds out the park's water attractions, all of which are watched constantly by a skilled team of lifeguards, EMTs, and swimming instructors. For visitors' convenience, Burdette Park carries a full line of swimming necessities and rents raft and flotation devices. There's a poolside snack bar for hungry swimmers, and large party rooms, which can hold up to 60, are located on the second floor of the Aquatic Center's entry complex.

Burdette Park offers much more. Its chalets, party houses, and pavilion are all available for rent at reasonable rates. The chalets are perfect for overnight stays of up to a week; they comfortably sleep eight guests. All have a breakfast bar, color television, microwave oven, fireplace, and most furnishings. Some have a Jacuzzi. The party houses are placed throughout the park. They can accommodate 25 to 200. The pavilion, which holds up to 1,000 guests, has facilities for catering service.

Craig offers a long list of other park attractions: "Tennis courts, batting cages, baseball diamonds, soccer fields, a miniature golf course, and a BMX racing track. Plus we have walking trails, RV camping, primitive camping, and two lakes for fishing."

In the summer, Burdette offers a day camp for children ages 6 to 12 and a Summer Discovery Camp for 10 to 14-year-olds interested in exploring the world around them.

Coliseum and Old Courthouse

The Board of Commissioners leases two of Evansville's historical landmarks to local organizations.

The Coliseum, which had been completed in 1917 as a memorial to veterans of the Spanish-American War, was remodeled in the 1930s as a

Autumn foliage in Burdette Park. Photo by L. Kent Whitehead.

cultural arts center. Scheduled for demolition in the 1970s, it was saved by local veterans groups, who leased the building for 99 years and agreed to renovate and manage it. The Coliseum is now used for meetings and a variety of entertainment events, including bingo, wrestling, and concerts.

The Old Courthouse was built in 1888-90 in the ornate Second Empire Renaissance Baroque style. It later fell into disrepair, and the Conrad Baker Foundation (later renamed the Old Courthouse Preservation Society) began preservation efforts in 1968. The majestic building is now home to a variety of small businesses and non-profit organizations. Two of the area's major craft shows are held at the Old Courthouse each year, one in the spring and one in the fall. Some county government offices are returning to the Old Courthouse, with the County Engineer and Veterans Affairs being the first. ▓

❈ CITY OF EVANSVILLE ❈

The City of Evansville operates three popular and unique entertainment facilities—Roberts Stadium, the Victory Theatre, and Mesker Amphitheatre. Although each facility is very different from the others, they share a common denominator: They were purposefully designed for multiple uses which means they can offer a wide variety of cultural and entertainment events that appeal to every segment of the regional population of more than one million. Ogden Entertainment, Inc. is responsible for the total management of these facilities.

Roberts Stadium

Roberts Stadium hosts a wide array of activities each year. With a capacity of 12,500, the stadium is home to the University of Evansville Purple Aces basketball team (NCAA Division I). In early 1999, Roberts Stadium also began hosting Division II games in the Great Lakes Valley Conference.

A performance by a dance troop from Tochigi City, Japan at the Shanklin Theater on the campus of the University of Evansville. These performers are rarely seen outside of Japan.

The Evansville Philharmonic, performing continually since 1934, performs before a capacity crowd in the beautifully restored Victory Theatre.

Thanks to a $19 million renovation in the early 1990s, the stadium is also an intimate concert arena. Entertainers from every music genre perform regularly at this venue.

The diverse event mix offers family entertainment that includes the Hadi Shrine Circus, professional wrestling (WWF and WCW), ice shows, rodeos, monster trucks, and theatrical productions. The stadium also hosts high school and college graduations and a variety of annual trade shows and conferences.

Roberts Stadium also offers full-service catering and a meeting room that can seat up to 400 people. Located along the Lloyd Expressway in between Highway 41 and Green River Road, the stadium is easily accessible from throughout the Tri-State. Parking for 4,000 vehicles is available.

Victory Theatre

The Victory Theatre was once a popular Downtown Evansville vaudeville theater and movie house. This historic facility underwent a $20 million renovation in 1998 that restored the theater to its former beauty. Now home to the Evansville Philharmonic Orchestra, the Victory Theatre seats 1,950 in an elegant atmosphere reminiscent of the 1920s while employing modern amenities such as an infrared hearing assistance headset system and wheelchair accessibility.

In addition to the orchestra, the Victory also hosts entertainment that appeals to the entire community, including plays, concerts of all formats, stand-up comedy, and children's programming.

The Victory Theatre is available for corporate gatherings such as annual meetings. A 200-seat banquet room is available for receptions and smaller business meetings.

Mesker Amphitheatre

Anyone searching for a night of entertainment under the stars can find it at Mesker Amphitheatre. Constructed in 1954 and recently modernized to enhance the setting and improve patron comfort, this outdoor venue hosts summertime entertainment events of many kinds. Concerts are always popular here, with performers of every format, including rock, blues, country, Christian, and classical. The summer Mesker Movies are offered to the community for free and attract families from a wide geographical area.

Mesker Amphitheatre accommodates 5,800 in reserved seats and 2,500 on the lawn. Ample parking is available.

Why are these facilities important? The events presented at these three venues create a significant economic impact on Evansville and the surrounding area. First of all, at least 65 percent of their patrons come from outside Vanderburgh County—which is a strong demonstration of their drawing power. Secondly, the musical groups, theater companies, and other groups who perform there usually include a number of people, sometimes several dozen, who stay in local hotels, eat in local restaurants, and patronize local businesses while they are here, often for stays of three or four days. The college sporting events, particularly tournament events, draw people from around the country and many of them stay overnight for one or more nights.

Entertainment venues such as Roberts Stadium, the Victory Theatre, and Mesker Amphitheatre enrich the quality of life in the Evansville area. By offering diverse cultural entertainment for the whole family, they encourage participation in the community. People find cohesion through a shared experience of the arts, and these venues, along with the City of Evansville and Ogden Entertainment, are proud to be a part of that. ▨

Fireworks can be observed on the riverfront at the Four Freedoms Monument. The fireworks display is part of the Annual Evansville Freedom Festival held each year on July 4th.

Evansville, a thriving city rich in history and diversity, is located on a scenic bend of the Ohio River.

❈ HILLIARD LYONS ❈

Dating back to pre-Civil War 1854, Hilliard Lyons had established a successful trade in gold shares and whiskey receipts. In the ensuing century and a half, the firm has grown to become the largest Kentucky-based securities firm in the Midwest and South. Headquartered in Louisville, Kentucky, Hilliard Lyons has approximately 100 offices in 15 states ranging from Michigan to Mississippi and Missouri to North Carolina. The company's Financial Consultants specialize in guiding the investment strategies and servicing the accounts of individuals and small businesses; they handle more than a billion dollars in securities transactions annually.

The Evansville office of Hilliard Lyons, located in the heart of the city's Downtown financial district, has been committed to the financial well-being of its clients for more than three decades. Always keeping in mind that "Our Best Investment is You," the Evansville offices' 30-plus Financial Consultants develop custom-tailored investment plans based upon the individual needs of their clients.

The Evansville office has been the firm's flagship office year after year, measured in terms of revenue and firm profitability. Many of its Financial Consultants have won individual awards. This kind of success does not just happen. The entire staff works diligently to bring its mission statement to life: "To be the most sought after brokerage office in the Tri-State because of our superior level of customer service."

The credo of Hilliard Lyons is to keep the needs of the client first and foremost, by taking the appropriate action and supplying the appropriate level of service. Alan Newman, senior vice president and manager of the Evansville complex, says, "Our company slogan, 'Our Best Investment is You,' can be a catchy phrase, or it can be something you breathe life into daily. It is by bringing these words to life that we have developed the wonderful client base, niche, and marketshare we enjoy here in Southwest Indiana."

In order to offer the highest quality of service, the firm has always adopted the most sophisticated tools available and positioned itself to provide every investment service its clients need. In addition, Hilliard Lyons offers very few proprietary products. "We don't ever want to be perceived as pursuing our own agenda," says Newman. "So rather than package our own products, it's incumbent upon our firm to provide our Financial Consultants with the best products in the marketplace to serve our clients and meet their investment objectives."

Wall Street on the Walkway. Photo by L. Kent Whitehead.

Hilliard Lyons plays an active role in the economic success of Evansville and the surrounding area. Members of the staff are active in economic development organizations and sit on the boards of many Southwest Indiana civic and philanthropic organizations. The firm provides capital through public markets by selling shares of stock, providing debt financing, and offering private placements. But, more than anything else, by helping to strengthen the financial position of its thousands of retail clients, it contributes to the financial health of the larger economy of Southwest Indiana. ❈

J.J.B. Hilliard, W.L. Lyons, Inc.
4th and Main on the Walkway.

❈ Evansville Convention & Visitors Bureau ❈

Long called the River City for its location on a strategic bend in the Ohio River, Evansville is the cultural and economic center for the Tri-State area composed of Southwest Indiana, Southeast Illinois, and Northwest Kentucky. This beautiful region offers a multitude of activities, events, historic locations, and entertainment attractions that draw hundreds of thousands of visitors each year. In addition, recent surveys show that many travelers to the area come to visit family and friends and that many of them stay in hotels and spend their travel dollars in other ways while they are here. In order to keep those numbers growing, The Evansville Convention & Visitors Bureau works diligently to promote tourism and to encourage the hospitality that brings guests back again and again.

Housed in the newly-renovated Pagoda on the downtown riverfront, The Evansville Convention & Visitors Bureau employs several strategies to keep Evansville in the minds of those thousands of leisure and business travelers as well as attract new ones. For potential leisure travelers, the bureau uses print advertising in the form of ads in major regional and national magazines plus direct advertising promotions. To attract convention-minded associations and professional groups, as well as leisure bus tours, they use direct mail and print advertising along with face-to-face meetings with those groups' decision-makers and meeting planners. Thanks to these efforts, each year they receive more than 30,000 phone, mail, and email inquiries asking for tourism information. Of that number of people who request information, it is estimated that 25 percent do visit the area and that 75 percent of those visitors return.

The number of conventions coming to the city is expected to improve greatly with the opening of the renovated and renamed Evansville Auditorium and Convention Centre. The Convention & Visitors Bureau is publicizing the advantages of this beautiful facility to groups and associations across the country. It will be the second-largest and most up-to-date convention center in Indiana, making Evansville more attractive to regional as well as state groups searching for a convention location.

Tourism plays a large role in the continuing economic success of the city. In 1998 alone, for instance, tourists added $248 million in direct tourism dollars to the local economy, 60 percent of which was spent on food and shopping. Clearly, the importance of the promotional efforts of the Evansville Convention & Visitors Bureau should not be underestimated. ❈

Evansville Convention & Visitors Bureau.

AMERICAN GENERAL FINANCE

American General Finance (AGF), headquartered in Evansville, is one of the leaders in the consumer lending industry. With more than $11 billion in assets, AGF is the consumer finance division of the $105 billion American General Financial Group of companies.

The story of AGF began with a one-man office in Evansville in 1920. Richard E. Meier called his company Interstate Finance, and in the beginning he kept his corporate funds in a cigar box! Under his pioneering leadership, which enabled the company to make astute acquisitions and establish strategic long-term plans, Interstate continued to meet the growing need for consumer credit as the century progressed. By 1957, there were 100 branch offices, and in 1964, the name was changed to CrediThrift to reflect its dual functions. Five years later, the company was listed on the New York Stock Exchange. In 1982, CrediThrift became part of American General Corporation of Houston, and in 1990, American General Finance became the official name of the Evansville-based operation. AGF reached the landmark of $1 billion of profitable internal growth in 1994.

Today, at the beginning of the 21st century, American General Finance is an industry leader with the vision that realizes the kinds of employees and consumers it seeks, the types of services it wants to provide, and where it intends to go as an organization.

AGF products and services include consumer loans, residential real estate mortgages, home equity loans, revolving lines of credit, retail sales financing, private label credit cards, credit insurance (life, accident and health, and property and casualty), and non-credit life insurance. In 1999, AGF acquired a federal savings bank in California, which will allow AGF to offer more banking services, including traditional bank products.

With 7,000-plus loan specialists in more than 1,300 local offices in 41 states, Puerto Rico, and the U. S. Virgin Islands, AGF serves more than 2.3 million low-to-middle income households every year.

The Evansville headquarters handles the administrative and support services for the front-line loan offices: including data processing functions (transmitted daily via satellite system), human resources, marketing, and accounting, to name a few. In all, there are more than 1,100 employees in Evansville. Four loan offices are also located here.

AGF is a strong philanthropic force in the community. The company sponsors major events, such as the Downtown Christmas Parade and a large soccer tournament to benefit the Red Cross; matches employee United Way contributions dollar for dollar; and allows employees two paid hours off each month to volunteer and encourages them to add two more hours of their own time. ▓

American General Finance serves over 2 million American households.

American General Finance corporate headquarters.

❖ OLD JAIL MANAGEMENT CORPORATION ❖

Old Jail Management Corporation is Downtown Evansville's largest supplier of commercial office space and property management services. OJMC owns and/or manages the Old Eagle's Home Building, 402 Court Street, General Cigar Building, Old Jail Office Building, Sycamore Building, Old Post Office Place, Civitas Insurance Building, Fifth/Main Financial Plaza, Curtis Building, CAPE Building, and Evansville Municipal Market—more than 400,000 square feet in Evansville's downtown business district. The company is well on its way to becoming the "premiere source for unique office space."

Many of OJMC's offerings are renovated historic buildings. Half of the company's offerings are on the National Register of Historic Places. For example, the Old Jail Office Building was formerly the Vanderburgh County Jail and Sheriff's Residence. Built in 1898, it was designed to look like an imposing castle to dampen people's desire for a stay there. In 1969, the building's functions were moved to the new Civic Center location. The Old Post Office was built in 1875 to house Evansville's main post office, federal courthouse, and customs house. It is a fine example of Richardsonian Romanesque architecture. The Evansville Municipal Market was built in 1916. OJMC renovated the structure and returned the Farmer's Market to the area with a grand opening in 1999.

OJMC President Scott Anderson characterizes the company's properties as "boutique buildings." All are small to medium-sized buildings, have lots of character and adjacent tenant as well as customer/client parking, and can easily be adapted to tenant specifications. "Each building has its own personality," he says. "We work with each prospective tenant to make sure we place them in an environment in which they can exceed, be profitable, and be proud of their office space." The company also oversees the property management of all of its buildings, offering personalized services with a team of design, construction, maintenance, landscaping, and administrative personnel.

OJMC's preservation efforts and quality of service have led to numerous awards. OJMC had received the Preservation Alliance of Evansville Historic Preservation Award, the Indiana Main Street Business of the Year Award, and the Metropolitan Evansville Chamber of Commerce Business of the Year Award. Scott Anderson has received the Governor of Indiana, Sagamore of the Wabash, and the Governor of Kentucky, Kentucky Colonel awards.

"We think our buildings deserve to be saved," said Anderson, an Evansville native. "That's one reason we do this work. The second is financial. We can more than compete with new construction because the cost to renovate our buildings is less than comparable new construction. And no new construction has the quality of materials and workmanship we offer in our buildings. We offer offices with limestone walls, stained glass ceilings, wainscot panels, 24-foot high ceilings, decorative wood trims, and all have completely modern plumbing, HVAC, and electrical systems." ❖

A few of the buildings managed by Old Jail Management Corporation. Photos by L. Kent Whitehead.

❈ R. O. Forster & Associates, Inc. ❈

Ask Randall Forster to describe the business sales and acquisitions industry, and he will characterize it by using the image of the Olympic torch relay. As president of R. O. Forster & Associates, it's his job to match small business owners who want to sell their companies with qualified potential buyers. The relay image is apt: "I want to make sure the torch reaches the right person, someone who will keep the business growing and take it to the next level," he says. "And then, I want to make sure that the hand-off is smooth and profitable for both buyer and seller."

Randall Forster, president. RO Forster & Associates.

Forster comes from a family of small business owners. He understands the special needs and concerns of privately-held business owners, particularly when it comes to transferring ownership of these enterprises. For that reason, he left a corporate career to open R. O. Forster & Associates. They specialize in the sale of privately-held companies with annual revenues between $1 million and $25 million. R. O. Forster & Associates is the Southern Indiana affiliate of the Business Brokers Network, which, as the largest business brokerage multi-list affiliation in the world, has more than 450 independently-owned affiliates nationwide and in Canada. As a Certified Business Counselor and qualified business broker, Forster takes a hands-on leadership approach to the entire selling process. His paramount objective is to educate and assist the business owners in preparing the most effective marketing tools and sales strategy that will produce the best price and payout structure for the sale of their business.

Forster prefers to use the services of a respected third party evaluation firm to determine the best selling price for a business. Using an unbiased independent third party that specializes in business valuations will help to assure that buyers and sellers are comfortable with the asking price. He then creates a customized marketing package for the business and presents the business nationwide only to qualified potential buyers. He emphasizes that strict standards of confidentiality are maintained at all times.

As a lifelong resident of the Evansville area, Forster understands the local business community and the appeal of the region, with its lower cost of living and current explosion in economic growth. "Part of my job is to sell (buyers from outside the area) on the Evansville market," he says. "We're on the economic fast track now, and I want to be sure they know the positives this region has to offer. We work closely with the Chamber of Commerce to get this image across."

Since the recent growth in the Evansville area shows no signs of slowing down, there are many opportunities for those interested in selling businesses as well as those wanting to buy. Forster's skills are in high demand, as shown by his ever-growing list of quality businesses for sale and his successful track record. "We facilitate the transfer from the outgoing owner to someone new," he explains. "It's the relay image again. The hand-off must be a smooth and profitable transition. Our firm will make sure the seller receives the best price and the best net payout, and also that the new owner will bring renewed energy to the business and can take it to the next level." ❈

The business hand-off must be smooth and profitable for both buyer and seller.

Photo by L. Kent Whitehead.

12

C H A P T E R   T W E L V E

PROFESSIONS

Fire House, Inc., 186-189

rsc THE QUALITY MEASUREMENT COMPANY, 190-191

Rainbow Communications, Inc., 192

Photo by L. Kent Whitehead.

❧ FIRE HOUSE, INC. ❧

There is nothing more important to the people of Fire House, Inc. than meeting the needs of their clients. It is a spirit of service and dedication that has long lived in old Hose House #5. The bell now hangs silent, the hose and ax are only decorations, but when a call comes into Fire House, it is certain that help is on the way!

"Helping our clients communicate their message effectively and jumping through hoops to make it happen, that's what we mean by meeting their needs," says Ron Bonger, president, CEO, and one of the founding partners of Fire House, Inc. "We're built on a new tradition of service and responsiveness, and we have the talent and passion to make our clients successful."

A New Tradition Begins

The "new tradition" began in 1990, with only four employees, a short list of potential clients, and a lot of dreams and determination. On the third day, they received their first project (compliments of Mead Johnson Nutritionals), and the adventure began!

Hose House #5, one of the last active old-style fire houses in Evansville, provided a wonderfully unique ambience to begin building a reputation for highly creative thinking and responsive service. "Clients enjoyed just stopping in to see the place," remembers Angie Besing, vice president and founding partner. "It's always been important to us to provide a fun atmosphere for employees and clients alike." The old fireman's pole (yes, it's really made of brass!), a conference room that used to be a hay loft, and a life-size statue of a Dalmatian ready to spring into action—all contribute to the rich experience of working for and with Fire House.

In less than a year's time the organization had more than quadrupled in size to 18 full-time staff members, and the client list continued to grow. Bristol-Myers Squibb relocated their pharmaceutical marketing operations to New Jersey, and Fire House, believing in the strength of their relationships, soon followed. "We took a big risk in September of 1992 by committing to open our first regional office in Princeton, N.J.," recalls Bonger.

The move to New Jersey put to the test Fire House's deeply held philosophy that relationships really do matter in business, and it resulted in a win-win situation for everyone. Says Bonger, "We continue to provide high quality marketing communications to BMS, and we were able to expand our own service area."

Ron Bonger, President & CEO.

Relationships Bring Results

At Fire House, "partnership" is not just a buzzword. Establishing strong relationships founded upon trust is key to everything they do. "It's all about being competent and having character. That's what trust is made of, and that's what we provide to every client we serve," says Bonger. "They can see from the proven track record of quality solutions that we are competent. And doing it at a fair price and on schedule takes character. That's why our customers trust us. That's why they continue to be loyal."

The result of building such strong relationships has been a solid base of loyal clients, some of which Fire House has had since the beginning. In an industry where switching agencies is more the norm than the exception, that kind of loyalty says a lot about the value of building relationships. Those relationships extend beyond their clients. Fire House works just as hard to build and maintain deep and lasting relationships with their vendors as well as their own employees. "We are dependent on our strategic partnerships with other companies to meet the needs of those we serve. They are an extension of this organization, and therefore the relationship must be solid," says Besing. "And our number one client is our own employees. If the trust and respect is lacking there, we will not be successful long-term." That commitment to those who work for Fire House has resulted in a staff that is seasoned, highly skilled, loyal, and happy. That's a pretty big return on investment.

Hose House #5 has seen a lot of action in its history. As Fire House, Inc., it still does.

How They Do What They Do

Another benefit of strong client relationships is the ability to truly understand the marketing needs clients have. Rejecting cookie-cutter approaches and assembly-line thinking, Fire House instead treats each customer and project as a fresh challenge. They categorize the work in one of three ways: Quick Response Graphics, such as minor changes to existing pieces; Creative Design, in which a project is built from an existing idea or specific objectives; and Creative Problem Solving, in which Fire House provides the full range of services from strategic planning through final execution. In categorizing projects in this manner, Fire House ensures that only those staff members who add the most value work on the appropriate projects. That means customers receive real value for their money. "The ability to provide added-value services at every level and doing it efficiently helps our customers rest easy knowing they have invested their money wisely with Fire House," insists Bonger.

Among the services Fire House provides are Creative Development, such as annual reports, consumer and trade advertising, sales promotion programs, corporate identity, and communications, etc; Direct Marketing and Copy Services; and Media Placement, among other specialties.

Fire House is constantly developing new and expanded services in order to meet their clients' specific needs. One example of that commitment was the addition of PenguinDesign.Com in 1996, their online marketing division.

Collaboration is the name of the game at Fire House.

A Different Approach

In a world where change is the only constant, nowhere is the pressure felt more keenly than in the realm of communications. The Internet has changed the way business communicates forever. That fact provided the motivation for Fire House to extend its capabilities into the area of Internet strategy and design through the formation of a new division called PenguinDesign.Com.

At Fire House, we say… "The uniforms may have changed, but the determination to serve hasn't."
That's what the "New Tradition" is all about.

Fire House has maintained the "old-style" charm of the original Hose House #5 (including the brass pole!) while redesigning the interior to create a unique and inspiring work environment.

Penguin's sole focus is to help their clients harness the power of online communications to their greatest advantage. By not dividing its attention among other traditional media, Penguin is able to devote its considerable expertise to the unique challenges of communicating via the Internet. "This is a new medium—it's not print; it's not radio or TV; it's brand new. That requires new thinking, new processes, and new tools, a completely different approach than we've applied to anything else," says Jim Hough, division founder. "Internet strategy and design isn't just another service that can be added to an agency's product line. It is different and requires a new organization to do it right."

Penguin has successfully combined the talents and experience of its staff to create compelling, tailored, and highly effective Internet communications. Within two years of its creation as a Fire House division, it had already won significant national and international awards. They attribute much of that success to the time invested into creating a unique three-phase approach to building effective online communication.

PenguinDesign.Com is dedicated to Internet strategy and design.

"It's like building a house. You don't start hammering studs together and pouring concrete until you have a detailed plan," explains Hough. "You have to begin with the end clearly in view in order to create something that will truly be effective." That plan is the result of Phase I in the "Penguin Process." This planning phase is where the mission of the project is clearly defined and specific goals and objectives come into sharp focus. Phase II: Design defines the content structure and creative look and feel of the site as well as the functionality it will have. Phase III: Construction is where it all comes together and springs to life. This process has served Penguin's clients well and has opened numerous opportunities for growth. "Our clients appreciate the attention to detail we give to every step of the project. It's really not that unique an approach. We just ask a lot of questions and listen carefully to what our clients tell us. They are the real experts, we just help them bring it all together," insists Hough.

A Common Goal

Although the medium Penguin works in is different than that of Fire House, there exists tremendous synergies within the organization. The same passion and commitment to meeting (and exceeding) the expectations of the client continue to drive them in a common direction. "Ultimately, we want every client and employee to feel that they have benefited in some significant way from their experience of working with Fire House," says Ron Bonger.

Whether that benefit comes in the form of increased sales, bigger market share, or just a job employees love getting up for every morning, Fire House and PenguinDesign.Com remain committed to their vision. Meeting the needs of the client no matter what, no matter how.

That kind of passion and dedication is what lasting traditions are made of. ▧

Ron Bonger and Angie Besing, Vice President, keep the vision alive at Fire House.

❈ rsc THE QUALITY MEASUREMENT COMPANY ❈

rsc THE QUALITY MEASUREMENT COMPANY—nestled in a quiet, shady corner of downtown Evansville's historic district—is one of the best kept secrets of this community. Quiet about its accomplishments and largely unknown here in its own hometown, this company has grown to become the global leader in advertising measurement.

rsc global headquarters are located in historic downtown Evansville.

In 1974, President Meg Blair co-founded **research systems corporation (rsc)**, a market-research firm specializing in measuring the persuasive power of television advertisements for some of the world's largest consumer-goods companies. The company's initial mission was to "provide advertising measurement worthy of becoming the industry standard." In 1987, when rsc's *ARS Persuasion*® metric had set the industry standard for quality, sales-related measurement, the company's mission was broadened to "helping customers continually improve advertising productivity."

Over its first 25 years of basic research, rsc has empirically discovered many important truths about how advertising works and as a result has set many of the current and evolving standards in advertising research, advertising measurement, and advertising improvement. Taking this empirical leadership role has not been inexpensive or easy, as so many of the findings have led to "breaking the rules" and "bucking industry convention." However, this rule-breaking has proven worth the investment—as rsc has evolved, its empirically driven quest for knowledge has continued to keep the company on the leading edge of advertising and research.

Because rsc attributes its success to excellent teamwork—a concept it takes very seriously—the company is organized into "teams" rather than "departments." Twenty-five years ago, the company employed only a small handful of "teammates" (rsc's

term for employees). Today teammates number more than 350 located in Evansville, Cincinnati, Dallas, New Jersey, Pittsburgh, San Francisco, Amsterdam, and Mexico City.

Teammates are encouraged to operate on cross-functional as well as functional teams and are given the opportunity to develop their skills with on-the-job and classroom training. This teamwork has benefited not only rsc as a company but the Evansville community as a whole: rsc has formed several teams that contribute to the needs of the Evansville community, including ACE Space, LUV Our Town, and the TAG teams. For instance, members of the LUV Our Town Team partner with new teammates who have relocated to Evansville to make them feel welcome and introduce them to the best the city has to offer.

rsc's attractive, restored buildings are the focus of another rsc team. In 1974, rsc purchased a property on the corner of First and Walnut Streets, beginning a long partnership in the revitalization of downtown Evansville. Twenty-five years later, the company operates its growing global business from its beautifully restored downtown campus of stately early twentieth-century buildings. The ACE Space Team is charged with ensuring that both the interior and exterior of these buildings are Attractive, Comfortable, and Effective. This team is comprised not only of individuals from rsc but also an interior designer, an exterior designer, and the owners of a facility maintenance company. Together, the team works on challenges like parking availability and how to best restore historic structures. In preserving its headquarters located at the heart of historic downtown, rsc has nicely balanced the creation of an attractive, comfortable, and effective work environment with the maintenance of its beautiful properties' historical significance. The

Visitors and teammates alike enjoy the open, attractive, and professional atmosphere at rsc.

company's commitment to downtown revitalization is evidenced by its recent application for the prestigious National Preservation Honor Award.

rsc is also proud of its involvement in a number of community efforts, including United Way. At their annual banquet on March 13, 1998, The United Way of Southwestern Indiana awarded rsc the prestigious *Chairman's Award* for running a model United Way campaign. The United Way's general eligibility requirements for the *Chairman's Award* include visible CEO support, employee meetings, special events, a thank-you program for employees, and campaign results that are above the community average of $60 per capita and 60 percent participation. While many companies met these requirements, rsc's campaign stood out because of its unique "bottom-up" approach. The campaign is run by the Teammates Advisory Group (TAG), which is made up of non-management teammates from all areas of the company. This "bottom-up" team concept was developed to create a positive work environment by demonstrating teammate and team empowerment. Since rsc began organizing the United Way Campaign through this approach in 1996, campaign goals have been exceeded each year. The company boasts 100 percent teammate participation and matches its teammates' contributions dollar for dollar.

The company and rsc President Meg Blair are also very active in supporting the University of Southern Indiana. In 1997, Blair made a personal donation to the University of Southern Indiana for the establishment of the Blair Chair in Marketing Sciences. According to Ray Hoops, the University's president, "She is the first individual to

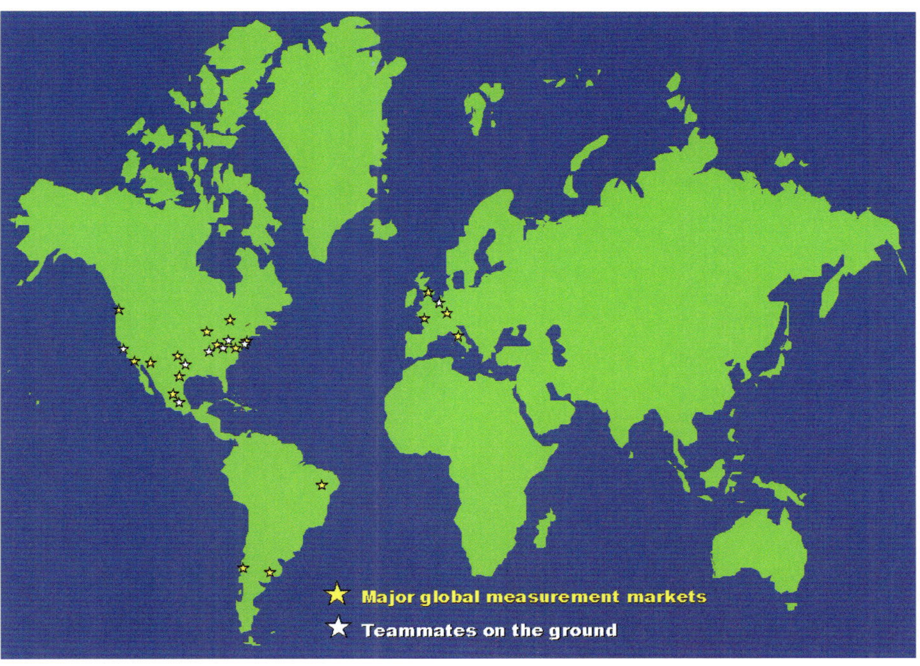

From its global headquarters in Evansville, rsc is continually expanding its markets across the world, providing exciting opportunities for its teammates.

establish an endowed academic chair [at USI], recognizing the value of nurturing this young discipline by bringing a marketing sciences professor and researcher of excellence to the University."

According to Blair, the intent of the gift is to further the advancement of marketing as an empirically-based discipline: "As marketers learn to apply rigorous measurement, as is the practice in the sciences, to areas where they traditionally have relied solely on their judgment, they will systematically improve marketing productivity.... It is my hope that the Blair Chair will further this emerging renaissance in marketing and build a lasting bridge between USI and the global business community."

As rsc heads toward the start of the twenty-first century, the company has empirical evidence that it can, in fact, satisfy its current mission, "to empower marketing leaders with Quality Measurement Feedback and Quality Process Tools for Revolutionary Improvement." Much has changed at rsc over the years, but some things remain the same. rsc remains committed to growing its and its customers' businesses, providing its teammates with both a great place to work and developmental opportunities, and being a good neighbor to the Evansville community. ▨

As rsc expands, the company remains committed to revitalizing downtown Evansville through renovating historic buildings. The global headquarters currently occupy three historic buildings on the corner of Walnut and First Streets.

ARS Persuasion® is a registered mark of rsc THE QUALITY MEASUREMENT COMPANY.

❖ Rainbow Communications, Inc. ❖

Joe Ellsworth never intended to go into business. He simply wanted a job where he could make films and videos. But in 1981, Ellsworth saw an empty niche in the Evansville media market. He started a company he dubbed Rainbow Productions and began creating video presentations for area industries. Before long, the name had been changed to Rainbow Communications, the company mission had expanded, and major corporations were hiring Rainbow to create media programs and events around the world.

In addition to corporate video presentations, the staff at Rainbow Communications today creates educational and documentary television programs, TV commercials, graphics for print applications, interactive CD-ROMs and DVDs, Web sites, and thematic media for conventions, meetings, and special events. Rainbow's craft is creating various media tools. But their uniqueness is in turning those tools into integrated communications strategies and awareness campaigns. These efforts have garnered them notice far beyond Southwest Indiana as their number of national and international clients grows quickly.

Rainbow Communications is guided by three principles:
- to give unparalleled client service,
- to offer continuously fresh creative ideas, and
- to perform proficiently using leading-edge technology.

They have used these principles to make magic in every major city in the United States, as well as Rome, Munich, Sydney, Monte Carlo, on Caribbean islands, and aboard ships at sea. In all these places, they have designed and produced corporate programs and events that have left attendees in awe. For instance, there was the convention where

Charles Darwin and a live elephant appeared in a ballroom to illustrate business evolution. Or the time a staged "earthquake" rocked a company's guiding principles. And the meeting where a flying saucer beamed the CEO onto a stage to deliver business advice from another galaxy.

But Rainbow Communications has not forgotten its original mission of creating corporate video from start to finish, from concept through final production. While their first Emmy was awarded in 1999 for an instructional television program about heart disease, Rainbow Communications has won many Telly Awards over the years for non-broadcast videos that assist companies with branding, marketing, training, and product introduction.

A major reason for Rainbow's success is that they nurture the creative spirit that allows their talented artists to perform with enthusiasm and skill. They spur each other on, they brainstorm in creative sessions, and they work constantly to push boundaries and improve their craft.

Rainbow Communications is a company whose job is creating tools that facilitate and enhance communication. From devising the concept to producing the entire package, they ensure a consistent and integrated message. The result? Better business through better communication. ❖

Photo by L. Kent Whitehead.

nk-Belt

13

C H A P T E R   T H I R T E E N

REAL ESTATE & DEVELOPMENT

Photo by L. Kent Whitehead.

❈ INDUSTRIAL CONTRACTORS, INC. ❈

It's rare today for large construction firms to self-perform most of their projects. Most contractors simply no longer accept the risks and responsibilities that go along with self-performance. Instead, they hire subcontractors, which dilutes the strength of their role and often results in less customer satisfaction. One major exception to this trend is Industrial Contractors, Inc., the Tri-State's largest contractor and, since 1978, one of *Engineering News Record's* Top 400 contractors in the country. ICI has always self-performed the great majority of its projects, believing that accepting this kind of responsibility is the best way to successfully fulfill clients' needs.

Owned and guided by the Braun family since 1964, ICI is a full-service construction company with the capabilities to handle all phases of a project, from design and engineering to start-up and commissioning. By maintaining such a comprehensive involvement in its projects, ICI exercises control of scheduling and ensures that the job will be completed on time and within budget.

In line with its full-service mission, ICI has affiliated with several other companies. Among this group is Professional Consultants, Inc., ICI's in-house engineering and architectural design group. Through their seamless partnering arrangement, ICI and PCI have created one of the best design-build construction firms in the Midwest. Other affiliates of ICI are Burch & Lamb, Inc. (conveyor engineering and installation), Industrial Equipment Inc. (construction equipment rental and leasing), Sprinkler Systems Inc. (fire protection), Tri-State Refractories Corp. (refractories associated with boilers, incinerators, carbon bake, and heat treat furnaces) and Metal Fabrication Division.

Casino Aztar - Pavillion, Hotel, and Parking Garage.

ICI has established a presence in the Midwest, including West Virginia, where it has opened a satellite office in Parkersburg to serve the large number of nearby clients. Yet 95 percent of its projects are located within 75 miles of Evansville. ICI has made a conscious decision to keep its headquarters in the area that has contributed so much to its success for nearly 40 years. The relationship between the Tri-State and ICI is clearly beneficial for both: ICI's motto of "We're Building Success" applies both to its role in the region's economic development as well as corporate growth. In addition to its professional role, ICI is also a proud supporter of local charitable organizations and events.

In the late 1990s, ICI completed or made significant contributions to the Tri-State's largest construction and renovation projects at the time, including Toyota Motor Manufacturing Indiana in Princeton, AK Steel in Rockport, Casino Aztar and the Vanderburgh Auditorium and Convention Centre in Evansville. Prior to that time, the firm played a major role in the construction or renovation of such projects as General Electric in Mt. Vernon, Indiana, Alcoa Warrick Operations near Newburgh, and Whirlpool, Bristol-Myers Squibb, and Roberts Stadium in Evansville. ICI has been on-site at the majority of these large industrial plants since their initial construction.

Other projects have included power, chemical, and processing plants; sophisticated health care facilities; highways; urban shopping malls; modern educational facilities; and a variety of other complex process structures. Many clients continue to choose ICI long after the original project to handle upgrades, expansions, and renovations. In fact, 90 percent of Industrial Contractors' business now comes from repeat customers.

Vanderburgh County Auditorium and Convention Center Additions and Renovations.

In order to remain a full-service, multi-craft construction firm, ICI has established contracts with nearly all the craft unions in the region: carpenters, ironworkers, laborers, bricklayers, cement masons, millwrights, plumbers/pipe fitters, boilermakers, sheetmetal workers, operators, teamsters, roofers, and electricians. ICI also employs experienced craftspeople from all these trades.

Plumbing and Piping

For more than three decades, ICI's plumbing and piping professionals have been designing and installing mechanical systems. A specialty is sanitary stainless steel piping for food, pharmaceutical, and nutritional processing facilities. They regularly install piping for HVAC systems, medical gas lines, and chemical and power plant process systems. They also retrofit renovations and repairs at a variety of facilities, often in record time.

Toyota Truck Plant - Foundations...

Electrical

It's unusual to find one firm that can handle the variety of electrical installations and special systems that ICI does. Some examples are: navigational lock and dam installations, high voltage distribution systems, lighting renovations for office complexes, and power and control systems for manufacturing plants. ICI also designs, fabricates, and installs automation systems utilizing programmable logic controllers, fiber optics, and electronic instrumentation systems.

Commonwealth Aluminum Cold Mill.

Boilermaker

This division specializes in construction, erection, repair, and replacement of pressure vessels and associated equipment. Its members perform certified welding in accordance with section IX of the ASME code, and the company holds "U," "S," and "R" stamp certification for pressure vessel and power piping work. They install and/or maintain a wide variety of equipment and systems in power generation facilities and in chemical, industrial, and processing plants.

Roofing

ICI's Roofing Division is the largest roofing contractor in the Tri-State, leading the way in one-ply or membrane roof systems. This division also has the expertise to design, re-roof, or install roofing systems. Projects include manufacturing facilities, commercial buildings, and power and chemical plants.

Sheet Metal and HVAC

The field group has installed HVAC systems up to hundreds of tons in size. The metals group works from modern, highly-mechanized shops, one of which houses machinery capable of working with 1/2 inch-thick mild steel, aluminum, and stainless steel. Trained designers and craftspeople design, fabricate, and install a wide range of applications.

Process Machinery

The Process Machinery Division evolved from the need for turnkey process installations. They have designed, engineered, fabricated, and installed machinery for industries as varied as coal mining and furniture manufacturing, and everything in between.

Equipment Setting, Conveyor Fabrication, and Installation

It's the job of this division to transport, set, erect, and install machinery, heavy equipment, and conveying systems for a wide array of industrial needs.

Indianapolis Power & Light.

Instrumentation and Calibration

Using full-service mobile units, the members of this team travel to the location with NIST traceable equipment and meets ISO and OSHA certification to handle every step of installing, checking, and calibrating process control equipment. Applications include fiber and copper, local area networks, voice/video/security systems, and process controls and programming.

Casino Aztar - Parking Garage, Hotel, and Pavillion...

❈ PROFESSIONAL CONSULTANTS, INC. ❈

Since 1972, Professional Consultants, Inc. has provided complete, full-service engineering and construction management services to some of the finest companies in the world. With projects ranging in scope from global giants such as Toyota Motor Manufacturing, AK Steel, and GE Plastics, to Evansville's own Casino Aztar and the historic Old Post Office, PCI has developed strong client partnerships based on unrivaled professional expertise and dedication to customer service.

A Solid Reputation in the Industry

PCI's clients have come to rely on this prominent Evansville design/build firm for several reasons. Over the years, PCI has built a solid reputation for overall reliability and engineering design excellence. With PCI's experienced team of in-house engineering professionals, its clients know that every project is undertaken with sound engineering design methodology and an eye toward innovative solutions.

Design/Build Partnership with ICI

A long-standing partnership with Industrial Contractors, Inc. has allowed PCI to offer its clients several seamless design/build strengths, including financial stability, technical and construction expertise, a network of valuable industry contacts, and ICI's reputation for high-quality construction and scheduling efficiency.

PCI Technical Services Division

In addition to its five main engineering design services—civil, electrical, mechanical, structural, and architectural—PCI offers clients a unique Technical Services Division which handles all system trouble-shooting, diagnostics, and testing on-site. An extremely fast-growing division, PCI's Technical Services provides on-call support by a team of individuals with professional degrees and the hands-on field experience to supply both the theory and the first-hand knowledge to solve any technical challenge. And PCI's Technical Services Division provides on-site testing using PCI's own diagnostic equipment.

Special Capabilities

In addition to traditional E/A Design and Technical Services, PCI offers its clients special capabilities that provide a variety of specialized services, including Construction Management, Communication and Alarm System Design, Machine Design, Computer-Generated 3-D Modeling and Animation, Information Management System Design, and Document Management and Control.

Experienced Professionals

And finally, PCI's clients rely on the firm's true strength—its growing team of dedicated and experienced engineering professionals. Any company can boast the latest technology or the largest staff, but PCI's clients enjoy something more: a personal relationship with highly trained engineers and technicians who take the time to understand the scope of the client's total project in order to provide the best, most cost-efficient design solution possible. PCI's team of professionals is dedicated to continuing education and skill development, which enhances their ability to provide value to their clients by utilizing the most advanced engineering methods and technology on every project.

PCI—Providing Engineering Solutions and Value

What sets PCI apart from other E/A consulting firms? In a word—Value. From the moment a project is under consideration, through project completion and beyond, PCI engineers take individual ownership of every project. And it is PCI's approach to project ownership that allows them to detect and find solutions to unforeseen design issues before, during, and after the project is completed. From day one, the PCI team begins analyzing and evaluating the entire scope of the project in order to find high-quality design solutions that also provide their clients savings in both time and money—they get it done right the first time, which makes PCI a valuable partner on every project. ❈

❈ J. H. Rudolph & Co., Inc ❈

Anyone who drives in the Evansville area is literally riding on the reputation of J. H. Rudolph & Co., Inc., the area's premiere asphalt and concrete paving contractor. Family-owned since 1940, the company has paved most of the area's roads and highways at one time or another. They have also handled Southwest Indiana's most demanding commercial and industrial paving jobs, like the new Toyota and AK Steel plants. In living up to their motto of "Do it right . . . no matter what it takes," Rudolph ensures that every project, no matter the size, is safely completed on time and within budget by experienced workers using the highest-quality materials.

With many second and third-generation employees on the job at Rudolph, clients receive the benefit of literally hundreds of years of experience. The craftsmanship and expertise that employees bring to their work have brought many honors to the company. Among recent projects that have won national quality awards are Runway 18-36 at the Evansville Regional Airport, State Road (SR) 145 from SR 64 to SR 56, and 13th Street in Jasper, Indiana. SR 145 was also named one of the top three paving projects in the U. S. And no wonder, when the Indiana Department of Transportation ran a profilograph to test the smoothness of this new "SUPERPAVE" highway, the test showed a variance of only 0.89 inches per mile, when the specified variance was 12 inches per mile—SuperSmooth! Thanks to this quality of work, Indiana and Kentucky have granted Rudolph unlimited prequalification for state road projects.

As a full-service paving contractor, Rudolph will build the entire road system from start to finish or will partner with other professional contractors, architects, and engineers to complete the highest quality pavements.

Concrete Pavement, State Road 69.

Rudolph also offers site development services, drainage and utility installation, and pavement patching with UPM (Unique Paving Material). Most importantly, Rudolph offers the right type of paving material for each job, whether it's a standard mix or custom-created. Rudolph has its own AMRL Certified Mix Design Laboratory to assure the right pavement for any application or traffic load. The company's Quality Certified high production plants produce conventional hot mix asphalt, the new SUPERPAVE (Superior Performing Asphalt Pavements) mixes, and RAP (Recycled Asphalt Pavement) mixes to strict quality standards.

Concrete Supply, LLC is Rudolph's sister company, with ready-mix and central mix concrete plants located in Evansville and Mt. Vernon, Indiana. Concrete Supply, LLC provides ready-mix concrete and related products made to rigid quality standards. With a large fleet of Advance concrete trucks, drivers can deliver concrete to any customer location.

With facilities in Dubois County near Huntingburg, Troy, and two locations in Evansville, J. H. Rudolph & Co., Inc. and Concrete Supply, LLC are ready to serve the home, commercial, and industrial paving and ready-mix concrete needs of Southwest Indiana. ❈

J.H. Rudolph & Co., Inc.

❈ REGENCY ❈

With more than 50 years of experience in real estate development and management, Regency can credit its success to these attributes: the ability to recognize and respond to economic change, the commitment to conduct business in a manner that benefits the community and the economy, and a strong belief in loyalty, integrity, fairness, and the highest ethical standards. Regency has grown from a small family real estate firm to a full-service real estate management and development company that has acquired, developed, managed, and invested in more than 2 million square feet of commercial space and more than 10,000 apartment units in Indiana, Illinois, Ohio, Kentucky, South Carolina, Michigan, and Latin America.

Parent company Regency Associates LP encompasses four affiliates:

- Regency Residential Associates, LLC and its management company, Regency Management Service LLC—apartment ownership, management, and development.
- Regency Commercial Associates, LLC and its management company, Regency Property Services LLC—shopping center ownership, management, and domestic development.
- Regency—Wyndclyff, LLC—international shopping center development and international and domestic retail real estate advisory services.
- Regency Investment Associates—the sum of various partnerships and limited liability companies that own specific real estate properties—equity real estate investment.

Founder Alvin Eades began Regency's tradition of establishing long-term relationships with financiers, residents, tenants, employees, and consumers. In the 1970s, the company expanded its focus to including investment partners; today, Regency uses continuous adaptation and improvement strategies to remain at the forefront of commercial and residential real estate management and development. The company has developed the following core competencies:

Regency's offices located in Cross Pointe Commerce Center. Photo by Cocchiarella Design, Inc.

- In real estate development, Regency represents the interests of its clients in every phase of development, from conception to opening.
- By taking a personal and comprehensive approach to its property management, Regency manages properties as assets for long- and short-term returns to investors, tenants, and the communities it serves.
- Regency's management services include personnel management, leasing administration, insurance claim processing, accounting, purchasing, maintenance, periodic site inspection, and reporting.
- The Asset Management functions include evaluation and analysis of proposed investments; development of budgets, long- and short-range operation plans, and models for strategic decisions; financial analysis of property operations; and analysis of capital dispositions.
- In Leasing, Regency's property owners are consistently impressed by high occupancy rates, proactive tenant retention policy, and Regency's continuous efforts to increase property value.
- In Acquisition and Disposition, Regency calls upon its belief that a property must be capable of achieving capital appreciation, long-term viability, and cash distributions.
- The in-house Financial Reporting and Accounting division prepares a wide range of reports for investors, customers, and partners.
- Equity Investment—the ability to build partnerships—is one of Regency's greatest strengths, a tremendous advantage in attracting equity investors for real estate projects.

Truly a full-spectrum commercial real estate firm, Regency's properties include community and neighborhood shopping centers, apartment communities, land subdivision and master-planned tracts, business park development, urban and suburban offices, and built-to-suit buildings. Through its management of properties for some of the largest institutional owners of commercial real estate, Regency has earned a reputation for increasing revenues and decreasing costs to yield enhanced asset values. ❈

University Shopping Center on Evansville's west side. Photo by Cocchiarella Design, Inc.

14

CHAPTER FOURTEEN
HEALTH CARE &
EDUCATION

Photo by L. Kent Whitehead.

❧ St. Mary's Health Care Services ❧

Health care today is dominated by change: in technology, in the kinds of services available, and even in the definition of "health care" itself. The only aspect that will never change is the need for experienced care delivered with compassion and understanding. For more than 125 years, St. Mary's Health Care Services has provided this kind of care while maintaining the highest standards of medical excellence within a tradition of innovation.

1894 - Doctors A.M. Owen and Edwin Walker open the Evansville Sanitarium, later to be named the Welborn-Walker Hospital.

When Evansville desperately needed a hospital in 1872, the Daughters of Charity responded to the call. St. Vincent de Paul had founded the order in 1633 to minister to the poor and under-served with medical care, and the sisters brought their ministry to Evansville. Today, the Daughters of Charity National Health System (DCNHS) operates one of the largest not-for-profit systems in the United States. All of its members support the same mission, vision, and values as their hospitals did in the 19th century, demonstrating respect, quality service, simplicity, advocacy for the poor, and inventiveness to infinity. Through their Catholic heritage, they share a tradition of community service and maintain a leadership role in uniting the communities they serve to respond to the unmet needs of disadvantaged populations.

The first St. Mary's hospital was located on Evansville's waterfront, in the building that previously housed the Marine Hospital. The State of Indiana had constructed this facility to take care of the medical needs of the many men who worked on the area's rivers; it had been closed for some time. St. Mary's soon became an integral part of the Evansville community and served people of all economic levels, with special consideration for the poor. It moved twice before finally locating on Washington Avenue. There, it grew to become a medical center and later the largest health care organization and one of the largest employers in the Evansville region. In recent years, it has acquired satellite health care centers, acute care hospitals, and related organizations, including Harrisburg (Illinois) Medical Center, St. Mary's-Warrick, and Seton Health Corporation of Southern Indiana.

The largest and most recent acquisition occurred in 1999, when St. Mary's purchased the assets of Evansville's Welborn Baptist Hospital and its Mulberry Center. The joining of these two faith-based, not-for-profit organizations offered many benefits, including greater cost efficiencies, integrated delivery of patient care, and better value and choice through affiliated health plans. One of the most important benefits was the ability to offer expanded services to the poor and under-served. As part of this mission, the money from the sale of Welborn was used to create two foundations to provide resources for community initiatives on quality-of-life issues such as health and education.

In 1999, DCNHS created Mission Health System, Inc., as the parent company to all the St. Mary's affiliates, uniting them into one organization that offers a cohesive system of care in a variety of settings and locations. Mission Health has streamlined the services offered through St. Mary's multiple locations and is the center of strategic planning for the growth of the health ministry. The strength of the Mission Health system supports the local health initiatives and adds value to its member organizations.

The aim of today's ministry at Mission Health is the same as when the Daughters of Charity first came to Evansville: to make a positive difference in the lives and health status of individuals and the community as a whole, including caring for the poor and the whole person. Implicit in the mission is the promise to keep health services accessible and affordable.

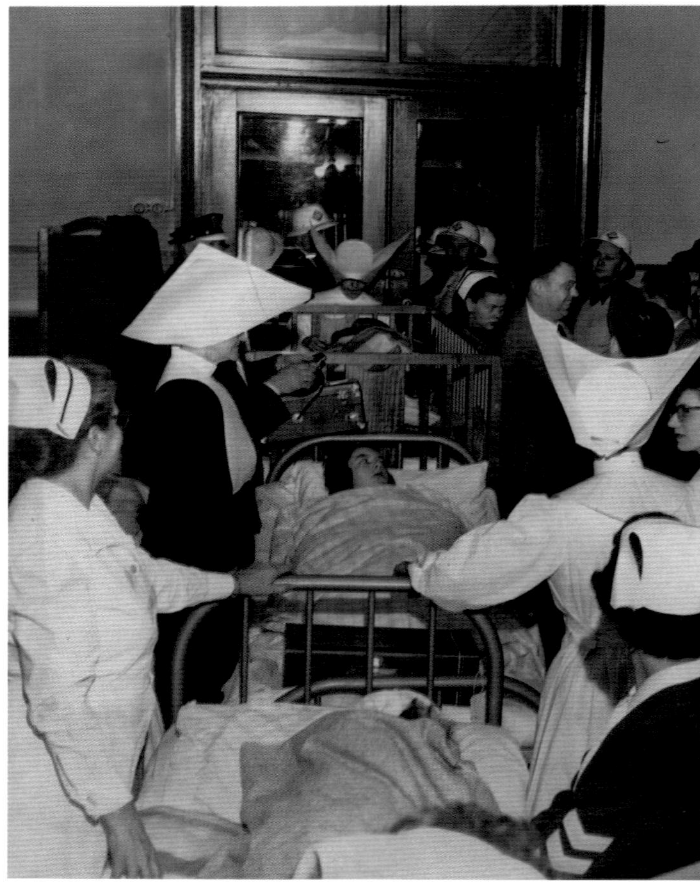

1956 - 800 volunteers and 5,000 vehicles move St. Mary's Medical Center to Washington Avenue. The one-day event is nicknamed "Operation Good Neighbor."

St. Mary's Health Ministry

The health ministry of St. Mary's flows from its Catholic heritage. As a ministry of Jesus Christ, the entire organization is dedicated to the health of every person—body, mind, and spirit. Within its integrated regional and community-based facilities, St. Mary's offers a broad spectrum of services. It is recognized for exceptional care in cardiology/cardiovascular surgery, women's health, laser surgery, renal disease, rehabilitation, oncology, geriatrics, occupational health, and mental health.

With all the changes occurring in health care today, the medical needs of a modern community extend far beyond the services offered by a single hospital. St. Mary's understands that effective health care at the beginning of the 21st century is a complex web of primary care services, specialized facilities, hospitals, and community programs, not to mention managed care, which is changing the face of health care across America.

In light of these many changes, St. Mary's has moved from the more traditional inpatient setting to a delivery that considers the full continuum of health care. New levels of care have been added to its services, including comprehensive outpatient rehabilitation, home care, long-term acute care and sub-acute care, plus a growing list of ambulatory services offered in a number of locations. These ambulatory services include a senior health center, a cancer center, two urgent care centers, a women's health center, a fitness center, an ambulatory surgery center, two renal dialysis centers, an occupational medicine center, and advanced emergency services.

The Daughters of Charity believe that the charity of Christ urges everyone to respond to the needs of the poor. St. Mary's has long practiced the values of inventiveness to infinity and advocacy in constantly finding new ways to serve the poor of all ages and contributes millions of dollars annually to the needs of the poor in its Tri-State communities.

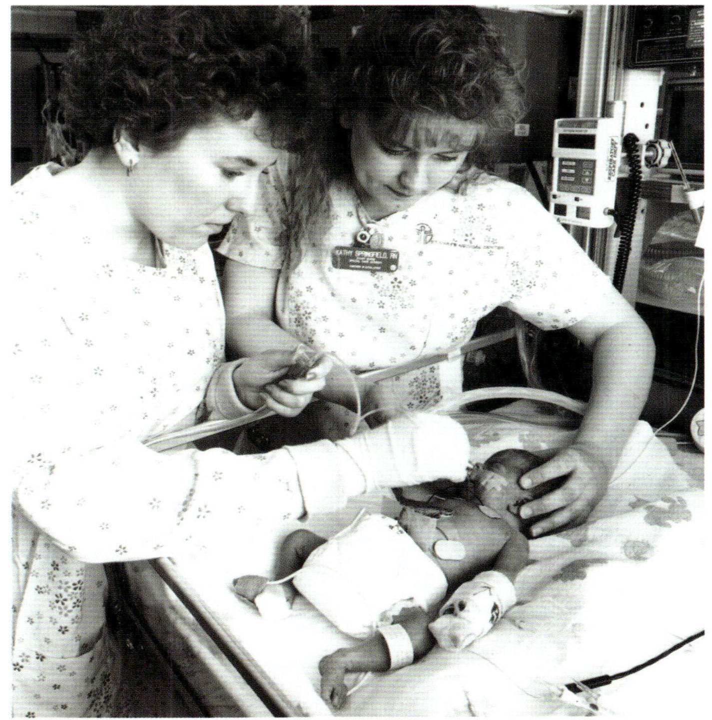

St. Mary's operates the only Level III Neonatal Intensive Care Unit in the region. Two clinical professionals tend to a patient in the NICU.

Innovation and Partnerships: Making a Positive Difference

While change always represents challenges to the health care industry, it also offers opportunities to step out in front with innovative solutions that offer better patient care, education, and technology—in short, the opportunity to make a positive difference. Over the years, St. Mary's has created an impressive list of services and programs that have made a positive difference in the lives of thousands of people. Many times, these innovations were later adopted by other hospitals in the Tri-State or by the entire health care industry. Here are just a few examples:

- In 1956, St. Mary's Hospital was the first in the United States to introduce Family-Centered Maternity Care that allowed the mother and father to remain together during labor and delivery and then provided close, frequent contact with the newest member of the family. By keeping the family together, St. Mary's was ministering to the people involved, not clinging to outmoded procedures. Today, this practice is commonplace in all hospitals.

1994-1996 - St. Mary's is named one of the top 100 hospitals by HCIA/Mercer Study. Partners in Excellence (employees) celebrate the accomplishment at an employee function.

1995-Present - St Mary's Partners, physicians, and friends travel to St. Ann's Bay, Jamaica to assist its 120-bed hospital in dire need of assistance. Hospital president, Jay Kasey helps build a needed expansion project at the mission.

- In the late 1970s, St. Mary's reached out to alcoholics, particularly among the poor. Its Alcohol Treatment Program was the first in Indiana to be certified by the Department of Mental Health, Division of Addiction Services.
- In 1997, the Mobile Outreach Clinic began bringing needed health care services to the under-served in the area. Housed in a large vehicle resembling a recreational vehicle, the mobile clinic makes regular visits to more than a dozen locations each week. St. Mary's staff members provide primary health care screenings, minor acute care, physical exams, immunizations, and health referrals. Services are provided according to income.

Crucial to St. Mary's mission of making a positive difference are the strong ties it has formed with the community. By partnering with values-based leaders, St. Mary's has been able to build a complete system of health services, including outreach efforts that take health care services to the neighborhoods where they are needed most.

Included among recent partnerships and outreach services are:
- The Joshua Academy—An alternative, non-denominational school, The Joshua Academy offers a curriculum designed to prepare children for life spiritually, academically, and socially. Its students are aged 3 through first grade, although the program will be expanded in the future. St. Mary's has made an extended commitment to help fund The Joshua Academy, which is located at Nazarene Missionary Baptist Church.

- Hoosier Healthwise Insurance (Medicaid) enrollment station—St. Mary's is one of two such stations in Vanderburgh County. This appointment reflects St. Mary's commitment to the Children's Health Matters program, which is a partnership of DCNHS, Carondelet Health Systems, and Catholic Charities, U.S.A. devoted to reducing the enormous number of uninsured children. Families can now enroll for Medicaid through St. Mary's, including the Mobile Outreach Clinic.
- Project site for Supportive Care of the Dying: A Coalition of Compassionate Care—The goal of this initiative is to change society's perceptions of care of the dying to ensure that individuals live and die well. This work ties into St. Mary's strategic initiative of "supportive care of the dying/palliative care." The coalition conducting this initiative comprises DCNHS, the Catholic Health Association, and several other Catholic health systems.
- Teen Health Care Clinic—A collaborative effort with the Vanderburgh County Health Department, the Teen Health Care Clinic provides acute and preventive health care services and education to a very at-risk population in Evansville: adolescents, particularly those who previously had no access to these vital services.
- Parish Nursing Efforts—Programs at area churches provide education as well as supportive and preventive health care services to parishioners. The parish nurses act as health educators, consultants, and referral sources, and they visit the housebound and hospitalized, provide relief to caregivers, and provide other services.
- Partnership with St. Ann's Bay Hospital—St. Mary's began a mission to this Jamaica hospital in 1996. Since that time, more than 100 Partners in Excellence (employees) have shared their knowledge, skills, and Vincentian spirit with the Third World hospital staff and patients. The number of volunteers for the annual mission trip continues to grow.

1999 - St. Mary's purchases Welborn Baptist Hospital, located in the heart of Evansville's downtown. Flying overhead is the LifeFlight helicopter, a service of Welborn, and now St. Mary's.

- Community Marriage Builders—A joint effort with the United Way of Southwestern Indiana, this project provides leadership to a coalition of community churches, organizations, and individuals committed to nurturing people toward lifetime marriages. This project provides workshops for training married couples to be marriage mentors for engaged couples, as well as premarital counseling.

St. Mary's also works in the community in other ways to promote health and wellness. One example is its Programs for Industry. These programs offer comprehensive, integrated services designed to assist employers in achieving well-managed health care programs that meet their unique needs. St. Mary's can provide all aspects of necessary and desired care, from managed care options to occupational medicine services.

Another important facet of St. Mary's mission within the community is education in wellness and preventive care. Comprehensive health care begins with keeping people healthy and providing early diagnosis when they do become ill. Not only do individuals have a higher quality of life, but also the entire community benefits from lower health care costs. St. Mary's accomplishes this task in a number of ways: offering simple health screenings at local shopping malls and other locations; offering on-site tests and education about cholesterol, blood pressure, heart risk factors, and more; offering fitness options through its Health Matters Fitness Center; and a comprehensive schedule of seminars and classes throughout the year that offer something for everyone.

St. Mary's in the New Century

In the mid-1990s, St. Mary's was ranked among the top 100 hospitals in the United States by the HCIA/William Mercer study—three years in a row. It was one of only 27 facilities in the country to be so recognized two years running, and only a dozen for three years. This rank placed St. Mary's within the top 2.5 percent of hospitals nationwide.

Many factors came together to create the atmosphere that led to these extraordinary rankings. The long healing tradition of the Daughters of Charity is one. St. Mary's dedication to providing all citizens in the community with the best care, regardless of their ability to pay is another.

1997 - St. Mary's celebrates its 125th anniversary. A six-story banner is erected on the side of the medical facility in honor of this milestone.

Ministering to the whole person—body, mind, and spirit— means taking time for a special greeting for patients and their families. Here, a volunteer takes time to talk with a resident of Regina Continuing Care Center on the St. Mary's campus.

Also crucial is the fact that employees at St. Mary's are Partners in Excellence who receive extensive training and ongoing evaluation, while offering their own suggestions for improvement (which have saved hundreds of thousands of dollars and improved patient care).

The new century is full of changes for St. Mary's. The acquisition of Welborn Baptist Hospital in 1999 presented opportunities which are just now beginning to be explored. Integration efforts have begun between the two tertiary centers, including mental health, heart services, rehabilitation, maternity services, and all support services. Current expansion projects include a new women's center which connects directly to St. Mary's Medical Center, a new adjacent cancer center, expansion of the surgery suites, and a new location for the bustling St. Mary's Family Practice Center and OB/GYN/Peds Clinic.

Perhaps one sentence best sums up the tradition at St. Mary's. It comes from the philosophy by which Partners in Excellence are evaluated each year: "Believe that all things are possible until proven otherwise." From its beginning in 1872, the staff of St. Mary's has believed exactly that and put it into practice every day. The old tradition combined with the newest technology and the latest knowledge—it is this kind of health care that will continue to sustain St. Mary's and Mission Health long into the new century. ▓

❧ THE UNIVERSITY OF EVANSVILLE ❧

The University of Evansville is best described by the people who know it well: students and alumni. Paul Hogle '87, vice president for development of the Baltimore Symphony, said, "At UE, I first experienced the tremendous possibilities that become available when a group of faculty truly takes the time to know their students."

From its beginning, the mission of the University of Evansville has been to provide a personalized, quality education to its students. The University of Evansville is an independent, comprehensive, liberal arts and sciences university affiliated with the United Methodist Church. The University originated in 1854 in a former United Methodist Church in Moores Hill, located in Southwestern Indiana. First named Moores Hill Male and Female Collegiate Institute, the school became Moores Hill College in 1887. In 1919, the school was moved to the city of Evansville and was renamed Evansville College when Indiana Governor James P. Goodrich signed the school's charter. In 1931, the college received accreditation from the North Central Association of Colleges and Secondary Schools, and in 1967 the name was changed to the University of Evansville.

An Academic Community

For seven consecutive years, the University of Evansville has been ranked by *U.S. News & World Report* as one of the top 15 outstanding Midwest regional universities and eighth in the category of best value. Attending UE is affordable; more than 90 percent of UE students receive some type of financial aid.

The vast array of majors, more than 80 areas of study, and the 13-to-one student to faculty ratio are just some of the reasons students study at the University of Evansville. "UE was one of the few small schools I found where I could pursue a degree in physical therapy and

receive the personal attention that would allow me to further develop my professional and people skills," said Brandi Doyle '98. She is an outpatient physical therapist, specializing with Broadway performers and professional dancers in New York City.

Students may choose from bachelor's degrees, certification programs, and selected professional programs. The University has four academic colleges and schools: the College of Arts and Sciences, College of Education and Health Sciences, College of Engineering and Computer Science, and School of Business Administration. There are two centers for special instruction: Center for Continuing Education, offering adult degree programs and credit and non-credit evening programs; and the International Institute, offering an Intensive English Program, English credit courses, and custom-designed programs with international universities.

Special academic programs taken by all students make the University of Evansville curriculum outstanding. Developed by our faculty, the World Cultures Sequence is a part of the general education requirement that focuses on the cultural achievements of selected societies throughout history, global awareness, values, and community consciousness and involvement.

The Honors Program gives an added challenge to students. Those who wish may conduct original research work with faculty through Advantage, the undergraduate research program. Often, students present their research at regional and national conferences. "The research and classroom projects I am doing at UE have helped me decide what direction to go in my career," said Ryan Brown, who plans to attend graduate school and study plant pathology.

Technology Centered

Using technology throughout the campus remains a priority at the University of Evansville. The entire University (including all 13 student computer labs as well as residence halls) is wired for campus-wide Internet access. The Foreign Language Lab, the first of its type in the nation, has 31 networked stations that allow professors to use video, audio, computer graphics, and information from CD-ROMs as a unique learning tool for students. UE's Center for Teaching Excellence encourages UE professors to strengthen their teaching abilities and try new classroom approaches such as integrating computer technology into the curriculum. "Interdisciplinary groups of faculty fellows meet weekly to share ideas and evaluate the strengths and weakness of different approaches," said Dr. Michael Stankey, director of the Center for Teaching Excellence. "Fellows are supported with seed grants to fund their ideas, and a full-time technology trainer is on staff to help them work through implementation."

Another innovative learning tool is the Internet Applications Laboratory where student teams create limited area search engines on the Internet so that users can access scholarly information without searching through the mass of irrelevant material on the Web.

A Career Advantage

UE students are preparing for their careers, and it is the University's goal to give them every advantage. "To continue to improve the educational experience for all students, we are focusing on effective teaching, student advising and retention, career placement, and experiential learning," said President James S. Vinson. UE JobLink, a free 24-hour on-

line Internet service, allows students and alumni to post their resumes on-line, and employers can search for job candidates and post job openings. Through UExperience Transcript, an official University document, UE graduates showcase their volunteer involvement and leadership activities. Many use them along with their resumes. Another option for students is UE MentorNet, a World Wide Web database linking UE students with mentors (UE alumni) via e-mail. Students gather information about an area of study or career interest and begin networking with professionals.

To give first-year UE students a head start on college, the University offers SummerStart, where students take classes, live in the residence halls, and learn how to succeed in college. The goal of UE 101: University Success is to help freshmen make the transition from high school to college and to succeed in college-level work. Freshman Connection provides personal and academic assistance and a social connection for all freshmen.

The World as a Classroom

Thirty-five percent of UE graduates have studied abroad, compared to the national average of only 1 percent. Many students choose to study in England at Harlaxton College, UE's British campus, listed as one of the top 25 best study abroad opportunities by The Student's Guide to the Best Study Abroad Programs.

UE students who venture to Harlaxton College are delighted at what they find. "Harlaxton was the most amazing experience—spending a semester abroad, living and traveling in Europe for a semester, and constantly being exposed to new ideas and situations," said Sara Rowe '99.

Located in the English midlands of Grantham, Harlaxton attracts students from colleges all over the U.S. who live and study in a 100-room manor many compare to a castle. Students take classes from both American and British professors. The centerpiece of the Harlaxton curriculum is British Studies, which combines history, literature, art, political science, and economics with field trips to cultural sites, ancient buildings, and other areas of natural beauty.

International programs prepare students for the global community in which we live. That is why the University offers international studies and global business degree programs, an extensive foreign language program, international internships, and study abroad at Harlaxton or at more than 100 exchange programs in 50 countries worldwide. The University also regularly offers summer study abroad programs to Tokoha Gakuen University program in Japan and Mexico; Franklin College in Switzerland; an archaeology excavation in Murlo, Italy; and Harlaxton College in England.

Stateside, linkages with international agencies, professionals abroad, and institutions are maintained through short-term training programs sponsored on-campus by the University's International Institute. Scholarships, language training, and support services for international students are more examples of the University's commitment to creating an international environment that encourages cross-cultural dialogue and understanding.

Athletics: A Winning Tradition

At the University of Evansville, a powerful combination exists—NCAA Division I athletics and a small, challenging academic environment. From the start, UE athletes are students first. A prime example of the caliber of students who attend UE is Australian native Karen Black, who received a UE tennis scholarship when she was just 16. In addition to being UE's all-time wins leader, Black graduated in only three and a half years, with honors. A recent graduate, Black is using her mass communications degree as an employee of a local marketing communications firm. The winning tradition at UE is based on a record of commitment to excellence. At Roberts Municipal Stadium, home to the Purple Aces, five NCAA banners are displayed that commemorate the years of Division II dominion: national champions in 1959, 1960, 1965, and 1971.

The University elected to upgrade its athletic program to Division I in 1977. In December of that same year, however, tragedy struck when a plane crash claimed the lives of the entire men's basketball team and coaching staff. Out of this tragedy came the resolve to maintain and strengthen the University's program at the Division I level.

In 1994, the University joined the Missouri Valley Conference (MVC), the second oldest collegiate conference, formed in 1907. Fifteen varsity sports compete in MVC championships: men's baseball, basketball, golf, soccer, swimming, diving, and tennis; and women's basketball, cross country, soccer, softball, swimming and diving, tennis, volleyball, and golf.

Since then, the Aces have enjoyed success throughout the athletic program; the men's basketball, baseball, and soccer teams have all qualified for the NCAA Tournament at least once and have won the MVC championships as well. In the 1998-99 season, both the men's and women's basketball teams and the women's soccer team qualified for the NCAA Tournament. The Aces have won Missouri Valley Conference championships in men's and women's basketball, men's and women's soccer, and they have been among the league's best in virtually every other sport.

After Hours: Student Life

Many University of Evansville students live on campus or nearby in University housing. There are seven residence halls on the University's 80-acre campus, and some offer thematic floors. For example, the Cultural Immersion Floor of Moore Hall has a no-English policy to encourage residents to develop language fluency and sensitivity to other cultures. The Fine Arts Floor allows students majoring in the arts to delve deeper in their areas of study, learning from each other. Twenty-five percent of students belong to a Greek life organization; there are six fraternities and four sororities at the University.

Outside of class, UE students are busy. There are more than 130 on-campus organizations, and 95 percent of students belong to at least one of them.

Nineteen percent of students volunteer in community programs. They play intramurals, attend sporting events, and participate in University sports and other University-sponsored activities such as Musical Madness, Winter Whispers Dance, movies, Talent Show, Sunset Concert, Bike Race, Masquerade Ball, Paoli Peaks Ski Trip, concerts, and UE Theatre productions. In the Patricia H. Snyder Concert and Lecture Series, students heard special guests Ray Bradbury, author; W.D. Snodgrass, poet; Naomi Wolf, author; Harry Wu, human rights activist; Julian Bond, chairman of the NAACP; and Mae Jemison, former astronaut. They enjoyed performances by world-renowned pianists Awadagin Pratt and Ralph Votapek, and child prodigy violinist Yura Lee.

Religious life is an active part of the UE community with 22 student organizations. Students participate in weekly on-campus worship services, retreats, conferences, and national and international mission trips and service projects with church-related agencies. They have served in South Africa, Brazil, Belize, Mexico, and Russia, as well as Jamaica and Miami, Washington, D.C., and Memphis in the U.S.

The mission of the University of Evansville is to provide talented and motivated students with the highest quality educational experience so that they develop worthy goals for a meaningful life, develop the skills to accomplish those goals with distinction, and by this process, realize their potential.

A UE education should prepare graduates not only for careers but also for life. Sometimes it is apparent that it does. Rebecca Lee Glancy '97 wrote this in her journal, reflecting on a UE mission trip she took to South Africa: "We have been given far beyond what we deserve. We must share with those born in less advantaged situations. There are two sides to every story.

You can learn from every person you come into contact with. Get out of your comfort zone once in a while.

Seek out joy; listen and learn. God will surprise you." ▓

❈ DEACONESS HOSPITAL ❈

The word "deaconess" is derived from a Greek word that means "one who ministers to the needs of another." For more than a century Evansville's Deaconess Hospital has lived up to its name by offering the utmost in patient care coupled with the latest in technology, all delivered by an experienced, caring staff. One of the largest hospitals in the region, Deaconess is a not-for-profit acute care teaching hospital that serves Southern Indiana, Southeastern Illinois, and Western Kentucky. From its main campus on the city's near-north side and many smaller locations throughout the region, Deaconess offers a broad range of inpatient and outpatient medical, surgical, and diagnostic services.

Deaconess has played a critical role in the health of the area since its arrival more than a century ago. Evansville's population had mushroomed from about 30,000 to more than 50,000 between 1880 and 1890. This rapid growth, caused mainly by immigrants coming to work at the local lumber, milling, and tobacco companies, overwhelmed the city's ability to provide adequate services, including health care. In 1892, a group called the Protestant Deaconess Association expressed its dream of bringing a second hospital to Evansville. They purchased a large house at the corner of Mary and Iowa streets and converted it into a 19-bed hospital. The home had earlier been the site of one of this country's first organized relief efforts when, in 1884, Clara Barton, founder of the American Red Cross, assisted the victims of the disastrous flood along the Ohio River while staying there.

When the Protestant Deaconess Nursing Home and Hospital opened in 1893, it was staffed with four physicians. Within the next few years, several deaconesses were added to the staff. They were young women who had received spiritual as well as nursing training before being consecrated as deaconesses. This tiny hospital cared for more than 100 patients during its first year. In 1895, the Association was planning to open a larger hospital by the turn of the century. Since that time, Deaconess has never stopped growing.

The Protestant Deaconess Nursing Home and Hospital was the beginning of the sprawling Deaconess campus and group of affiliated satellite offices that exist today. Deaconess services and regional specialist clinics can be found in Vanderburgh, Warrick, Daviess, Pike, Spencer, Perry, and Gibson counties in Indiana; Crawford, Richland, Wayne, Edwards, White, Saline, and Gallatin counties in Illinois; and Henderson and Union counties in Kentucky. Deaconess is one of the major employers in the Evansville area, with more than 2,500 on staff. The hospital is a member of VHA, a nationwide network of nearly 1,850 health care organizations. This alliance provides benefits such as shared insurance, group purchasing, access to capital, and shared research, education, and communications.

Long recognized locally for its high levels of care and excellence in its operation, Deaconess has several times been ranked among the top 100 hospitals in the country and was recently noted as one of America's Best Hospitals by *U. S. News & World Report*. It has also been ranked among the top 25 teaching hospitals with 250 or more beds in service. Deaconess is among the Midwest's most progressive hospitals, always searching for ways to improve and enhance service. This attitude has led to many changes over the course of its history, but one aspect of Deaconess will never change: the compassionate expertise that

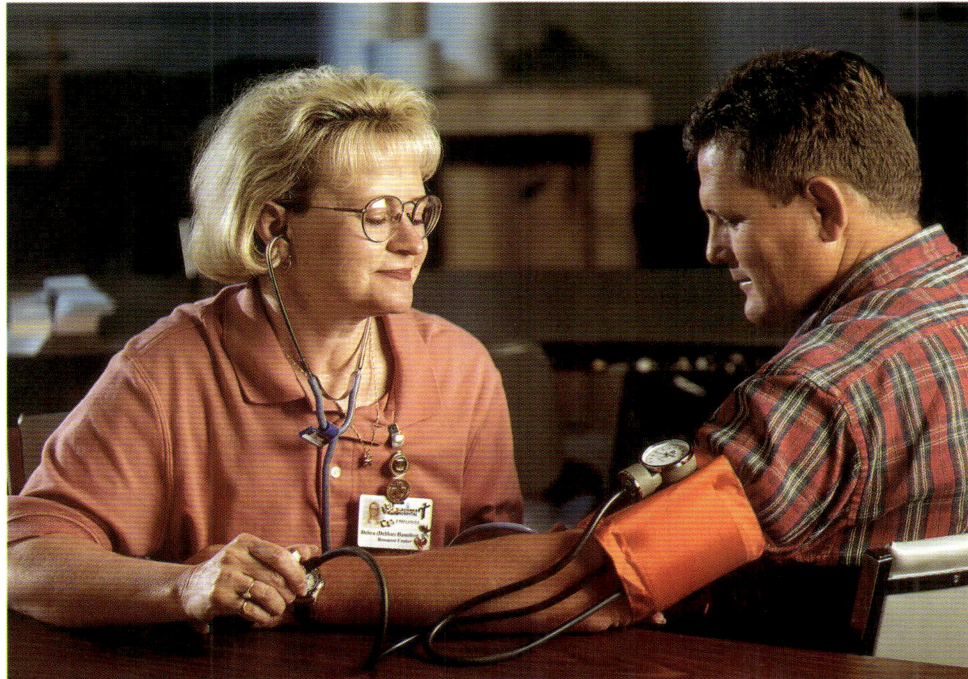

Deaconess operates a significant community outreach program, with many services targeted at various segments of the community. The LifeQuest wellness program and the Resource Center for Healthy Living work to promote healthy lifestyles through an extensive curriculum of prevention programs and health screenings. Senior services include the Helping Hand program with assistance in filing insurance claims, transportation, prescription drug discounts, and other benefits; the Connections for Caring program assists those who care for an older family member or friend; Deaconess Medicare SELECT offers a competitively priced Medicare supplement; and Companion Service provides an emergency response service. In addition, two MedWise Centers are designed and located to offer comprehensive primary care exclusively to people 65 and older.

guides the care of patients. From the days when the first Evansville deaconesses answered a spiritual call to minister to the sick and came to the city on the bend in the river to put their beliefs into action, Deaconess Hospital has always kept the needs of its patients as the highest priority.

In keeping with the hospital's not-for-profit mission, the Deaconess Foundation supports various programs, services, and advanced technology at Deaconess. In addition, thanks to the generosity of many individuals, the Foundation supports activities to improve access to health care throughout the Tri-State.

Deaconess maintains the area's largest physician network, Deaconess Health Partners, a Preferred Provider Organization (PPO), and recently was one of four Indiana hospitals to jointly sponsor a new managed care company, The Health Care Group, LLC. Area employers also partner with Deaconess for custom-designed wellness and prevention programs.

For many years, the hospital ran a nursing school, which graduated its first class in 1895 and its last class in 1990. In the late 1980s, the Indiana Commission on Higher Education recommended that the University of Southern Indiana, located in Evansville, establish a baccalaureate nursing degree program. In 1988, Deaconess decided to close its School of Nursing and turn the tradition of teaching excellence in nursing care over to USI.

Services and Firsts

Deaconess offers a wide array of services. Its areas of excellence include cardiac care, cancer care, pulmonary care, ortho-neuro surgical care, and emergency medicine.

Other services include hospice care; family-centered maternity care; women's and children's services; medical, surgical, and cardiac intensive care units; outpatient surgery; comprehensive rehabilitation; a pediatric cardiology clinic; and the area's only cystic fibrosis clinic.

Deaconess also offers a variety of specialized services to area business and industry. A comprehensive occupational medicine program is offered through the Deaconess COMP Center, which provides injury care, rehabilitation, X-ray capabilities, pre-employment testing, and laboratory services in one convenient setting. Deaconess CONCERN, an employee assistance program, offers assessment and short-term counseling to employees and members of the families who want assistance with personal problems. Complete clinical laboratory and drug screening services are available to local employers at competitive prices.

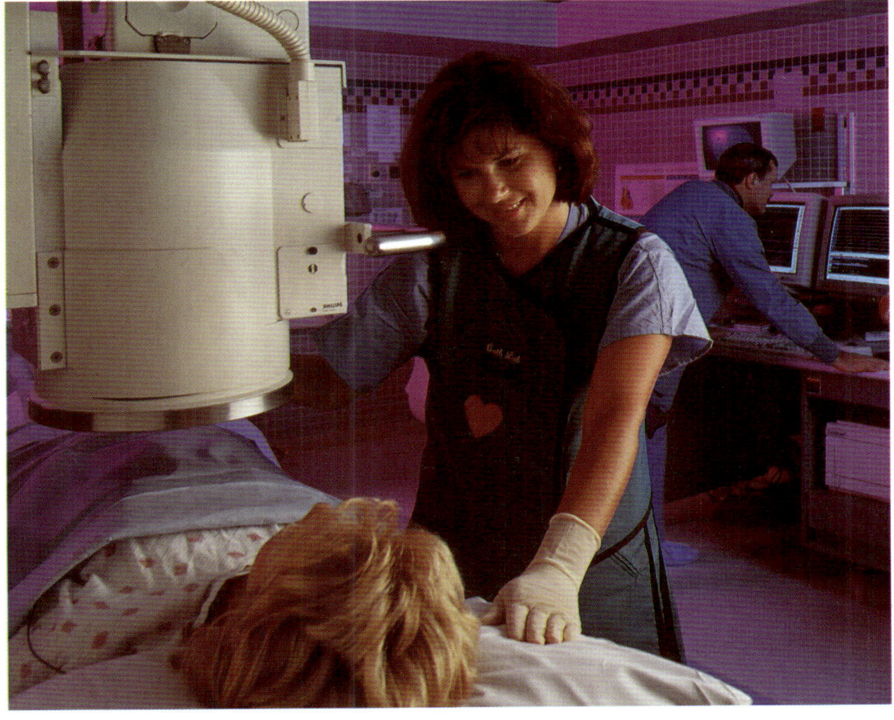

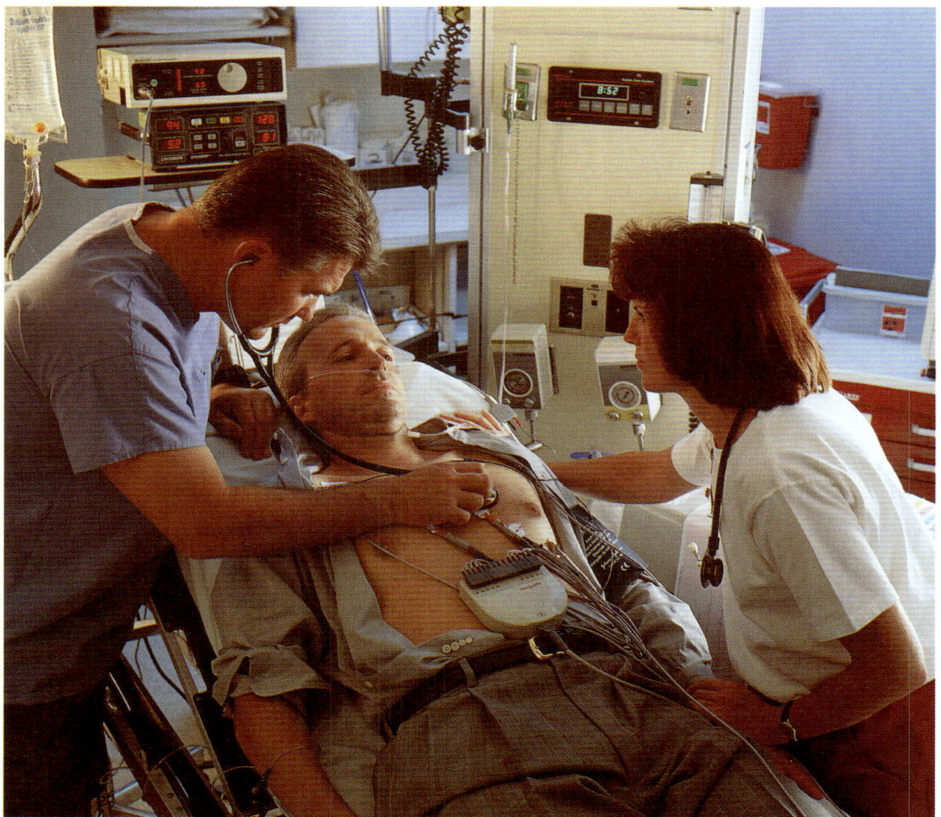

Deaconess has long been a pioneer. Among its "firsts" in the Evansville area:

- During the polio epidemic that began in the 1940s, Deaconess physicians were among the first in the U. S. to use the techniques developed by Sister Elizabeth Kenny, an Australian nurse, to treat the severe muscle spasms suffered by those who contracted this insidious disease.

- In 1972, Deaconess opened the area's first cardiac catheterization lab. The following year brought approval to begin a heart surgery program, which required bringing in supporting heart team members and specialized equipment from a hospital in Pennsylvania. By late 1978, the hospital had its own dedicated heart team and the equipment necessary to perform delicate and complicated open heart surgeries. By 1980, Deaconess was among only 100 hospitals in the world performing percutaneous transluminal coronary angioplasty, more commonly known as balloon angioplasty. Today, the comprehensive cardiac program offers a full range of advanced cardiac services ranging from prevention and wellness to chest pain management, diagnosis, treatment, and rehabilitation. Heart patients throughout the region have easy access to care close to home at satellite clinic locations.

- The area's first specialized emergency physician joined Deaconess in 1976; within three years, the hospital had added three more emergency physicians—giving the hospital four of Indiana's 12 emergency physicians at the time. Today, eight board certified emergency physicians provide treatment for approximately 50,000 patients a year at the

Deaconess is also well-respected for "teaching" family practice physicians, who receive excellent training as residents and medical students in family practice, obstetrics and gynecology, internal medicine, surgery, and other specialties.

Some of the newest specialized facilities at Deaconess include:

- Deaconess Crosse Pointe opened in 1999. This 60-bed facility features behavioral and chemical dependency inpatient and outpatient services for adults, adolescents, and children.

- The Deaconess Cardiovascular Care Center, also opened in 1999, offers advanced inpatient cardiac services. It features single-bed rooms, a system able to monitor patients from almost anywhere in the hospital, nurses equipped with palmtop computers for bedside care, buffet service for patients, and a technology center for improved communications and services for health care providers.

- Deaconess Cardiac Rehab offers outpatient services for patients recovering from heart attacks and other cardiac illness. The program features continuous heart monitoring in conjunction with a personalized exercise program. There are also support group meetings and classes to help patients reach a full recovery.

- The Deaconess Women's Hospital of Southern Indiana, LLC, is scheduled to open in the summer of 2000. Located at Deaconess Gateway Center near Interstate 164 and the Lloyd Expressway, the Women's Hospital will provide specialized, comprehensive women's care in a dedicated setting. These services include obstetrics, nursery (including facilities for high-risk infants), surgery, breast center, urodynamics, infertility services, diagnostic services, preventive health care, and educational services. The Hospital is designed to handle up to 2,500 births each year, with patients remaining in one room for labor, delivery, recovery, and postpartum.

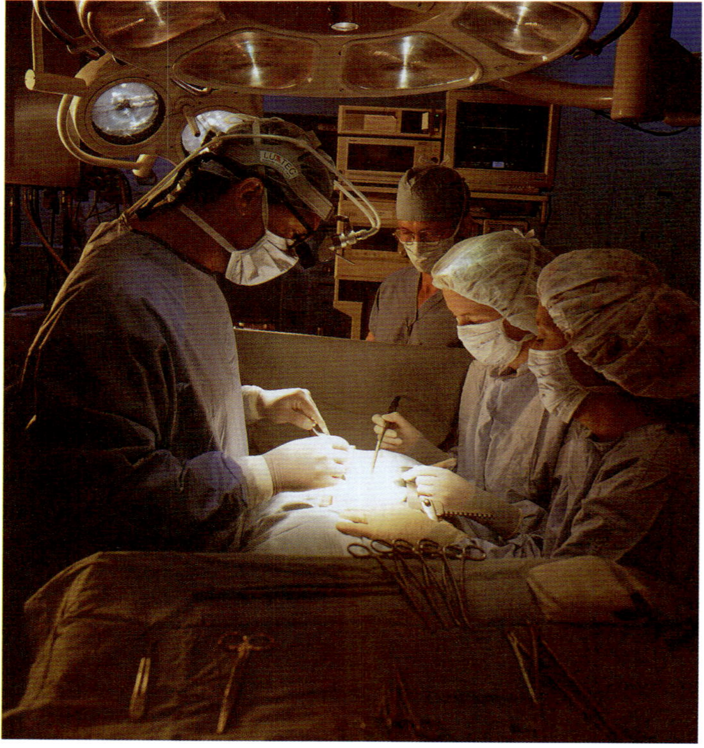

Deaconess Emergency Center, which houses three trauma rooms, a dedicated chest pain/observation area, and other specialized treatment rooms. It is the only emergency facility in Evansville with a board-certified emergency physician on duty 24 hours a day, 7 days a week. Furthermore, a specially trained team is prepared to handle any emergency situation that arises.

- In 1985, Deaconess opened Evansville's first Women's Center to address the special health care needs of women. It was the first breast screening center in Evansville to be accredited by the American College of Radiology and the first to acquire a densitometer to measure and detect osteoporosis. A more specialized facility opened in 1999. The Deaconess Breast Center today offers complete breast care, including stereotactic breast biopsies, breast ultrasounds, mammography, osteoporosis screenings, and breast ultrasound guided biopsies.

- Also in 1985, Deaconess was the first hospital within 150 miles to install a hyperbaric oxygen chamber, which uses highly concentrated oxygen to treat a variety of conditions, such as gangrene, carbon monoxide poisoning, and slow-healing wounds.

- The Deaconess Holistic Resource Center, which provides tools for healing body, mind, and spirit, was the first in the region when it opened in 1997. The center's holistic services include educational materials, a lending library, and ongoing classes on relaxation techniques, stress management, meditation, yoga, massage therapy, acupuncture, and much more.

The Future of Deaconess Hospital

Medicine and health care are constantly changing, and all health care facilities face the daunting challenge of simply keeping up. Yet Deaconess is able not only to keep up with change but also to embrace and initiate it. Through unique partnerships with other health care providers, some exciting new innovations are underway—and they promise to improve Evansville's health scene even more. For instance, the addition of the Deaconess Women's Hospital means that obstetric and maternity services, along with the newborn nursery, will be located on the city's east side. This move of women's services will open up more space within the acute care hospital to convert more patient rooms to private, single-bed accommodations.

Also, working in partnership with Welborn Clinic, Deaconess will open a freestanding diagnostic and treatment facility for the outpatient care of cancer patients.

From the late 19th century into the dawn of the 21st, Deaconess Hospital has maintained an unbroken record of excellent care while embracing community needs with expertise and compassion. ▨

❖ University of Southern Indiana ❖

Mission

The University of Southern Indiana is a comprehensive public university, founded in 1965 to bring affordable higher education to Evansville and southwestern Indiana. The University remains true to that mission today, meeting the needs of increasing numbers of students and preparing those students for jobs in the area's evolving economy. USI is a service-oriented institution that is accessible and responsive to regional and state educational needs.

Academic programs

The University offers 60 undergraduate majors in five schools including the School of Business, Bower-Suhrheinrich School of Education and Human Services, School of Liberal Arts, School of Nursing and Health Professions, and Pott School of Science and Engineering Technology. Selected master's degrees serve persons in business, professional, and technical studies.

Enrollment

Enrollment exceeds 8,600 students with more than 90 percent of those students coming from Indiana. The University has experienced rapid growth, almost doubling enrollment in the 1990s. As the most affordable four-year institution in the state, USI attracts families who want quality programs within their financial reach.

Teaching focus

USI President H. Ray Hoops emphasizes that the University is an institution where teaching matters above all else. Most classes have 25 or fewer students, allowing close interaction between faculty and students. Qualified faculty members dedicated to teaching undergraduate students are in the classroom every day. The student/faculty ratio is 18:1.

Study abroad

Study-abroad opportunities are available at more than 100 institutions in 38 countries. One of the most popular study-abroad experiences for USI students is in England at Harlaxton College, located an hour by train from London. Harlaxton College is a cooperative program with the University of Evansville.

Facilities

The University is proud to serve students in modern classrooms with advanced technology in appropriate space for all academic and student life functions. Nine major buildings plus apartments and suite-style housing for nearly 3,000 students are located on the 300-acre suburban campus.

Athletics

USI is a member of the Great Lakes Valley Conference of the National Collegiate Athletic Association (NCAA) Division II. The men's and women's basketball programs are the flagships of the athletic program. In 1995, the men won the University's first NCAA Division II National Championship. The women's basketball team has gone to the NCAA Division II Tournament four straight seasons and was a 1997 NCAA Division II finalist. Other varsity sports for men are baseball, cross country, golf, soccer, and tennis. Other women's varsity sports are cross country, golf, soccer, softball, tennis, and volleyball. The Physical Activities Center seats 3,300 in the Eagles' home court and provides swimming in an Olympic-sized pool.

USI Foundation

The USI Foundation is the official gift-receiving agency for the University of Southern Indiana. The mission of the USI Foundation is to develop, implement, and coordinate a comprehensive fund-raising program, manage assets, and administer the resources for the benefit of USI.

Cultural life

USI programs enrich the cultural and intellectual life of the community. Recent speakers or visiting scholars have included Stephen Jay Gould, Harvard University professor and prominent author on the topic of evolution; Julia Hare, educator and author who is executive director of The Black Think Tank; and Dr. Richard M. Zaner, the Ann Geddes Stahlman professor of medical ethics and professor of philosophy at Vanderbilt University Medical Center.

In addition to its own theatre program, the University directs New Harmony Theatre, a professional summer theatre program, and sponsors Lincoln Amphitheatre in Lincoln City, Indiana, in cooperation with the Indiana Department of Natural Resources. USI manages Historic New Harmony, the home of two 19th century communal societies, and Historic Southern Indiana, a project to preserve regional history and promote tourism.

Community partnerships

The University prides itself on being responsive to the changing needs of the area it serves. Many faculty perform applied research to advance knowledge and solve problems in the community. Faculty serve as consultants to public schools, business, industry, and governmental agencies. Every two years, USI publishes a new edition of the *Evansville Factbook*, a comprehensive source of economic, social, and demographic data on the city of Evansville and the surrounding area. USI also works with area employers to tailor specific educational programs for their employees. The School of Business, accredited by the AACSB — The International Association for Management Education, offers strong academic programs that build skills needed for success in today's business environment, including communication, teamwork, and problem-solving capabilities.

To ensure it stays in touch with developments in the business world, the School of Business has established a Board of Visitors with nearly 40 senior executives who advise and support the school. Within the School of Business, the Accounting and Business Law Department and the Master of Business Administration program have similar advisory groups. School officials often implement changes in curriculum and course content in response to recommendations from these groups.

The Bower-Suhrheinrich School of Education and Human Services is also active in community partnerships. The Teacher Education Department offers courses on site at area schools, providing for seamless integration of theory and practice. The School of Nursing and Health Professions joins with area healthcare providers for practice and research. As a public service, faculty and staff extend their expertise to numerous regional organizations that enhance the quality of life in southern Indiana.

Additional Educational Services

The University of Southern Indiana embraces programs that support the business community and enhance the knowledge and skills that employees offer to their employers. Through the Office of Extended Services, USI sponsors a number of organizational and professional development programs in quality management, human resource development, and other areas of continuing education. Through the USI Learning Network, the University offers distance education courses that allow busy professionals to enroll in classes that fit their time and travel needs. The School of Nursing and Health Professions offers a certificate program with Internet-delivered instruction that teaches the skills required to develop a wellness program in the workplace, a need recognized by many companies today. USI also provides instruction in English as a second language, organizes and facilitates programs for the Tri State World Trade Council, administers the Southern Indiana Japanese Saturday School, and offers classes at the Signature Learning Center.

Commitment to Indiana

The University of Southern Indiana is committed to the progress of southwestern Indiana and the entire state. In recent graduating classes, more than 85 percent of the students earning degrees have remained in Indiana to live and work, contributing to the accumulation of human capital and the increased level of post-secondary educational attainment in the state. A USI education is a wise investment for the individual and for Indiana. ▧

❖ Ivy Tech State College ❖

The thriving economy of Southwest Indiana requires a huge pool of qualified workers able to function in industries ranging from vehicle manufacturing and steel fabrication to visual communication and healthcare. Individuals in this varied workforce must possess the "hard" skills that enable them to operate complex, high-tech equipment as well as the "soft" skills needed for effective communication and teamwork. A growing number of students and employers alike turn to Ivy Tech State College-Southwest when they need assistance in gaining these skills or in recruiting employees who possess them.

Ivy Tech is Indiana's third largest college, with 22 campuses across the state. The Southwest campus has long been recognized as the Evansville area's provider of choice for workforce education, thanks to its responsiveness to local workforce development needs and its preparation of the region's technical workforce.

Prominent Washington, D. C. newsletter, *The Kiplinger Washington Letter*, has recognized Ivy Tech-Southwest as a significant factor in the region's recent industrial and economic growth. The editors explained reasons for this growth to include, "Location…gateway to the Midwest and South. A good workforce and vo-tech center for training" namely, Ivy Tech-Southwest.

Ivy Tech-Southwest works hand in hand with employers of the Tri-State region, partnering with them to tailor services to their needs. The Industry Advisory Task Force, a consortium of area employers, educational institutions, and the Metropolitan Evansville Chamber of Commerce, is one example of such a partnership. The task force secured a $200,000 grant and matching funds to create a joint curriculum development process that will serve employment needs in electronics and industrial technology.

Ivy Tech-Southwest has taken the lead in helping employers to manage their most important resource: employees. Ivy Tech-Southwest believes this market niche will only continue to grow as the region's tight labor market makes employee recruitment and retention even more critical. Thus Ivy Tech-Southwest offers a wide variety of services to the region's employers through its Business and Industry Training Center.

Among the services offered through BIT are apprenticeship programs tailored to the individual industry, workforce skills testing evaluation, economic development services, customized training programs, continuing education coursework, public seminars and conferences, management of extension site course offerings, and support services.

BIT can assist with all stages of plant start-up, pre-employment training, and quality management.

BIT also offers an advanced, computerized job analysis system, called the Work Profiling System (WPS). WPS makes it faster and easier to accurately perform human resource functions such as employee selection, job analysis, performance appraisal, training profiles, and job restructuring. Many employers use WPS to help develop job descriptions to meet ISO/QS 9000 requirements.

The college also partners with other educational institutions in the area, including the University of Southern Indiana and Evansville's high schools, to share resources and form cooperative educational ventures. These partnerships allow Ivy Tech students to succeed in the world of high-tech employment or in continuing their education at other institutions.

Computers are integral to the curricula of Ivy Tech State College's degree programs and business training.

Students can choose from associate of science degrees, associate in applied science degrees, technical certificates, and continuing education services. Ninety-eight percent of Ivy Tech graduates will find jobs within six months of graduation, and 86 percent of those will be hired in positions directly related to their training. Their average wage has increased 25 percent in recent years.

The student body reflects the regional population as a whole. It includes members of every socioeconomic level: Students have GEDs through post-graduate degrees and come from the working poor through the upper income levels. Many students already have significant work experience, but they come to Ivy Tech to gain new job skills or re-training that will qualify them for many of the area's high-tech positions. Regardless of their age or educational background, Ivy Tech students are attracted by the school's dynamic nature, personal attention, and the promise of a solid, practical education that can be completed within two semesters or two years. They are taught by master-credentialed faculty who hold many years of professional experience in their fields.

Ivy Tech-Southwest is growing rapidly. From 1997 to 1999, enrollment grew by 12 percent, with approximately 3,600 students attending Ivy Tech. To accommodate this growth, Ivy Tech is expanding its main campus on First Avenue in Evansville. The 200,000-square-feet design includes high-tech labs, distance education facilities, and an auditorium. An expanded Carter Library will allow students to use state-of-the-art multimedia technology and to participate in distance education programs.

By forming strong, enduring partnerships with employers, educational institutions, and students, Ivy Tech-Southwest has become and will remain the provider of choice for workforce education in Southwestern Indiana. ▓

Technology is the core of Ivy Tech State College's facility. Students and area employers train on industry quality equipment.

❈ Evansville Surgery Center ❈

In the mid-1980s, a group of Evansville physicians developed the first surgery center in the Tri-State area. With all the changes beginning to happen in health care, they knew there was a growing need for a place where patients could go for surgery without having to be admitted to a hospital. Today, thousands of patients each year come to the Evansville Surgery Center. The convenience, personalized care, up-to-date technology, and experience of more than 100 physicians has made it the premiere surgery center in the Tri-State.

At the Evansville Surgery Center's three locations, the emphasis is on wellness. They specialize in ambulatory, outpatient surgery, and their goal is to return patients to the activities of daily living as quickly as possible. Most patients are able to have their surgery and return home on the same day. However, those patients needing more complex procedures can stay in one of the tastefully decorated overnight suites, each with a private bath.

The friendly, professional staff provides excellent care for patients and their families from the minute they walk in the door. The comfortable atmosphere makes everyone, especially children, feel more comfortable than in a large, more impersonal hospital. Children can stay with their parents right up until the surgery and rejoin them immediately afterward. Patients of all ages appreciate knowing that their families are always welcome.

Evansville Surgery Center performs a variety of surgical procedures: gynecological, otolaryngological, ophthalmological, general surgery,

The Evansville Surgery Center is conveniently located on the Deaconess Hospital Campus. The Center is fully equipped with the latest medical technology and staffed by professionally licensed nurses and physicians.

orthopedic, and cosmetic. More cosmetic surgery is performed here than at any other location in the area. Cosmetic surgery patients appreciate the confidentiality and uncompromised privacy they receive, along with the experienced skill of the physicians and nursing staff. Even more importantly, though, the staff at the Evansville Surgery Center understands the importance of elective cosmetic surgery to the individual, and this adds to patients' comfort.

Patients find other advantages in coming to the Evansville Surgery Center, which is supported and reimbursed by major health carriers. First and foremost, it is usually more economical than a hospital. Hospital surgical patients often experience long delays before their surgeries begin, but at the Evansville Surgery Center, procedures begin on time. And, to ensure the peace of mind of patients and their families, the Evansville Surgery Center maintains a high ratio of nurses to patients, often one-to-one, and nurses are always just a few steps away from their patients.

More than 100 physicians from throughout the area have privileges at the Evansville Surgery Center. Managed and directed by a local board of directors, the center is partnered with Deaconess Hospital and Healthsouth Corporation. It is fully licensed by the State of Indiana and accredited by the Joint Commission for the Accreditation of Healthcare Organizations. ❈

Evansville Surgery Center offers convenience, a friendly environment, and personalized care before and after surgery.

Photo by L. Kent Whitehead.

DOVE RIDGE FARM
CERTIFIED ORG'IC PRODUCE
VEGETABLES
HERBS
FLOWERS

15

C H A P T E R   F I F T E E N

THE MARKETPLACE

Photo by L. Kent Whitehead.

❧ DUNN HOSPITALITY GROUP ❧

When Southwest Indiana entered the economic development boom of the late 1990s, Dunn Hospitality Group was ready to accommodate the growing number of business and leisure travelers visiting the Evansville area. The company began on Evansville's East Side in 1978; by the end of 1999, the number of hotels owned and operated by Dunn Hospitality Group was approaching 20, scattered across Indiana, Illinois, and Kentucky. Six are located in Evansville, comprising more than 700 rooms. All hotels included within the Dunn Hospitality Group are rated in the top 10 percent in their brand across the country, based on customer satisfaction and quality index scores.

The hospitality industry has always been highly competitive, but never more than now. Today's traveler has numerous and varied lodging options in many price ranges, yet rarely does a traveler make a decision about where to stay based on price alone. Having become more discriminating than ever, today's traveler takes into account many other considerations—quality of service, safety, location, and special touches that make them feel valued as a guest. Dunn Hospitality Group understood this from the beginning and fashioned its business strategy around a vision based on quality at all levels. By carefully choosing their brand of hotels, locating at strategic and convenient sites, and then staffing their hotels with quality, trained associates, Dunn Hospitality Group is able to continue attracting travelers who expect—and receive—the best. Whether traveling for business or pleasure, whether first-time or returning, guests of the Dunn Hospitality Group can be assured that their needs will be met.

The corporation's six hotels in Evansville represent a variety of options that appeal to a broad base of guests. The Hampton Inn, Fairfield Inn by Marriott—East and West, Residence Inn by Marriott,

In 1999, Dunn Hospitality Group entered the economy-priced hotel market by opening a new prototype of the Red Roof Inn. With a new design and focus on quality at a low rate, this brand is sure to become an industry leader.

Red Roof Inn, and Holiday Inn Express offer travelers their own unique personality and amenities. The Hampton Inn, a mid-priced, limited service hotel, is the leader for the hospitality industry across the United States. Dunn Hospitality Group is proud to fly its flag and enjoys the success associated with its nationwide reputation for "100 Percent Guaranteed Satisfaction." In 1999, Dunn Hospitality Group entered the economy-priced hotel market by opening a Red Roof Inn; with its new prototype design, this economy-market leader is expected to experience rapid growth in the early years of the new century. The

The "just like home" atmosphere of the Residence Inn by Marriott provides their extended-stay guests with all the amenities of being at home, but with housekeeping service, indoor pool and spa, an on-site fitness center, grocery shopping service...

Dunn Hospitality Group's Fairfield Inns are consistently recognized with distinguished honors for Guest Satisfaction. Our staff training is a continual process to ensure the highest level of quality service.

Residence Inn by Marriott, which offers "room to relax, room to work, room to breathe," is the premiere extended stay hotel in the country. Designed primarily for business travelers, who stay an average of 11 days, Residence Inns are composed of suites with separate living and sleeping areas, fully equipped kitchens, plenty of room for meeting and entertaining colleagues, and the space to set up an office while on the road. With its manager's weekly barbecue, daily complimentary breakfasts, and Sport Court, it offers its guests all the benefits of a community away from home. The Evansville Residence Inn has maintained exceptionally high guest satisfaction ratings since its opening in 1998.

Dunn Hospitality Group was among the first in the industry to recognize the growing number of women travelers and their special concerns. In the late 1970s, research showed that women made up only 10 percent of business travelers, but that number was expected to grow considerably. It was at this time that Dunn Hospitality Group launched its "We Treat Women Differently" campaign, aimed at creating a loyal following from an excellent customer base. Guest rooms were personalized for women travelers. The rooms were near the front desk to offer added security and special amenities became regular features of these rooms—irons with ironing boards, shampoo, and shower caps. Today, when nearly half of all business travelers are women, these features have become standard at many hotels—along with non-smoking rooms and complimentary premium movie channels, two other features Dunn Hospitality Group introduced early on.

Historically, Dunn Hospitality Group focused primarily on constructing new hotels. In more recent years, however, as the company opened nearly 20 hotels and expanded outward from Evansville into Northern Indiana, Kentucky, and Illinois, this strategy had to be amended. Quality sites in many major markets are becoming harder to find, particularly at prices that can be justified within the area. To overcome this obstacle, Dunn Hospitality Group started evaluating opportunities to purchase older hotels for the purpose of modernizing and renovating them. This strategy has many excellent advantages: securing a piece of choice real estate, reduced construction costs when renovating rather than building from the ground up, plus eliminating a competitor from the market.

Given the intense competition within the hospitality industry today, the choice made by potential guests often rests on the quality of service they receive. In turn, that quality of service depends upon the attitude, training, and expertise of the hotel staff, all the way from housekeepers to managers. Therefore, Dunn Hospitality Group understands that its strength is to be found in its more than 400 associates. Its commitment to excellence includes a pledge not only to customers, shareholders/partners, and the community, but to associates as well. Put into action, this philosophy helps to build associates' loyalty to the company and pride in a job well done, which they communicate to guests through their actions and high quality of service.

All Dunn Hospitality Group associates receive an orientation into the corporate culture, instruction in brand awareness, personnel sensitivity, and safety training, in addition to annual job-specific classes and diversity/cultural training in response to the dynamics of the industry and awareness of changes in the marketplace. Additionally, the company is committed to providing a comprehensive wage and benefit package that is regularly evaluated to maintain the best programs available for its associates. This includes a company-matched 401 (k) plan; health, dental, accident, and cancer insurance plans; online computer training for front and back office positions; and one-on-one mentoring programs. Associates also have numerous opportunities to grow professionally and financially within the organization.

Fairfield Inns are Marriot's brand in the limited-sevice market. Our locations on the east and west sides of Evansville provide the exceptional style and service associated with the Marriot name.

Dunn Hospitality Group's presence within a community is recognized not only by monetary contributions to charitable and civic organizations but also by the involvement of its associates. All management associates are required to join and be active in their local Chamber of Commerce, convention and visitors bureaus, and at least one service club of their choice. They encourage their associates to participate in the local United Way and other charitable or community service functions, such as Rotary, Jaycees, Civitan, and Kiwanis clubs. In Evansville, Dunn Hospitality Group is a proud supporter of the arts, including the Evansville Philharmonic Orchestra, Museum of Arts and Sciences, Southwestern Indiana Arts Council, and the arts program at Oakland City University, which resulted in the presentation of the 1998 Mayor's Corporate Art Award by the Metropolitan Evansville Chamber of Commerce.

Setting goals high—and exceeding that commitment—has made Dunn Hospitality Group the "Premiere Hospitality Company in the Midwest." To maintain this status, the company must:

- Have the very best people, trained and empowered to deliver excellent service to every guest, every time.
- Maintain a results-oriented plan fostered by quality performance through team work that will achieve effective cost reductions while improving productivity.
- Develop a plan for extension into selective, well-defined, yet under-served markets that encourage future profitable growth; and
- Continue to develop limited-service hotels, primarily the Marriott and Hampton brands, that recognize the importance of meeting the changing needs of tomorrow's customers in order to stay competitive in today's market.

The Holiday Inn Express has been the recipient of many prestigious awards for quality service and excellence in product. This long-established east side hotel has just completed an extensive renovation to keep pace with their guests' expectations.

Now Evansville's largest hotel group, the company that began with one hotel more than 20 years ago has never experienced an unprofitable year. Not only has the company kept pace with industry changes, it has successfully introduced many innovations of its own. In establishing and maintaining its commitments to guests, associates, shareholders/partners, and the communities it serves, Dunn Hospitality Group has created a successful strategy to carry it proudly into the 21st century.

The quality and success of this Hampton Inn has been unprecedented. It continues to be a favorite with business people, and leisure travelers will drive several miles out of their way to stay at this award-winning hotel.

❖ EAGLE CREST COMMERCE CENTRE ❖

When planning began for the Eagle Crest Commerce Centre in 1990, residential neighbors feared the attractive and peaceful setting of their neighborhoods would be changed into a loud, bustling commercial nightmare. However, the developers wrote strict standards to ensure that the beauty and tranquility of the area would be maintained. Today, Eagle Crest Commerce Centre is among the most professional and beautifully maintained business complexes in the area.

This office and light retail development is nestled in the curve of a new highway and built around 12-acre Eagle Lake, which is surrounded by wide, green spaces, tree-lined boulevards, and unobtrusive lighting. All utilities, including natural gas and electricity provided by Southern Indiana Gas and Electric Company, are located underground to maintain a pleasant, uncluttered appearance. It blends perfectly into the upscale residential neighborhoods to which it is adjacent.

Eagle Crest Commerce Centre at sunset. Eagle Lake provides Eagle Crest tenants, as well as nearby residents, with a sense of peace and tranquility within a thriving business center.

The restrictive covenants for the subdivision were written to prohibit construction of any business that might intrude upon the tranquility of the area. Fast-food restaurants or any business utilizing drive-up windows, gas stations and truck stops, large specialty/discount stores, and even billboards have been specifically designated as unwelcome at Eagle Crest Commerce Centre. All buildings are tastefully designed and compliment each other and their surroundings. Each structure must meet the high specifications and standards that Eagle Crest demands of its tenants, including consistent finishes on all sides of the buildings and trash receptacles enclosed by a solid decorative screen.

Located at Interstate 164 and Highway 66 (Lloyd Expressway), Eagle Crest is situated at "Evansville's New Front Door" as the premiere business and office park among the many such developments in and around the city. A variety of hotels currently occupy the subdivision: Hampton Inn, Fairfield Inn by Marriott—East, Residence Inn by Marriott, Red Roof Inn, and Studio Plus. Other tenants include Southwestern Indiana AAA Regional Headquarters, Cracker Barrel Restaurant, and Pasta Grille Restaurant. You, too, can make Eagle Crest Commerce Centre your business address and "soar on the wings of success." ❖

In 1990, Eagle Crest Commerce Centre established the "new front door" to Evansville on the city's Eastside.

❈ CASINO AZTAR ❈

Casino Aztar fits into the landscape of the Ohio River as naturally as the bend in the river on which it sits. However, first time visitors to the mid-sized family town of Evansville may not realize what an asset Casino Aztar has been to this Ohio River community. A riverfront park, in the past marked more by graffiti than grandeur, is now a beautiful recreation area in which to take pride. A riverfront once little more than a littered boat dock is now home to a grand pagoda and a museum transportation center. The Dress Plaza area along the riverfront will soon receive an $11 million face-lift to make it more "citizen-friendly"—with terraced seating, three overlooks, and an improved esplanade.

Regent Court, located in Casino Aztar's Riverfront Pavilion offers fine dining overlooking the Ohio River.

A historic downtown once in the midst of economic distress is now an area of thriving businesses both new and old. And a city with a stagnant influx of new money is now experiencing unprecedented growth as a regional tourist destination, entertaining guests from throughout the Midwest. You don't have to look far to see the positive impact Casino Aztar has had on the Evansville community…and you don't have to go far to get in on the fun.

Historical Significance of Casino Aztar's Presence

Before 1993, the only way Tri-state residents could experience the entertainment and excitement that casinos offer was to hit the road or hop on a plane and head east or west. But the legalization of riverboat gaming by the State of Indiana in June 1993 gave Indiana communities the opportunity to decide for themselves whether or not they wanted to take advantage of the benefits riverboat gaming could offer.

Evansville residents realized the many ways a riverboat casino could benefit the community. The passing of a referendum on November 2, 1993, officially put Evansville's name into the hat to receive one of the 10 gaming licenses to be awarded in Indiana by the Indiana Gaming Commission, and one of five on the Ohio River.

Soon after, former Mayor Frank McDonald II appointed a riverboat casino evaluation committee, comprised of various city and county officials and corporate leaders representing various public interests, to evaluate the corporations vying for one of the much-coveted Indiana gaming licenses. After a grueling 16 months that included preparation and research and two rounds of proposals by casino corporations, the riverboat casino evaluation committee ranked the six casino contenders in order of their preference to win the Evansville casino bid. Aztar Corporation was the committee's overwhelming choice to bring gaming to Evansville.

While the Indiana Gaming Commission was not bound under the state's riverboat gaming law to consider the city's preferences, Mayor McDonald submitted the city's final recommendation to the Gaming Commission firm in the belief that Aztar could deliver what it promised.

It took the Indiana Gaming Commission less than one hour to agree with what the Evansville commission firmly believed already—Aztar would be a good fit in the Evansville community. In a five to two vote, Aztar Corporation received the nod from the Indiana Gaming Commission and was awarded a certificate of suitability. Evansville became the first Indiana community to offer legalized riverboat gaming, and Casino Aztar Evansville became the first casino riverboat to operate in the state of Indiana.

Aztar Corporation

Aztar Corporation has the industry knowledge and experience necessary to make such a venture successful in Evansville, Indiana. The company has been in the gaming business for more than 20 years and operates three casino hotels in major gaming markets and two riverboat casinos. Operating casinos and entertainment resorts solely in the United States, Aztar Corporation had approximately $1 billion in assets and 1999 revenues of $800 million. In addition to Casino Aztar Evansville, Aztar Corporation owns and operates Tropicana Casino and Resort in

Casino Aztar's Hotel features luxurious accomodations such as this suite.

Casino Aztar's Crystal Salon gives table game players the great gaming action and individual attention they deserve.

Atlantic City, New Jersey; Tropicana Resort and Casino in Las Vegas, Nevada; Ramada Express Hotel and Casino in Laughlin, Nevada; and Casino Aztar in Caruthersville, Missouri.

Good corporate citizenship is a cornerstone of Aztar Corporation's philosophy. Chairman of the Board, President and Chief Executive Officer Paul E. Rubeli believes that while revenue growth is important, it is not important for its own sake. It is for this reason that Aztar managers work hard to provide quality products, services, and facilities, as well as community support, to customers who appreciate and deserve them.

Property Facts Including Casino

Casino Aztar Evansville is located on the Ohio River in historic downtown Evansville. Located on an 841,848-square-foot area at Riverfront Park, the entertainment facility includes a 2,700-passenger riverboat casino, a 250-room hotel, a 1,660-vehicle parking garage, and a riverfront pavilion complex featuring five restaurants, two lounges, and ticketing and boarding facilities, along with expansive views of the Ohio River.

Known as the *City of Evansville*, the vessel is Robert E. Lee on the outside, pure Las Vegas on the inside. The vessel's Civil War-era ambiance is evoked by the intricate details and old world craftsmanship of the *City of Evansville*—a replica of the historic *Robert E. Lee* racing side-wheel steamboat crafted nearly 130 years ago. Inside the entrance of the vessel, the historic ambiance gives way to 47,863 square feet of public space masterfully designed to

showcase the Las Vegas-style glamour that truly defines the *City of Evansville* as one of the finest fully-functional gaming vessels in the Midwest.

Brocade, marble, and gold finishes adorn the interior of the boat's three gaming levels to create an atmosphere that is rich and elegant, while at the same time bright and colorful. The feeling of grandeur is further enhanced by lavish glass chandeliers imported from Italy, Greek-style columns with gold leaf etched glass, and custom hand-painted wallpaper with an inlay of gold mirrors. The observation deck on the top level of the vessel offers riverboat guests the perfect break from the gaming action with a scenic view of the Ohio River.

Day and night, the non-stop casino action hums against this elegant background. Casino Aztar offers something to entertain every riverboat visitor with over 1,300 slot and video poker games and more than 60 table games, including blackjack, craps, roulette, and a full-size poker room, along with many other table game favorites. For those more interested in taking in the sites, the *City of Evansville's* observation deck offers breathtaking views of the majestic Ohio River.

The Casino Aztar Hotel—built with the same attention to detail and adorned with the same touches of splendor as the *City of Evansville*—opened its doors in December 1996. Overlooking Casino Aztar and the Ohio River, the hotel, with its warm, hand-rubbed woods and rich, serpentine marble, provides a feeling of the past while offering all of today's modern conveniences. The hotel has 250 guest rooms and suites, meeting, conference, and banquet facilities, a fitness room, and a 190-seat restaurant.

Casino Aztar's Riverfront Pavilion is designed to reflect the turn-of-the-century charm of downtown Evansville and is home to a variety of dining and entertainment opportunities, including pre-boarding facilities, retail shops, restaurants, and a lounge area. An enclosed walkway links the pavilion to the Casino Aztar Hotel and the parking garage. Riverfront Park, adjacent to the pavilion, features pathways for bicycling, jogging, and walking, an amphitheater, events plaza, picnic areas, and lush landscaped grounds, as well as a great view of the Ohio River. The park is open for the general public to enjoy year-round.

Casino Aztar's manicured riverfront property features an outdoor amphitheater.

The *City of Evansville* cruises on the Ohio River near Casino Aztar's Riverfront Pavilion.

Casino Aztar Evansville also has five outstanding restaurants. Guests can savor the best steak and seafood Evansville has to offer at the elegant Regent Court restaurant. Located on the second level of the pavilion, Regent Court has a spectacular view of the Ohio River. Corky's BBQ, located on the first level of the pavilion, serves its world famous Memphis-style barbecue. Located conveniently on the second level of the Casino Aztar hotel, New Mandarin Garden features delicious Chinese cuisine. In addition, the pavilion is home to the River City Grille and the Sidewalk Café for those who want good food but don't have a lot of time.

Also located in the pavilion is Casino Aztar's Hoosiers Lounge, which offers the best in headline entertainment. Hoosiers Lounge has already hosted such legendary acts as Juice Newton, B.J. Thomas, Sha Na Na, the Fabulous Thunderbirds, and the Marshall Tucker Band, along with many local favorites, including the Duke Boys.

Casino Aztar's Positive Impact on the Community

From day one, Casino Aztar has made a positive impact on the quality of life in and around the Evansville area. In the first four years of operation, Casino Aztar has already contributed over $300 million directly back into the local economy through payroll, purchases, and payments to city and county government.

Casino Aztar also made $123 million in direct project investments in the first three years of operation—$23 million more than the original commitment. Included in the investment was the construction of the $20 million *City of Evansville* riverboat by Jeffboat Shipyard in nearby Jeffersonville, Indiana. Other major physical project components include the 250-room hotel with convention and banquet facilities, the

44,000-square foot passenger pavilion, the Riverfront Park, and the 1,668-space parking garage. Construction of these facilities represented over 1,000 construction jobs, primarily for Indiana residents.

Design and construction of the Casino Aztar Evansville facility was handled by Evansville firms. The primary architect was the Evansville architectural firm of Edmund L. Hafer Architect, Inc. and construction was completed by the Evansville construction firm of Industrial Contractors, Inc. The American Society of Civil Engineers presented their 1996 Indiana Civil Engineering Project of the Year award to both Industrial Contractors and Aztar for the Casino Aztar facility.

Aztar contributes to the financial stability of the City of Evansville, Vanderburgh County, and the State of Indiana through a number of direct and incentive payments each year. A total of over $153 million was paid to the city, county, and state through admission, wagering, and property taxes and lease payments through February 2000.

In addition, Casino Aztar donated amounts ranging from $200,000 to over $6 million to various special projects that directly benefit the city of Evansville and the residents of Vanderburgh County. Those projects and

Casino Aztar's Premier Slot Lounge features the newest, most popular slot machines in a luxurious environment.

donation recipients include the Downtown Revitalization Fund, Project Riverfront, Victory Theatre Renovation Project, Downtown Learning Center, Evansville Auditorium and Convention Center renovation, Burdette Park, Evansville One, Pigeon Creek Greenway Project, and United Way. As of February 2000, more than $16.1 million had been donated to these and various other projects.

The Private Industry Council of Southwest Indiana has twice honored Casino Aztar as its Vanderburgh County business of the year. The award, which is given annually, recognizes the business that "most contributes to the improvement of workforce development." Aztar's employee base of 1,200 local residents is comprised of 55 percent women and 20 percent minorities, which is double the Vanderburgh County minority population of 8.9 percent. Ninety-one percent of Casino Aztar's workforce are Indiana residents, 80 percent of which reside in Vanderburgh County. Along with its broad community representation, the Casino Aztar staff is well known for their bright smiles, friendly greetings, and outgoing personalities.

In addition to hiring locally, Casino Aztar has upheld a firm commitment to responsible purchasing from local and Minority and Women Business Enterprise (M/WBE) vendors. To-date, over $83 million of goods and services have been purchased from local vendors. In addition, Casino Aztar boasts millions of dollars in purchases from minority-owned, women-owned, and Downtown businesses, and has received numerous awards and recognitions.

Casino Aztar doesn't draw only the attention of the Evansville community; the majority of Casino Aztar's visitors come from over 50 miles from Evansville. These visits result in increased hotel, restaurant, shopping, and other revenues for the entire Evansville community. As a testament to the influence Aztar has had in increasing area tourism, the Evansville Convention and Visitors Bureau presented Casino Aztar with the William L. Brooks Hospitality Award in May 1996 as the business having the most positive impact on area tourism.

Key among Casino Aztar's goals has always been to vigorously promote Downtown Evansville. Casino Aztar has developed and implemented marketing cross promotions, funded advertising campaigns, and supported a variety of efforts to increase the awareness of Evansville's Downtown area. In addition, Casino Aztar has been the title sponsor of

The Regent Court Piano Bar, located in the Riverfront Pavilion is a relaxing, elegant atmosphere.

four of the most well-attended annual Downtown events: Center City's Evansville Riverfest, Evansville Thunder Festival's July 4th Fireworks Spectacular, Downtown After Sundown, and the Ohio Valley BBQ Cookoff & Festival.

Casino Aztar continues to be an honorable corporate citizen with members of its senior management team actively serving on many area boards and councils. Time, energy, and monetary support has also been generously given to many local agencies, organizations, and other worthy causes. They also recognize their duty to ensure that casino gaming serves as an entertainment alternative for responsible adults. Casino Aztar takes a highly proactive approach to the identification and prevention of problem and underage gambling and has been nationally recognized by the American Gaming Association for their on-going efforts in this area.

Future of Aztar in the Community

When Aztar Corporation was awarded the first gaming license on the Ohio River in 1995, Aztar made a commitment to the people of Evansville to have a positive impact on this community. That commitment remains as fervent as ever. Casino Aztar Evansville intends to remain a positive fixture in this community by providing long-term benefits to Evansville and its surrounding areas for many years to come.

Casino Aztar Evansville…bringing fun, fantasy, and excitement to Evansville's doorstep. █

Aerial view of Casino Aztar bordering downtown Evansville on the majestic Ohio River.

❖ RADISSON HOTEL ❖

Downtown Evansville saw some major positive changes take place in the last years of the 1990s. Beautiful new buildings rose up as historic structures were restored and renovated, cultural and entertainment options blossomed, and one hotel, long an integral part of the Downtown scene, took on a new look and a new attitude. The newly-christened Radisson made itself ready to enter the new century, fully prepared to offer the best hospitality experience in the city. Whether traveling for business or pleasure, whether staying one night or again and again, guests at Evansville's Radisson can expect to enjoy a wonderful stay with all the comforts of home and more.

Along with the new name came a new, experienced management team, a staff of 175 team members thoroughly trained in Radisson's "Yes I Can!®" customer service program, $10 million worth of renovations, and expanded facilities.

The hotel that eventually became the Radisson was built in 1963 as a 250-room Ramada Inn. Bob Green purchased it in 1969 and re-named it The Executive Inn. In 1972, he expanded the building to include shops, an atrium, salons, and the Time-Out Bar. Green sold his hotel in 1981 but repurchased it two years later. After his death in 1995, his family sold the hotel to new owners. They made the conversion to Radisson, which was officially revealed to the curious city in May 1997.

The massive renovation brought the building up to the high standards of the Radisson chain, one of the world's leading upscale hotel companies. The 429 guest rooms received new furnishings and carpeting; 25" televisions with cable, pay-per-view, and Nintendo; hardwired smoke detectors; and two dataport telephones. Ninety-three of the guest rooms are parlor

The luxurious Radisson Hotel Evansville located in the heart of beautiful downtown Evansville. Photo by L. Kent Whitehead.

suites with separate living areas. Another seven are three-room luxury suites that include meeting areas complete with wet bar and conference table. An electronic system and card key access secure all rooms.

The hotel now has 14 meeting and convention rooms, totaling 35,000 square feet of space. The Bentwood Room seats 170 for meals. The International Ballroom holds up to 900 theater-style, but it can be divided into three salons when need dictates. Atrium Hall seats 800 for a meal and also functions well for exhibits and meetings. A staff of experienced meeting specialists is on hand to help plan gatherings and to ensure complete satisfaction. A Business Center offers copy, fax, and audiovisual services.

Both the hotel's indoor, Olympic-sized swimming pool and nearby hot tub are free to guests. So is use of the Advantage Health & Fitness Center, located on the top floor of the parking garage across the street, which offers three tennis courts, aerobics classes, state-of-the-art cardiovascular and weight training equipment, dry and steam saunas—even a massage therapist. Garage parking is also free.

The food service at the Radisson is among the best in the area. Guests can choose snacks or full-course meals from a mouthwatering room service menu. They can get a taste of the authentic Southwest at Chili Pepper's Cantina, which serves delightful entrees in a casual, fun atmosphere. The elegant Angus O'Leary's specializes in juicy steaks and the freshest seafood, while the gorgeous Lobby Bar offers refreshing beverages.

Yet even with all these improvements in the facility itself, the hotel's transformation would not have been complete without the proper attitude among the team members. Radisson Hotels Worldwide has pledged to distinguish itself in the hospitality industry through its commitment to delivering personalized service and genuine hospitality. The Evansville Radisson is no exception to this rule.

The exquisitely decorated lobby provides a relaxing atmosphere for pleasure or business. Photo by L. Kent Whitehead.

The elegant Angus O'Leary's restaurant specializes in juicy steaks and fresh seafood and can accomodate up to 175 people. Photo by L. Kent Whitehead.

Therefore, in order to ensure complete customer satisfaction, all team members there receive thorough training in how to interact with guests and other team members in every area from conflict resolution to dealing with stress. Called "Yes I Can!®," this training is the reason why Radisson leads the hospitality industry with a winning attitude. This program is based on a simple yet crucial premise: If a guest makes a request, or a team member asks for help, there is no doubt in the response that should be given: "Yes I Can!"

Evansville's Downtown hotel was meant to be a convention hotel. As the Executive Inn, it was supported in this aim for several decades by the former Green Convention Center and the Vanderburgh County Auditorium, both located across the street. When the convention center was closed, the hotel suffered. Fortunately, the county auditorium, now called The Centre, underwent an extensive, two-year renovation that turned it into Indiana's second-largest convention center and an excellent venue for a wide variety of cultural events. Completed in late 1999, this $35 million renovation injected new life not only into Downtown Evansville but into the Radisson as well. The hotel's dynamic marketing staff works diligently with other local organizations, such as the Evansville Convention & Visitors Bureau and the Metropolitan Evansville Chamber of Commerce, to attract a wide variety of groups for conventions, trade shows, meetings, and cultural events centered around The Centre and the Radisson.

Another large market for the Radisson is sports-minded visitors. With two universities and many area high schools that have excellent basketball teams; the Otters, the city's minor league baseball team; and many enthusiastic amateur soccer teams, Evansville plays host to thousands of visitors who come for athletic events. Other local events like Thunder on the Ohio and the Frog Follies bring many more thousands of folks to Evansville for stays of several days. Thanks to the Radisson's excellent reputation as a well-run luxury hotel and a solid marketing program, many of these visitors choose to stay at the Radisson.

Regardless of the reason for their visit to the city, guests can depend on the Downtown Radisson for the best lodging experience with the best service. There, "the difference is genuine." ▧

The gorgeous Lobby Bar offers refreshing beverages and relaxing atmosphere for any occasion. Photo by L. Kent Whitehead.

❧ WOLF'S BAR-B-Q RESTAURANT ❧

More than 70 years of experience have gone into making Wolf's Bar-B-Q Restaurant an Evansville dining tradition. Creators of some of the tastiest barbecue around, Wolf's now proudly serves nearly 300,000 customers every year — a sure sign that this family-run restaurant has found the secret to success.

The business that became Wolf's Bar-B-Q Restaurant began in 1927, when Nicholas Frank Wolf opened a wholesale meat packing plant on First Avenue. Before long, he was distributing his products to local groceries and taverns. The company quickly grew to three plants, including locations in Illinois and Kentucky. When Nicholas Frank died tragically at an early age, his sons Nicholas II and Charles continued the business. In 1953, they opened the first Wolf's Bar-B-Q Restaurant on First Avenue, with a seating capacity of 60. In 1968, Charles died in a boating accident. The next year Nicholas II doubled the capacity of the restaurant. Its reputation for quality barbecue and delectable pies continued to grow, and in 1979, he expanded the capacity to 360, making it the largest restaurant in Evansville at the time. Wolf's added a second location on Vogel Road in 1998.

Evansville recently witnessed explosive growth in the number of restaurants, but Wolf's has remained a popular destination for hungry diners. Its longevity is directly related to the high value the staff places on their customers. "We never lose sight of that," says Terry Wolf,

Nicholas Frank's grandson and current co-owner, along with his sister, Kim. "We are always working to improve the quality of our product, but we maintain what customers come here for — the barbecue." Being located far out on First Avenue means that "if people come here, it's because they want to come here," asserts Wolf, "not because it's close." With great food and a customer service policy that guarantees 100 percent satisfaction, it's no surprise that guests make Wolf's their dining destination.

Also operating under the Wolf's roof are a retail carry-out business, a full-service catering operation that can serve everything from hot dogs to prime rib for two to 10,000, and a wholesale distribution business that provides local groceries along with Wolf's Bar-B-Q and its famous potato salad. Keeping all these outlets supplied keeps the food preparation staff busy. Each week, they turn out 5000 pounds of award-winning pork, pork ribs, chicken, and beef barbecue; 700 gallons of potato salad; and more than 1000 pies.

Even with a long tradition behind them, Wolf's stays current with new dining trends. Wolf's is also exploring the possibility of expanding outside of Evansville. When that happens, people elsewhere will know what Evansville has known for decades — When you want great food, go to Wolf's Bar-B-Q, where customers are number one. ❧

❈ Eastland Mall ❈

For nearly 20 years, Simon's Eastland Mall has played a leading role in transforming the community of Evansville into one of Indiana's major business centers. The quest to develop Eastland Mall began in the late 1960s when developers marked 90 acres of farmland located on the east side of town to build the largest enclosed mall in the Tri-State area.

Anchored by JC Penney, Ben Snyder, and De Jong department stores, the $50-million Eastland Mall welcomed more than 60,000 Tri-State residents through its doors for the first time in August 1981. During the mall's first eight months of operations, Eastland Mall surpassed its original sales projections three times, stabilizing at more than $200 of sales generated for each square foot of retail space, becoming one of the nation's most profitable malls.

In 1982, Eastland Mall celebrated the completion of its final phase of construction with the opening of 34 additional retail stores, including the mall's fourth anchor, Lazarus. With the completion of this phase of construction, Eastland Mall, which now encompassed more than 750,000 square feet and housed 119 retail stores, fulfilled its initial vision of becoming the largest enclosed mall in the Tri-State area.

As part of its commitment to provide customers with a quality shopping experience, Eastland Mall began renovations to further expand its retail offerings in 1996. Eastland Mall added an additional 45,000 square feet of retail space, expanded and beautified the food court, as well as replaced

As part of its commitment to provide customers with a quality shopping experience, Eastland Mall renovated and expanded its retail offerings in 1996.

the original 70,000-square-foot Ben Snyder with an 180,000-square-foot Famous-Barr department store. By the end of the year, Eastland Mall had increased its size by 25 percent to encompass more than 912,000 square feet of space.

In 1998, Indianapolis-based Simon Property Group, the nation's largest owner and manager of mall properties, including such marquee properties as Mall of America and The Forum Shops at Caesars, acquired the management of Eastland Mall's operations. As part of Simon's national portfolio of malls, Eastland Mall was now able to provide Evansville-area residents with unique offerings, promotions, and events by leveraging Simon's national partnerships with global brands like the Pepsi-Cola Company and Visa.

That same year, as part of Simon's commitment to play an active role in the communities where it does business, Simon's Eastland Mall was instrumental in establishing the Komen/Evansville Race for the Cure, the second largest inaugural event in the history of the race, with more than $267,000 raised to benefit breast cancer research.

As Simon continues to redefine the shopping experience, Eastland Mall continues to evolve as well. In March 1999, Eastland Mall became one of the 145 Simon malls nationwide selected to participate in the company's landmark branding campaign that creates a link between the quality shopping experience available at these malls and the Simon brand name. Simon's Eastland Mall will strive to continue evolving its role within the Evansville community as both an economic and social leader by providing area residents with its unique shopping environment, entertainment, and products that cannot be found anywhere else. ❈

Offering the tri-state the latest in retail shopping concepts, Eastland Mall has always strived to provide the best shopping there is.

❈ Evansville Enterprise Index ❈

❈ BIBLIOGRAPHY ❈

Banta, R.E. *The Ohio*. New York: Rinehart & Company, 1949.

Bigham, Darrel. *An Evansville Album*. Bloomington, Indiana: Indiana University Press, 1988.

Bigham, Darrel. *Images of Evansville*. Charleston, South Carolina: Arcadia Publishing, 1998.

Evansville Courier & Press Archives.

Hebron Elementary Fifth Grade Students. *Green River Road: From Cornfields to Concrete*. Mt. Vernon, Indiana: Windmill Publications, Inc., 1993.

Klein, Benjamin F. *The Ohio River Handbook and Picture Album*. Cincinnati, Ohio: Young and Klein, Inc. 1958.

McCutchan, Kenneth P. *At the Bend in the River: The Story of Evansville*. Woodland Hills, California, 1982.

Overbeck, Thelma. *Evansville and How It Grew*. Evansville, Indiana: Evansville-Vanderburgh School Corporation, 1963.

Patry, Robert P. *City of the Four Freedoms: A History of Evansville, Indiana*. Evansville, Indiana: Friends of Willard Library, 1996.

Wooden, Howard E. *Architectural Heritage of Evansville: An Interpretive Review of the Nineteenth Century*. Evansville, Indiana:
        Evansville Museum of the Arts and Sciences, 1962.

❈ INDEX ❈